FOOTPRINTS OF JESUS

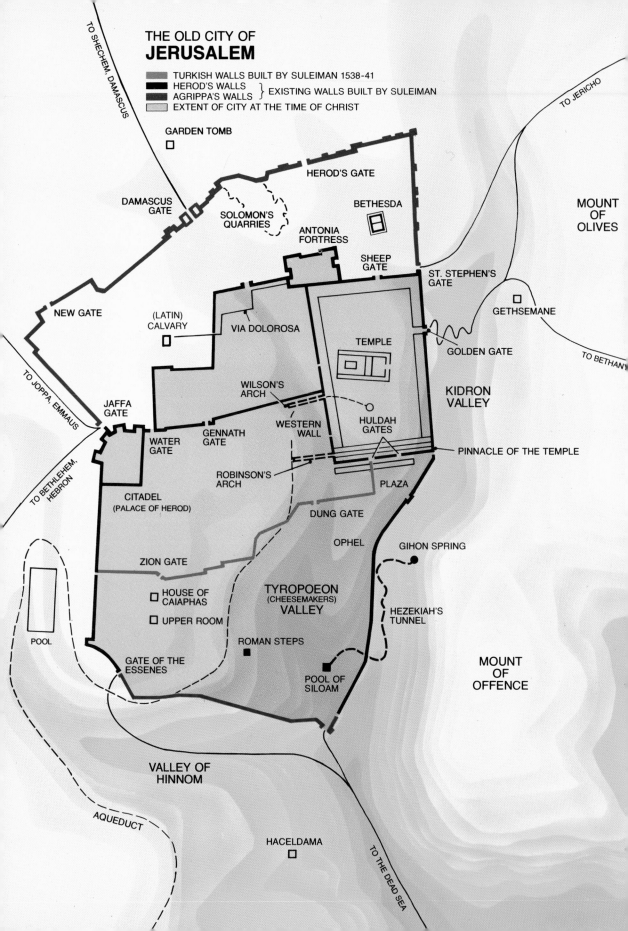

THE OLD CITY OF
JERUSALEM

TURKISH WALLS BUILT BY SULEIMAN 1538-41
HEROD'S WALLS
AGRIPPA'S WALLS } EXISTING WALLS BUILT BY SULEIMAN
EXTENT OF CITY AT THE TIME OF CHRIST

TO SHECHEM, DAMASCUS

GARDEN TOMB

TO JERICHO

HEROD'S GATE

DAMASCUS GATE

SOLOMON'S QUARRIES

BETHESDA

MOUNT OF OLIVES

ANTONIA FORTRESS

SHEEP GATE

ST. STEPHEN'S GATE

NEW GATE

(LATIN) CALVARY

VIA DOLOROSA

TEMPLE

GETHSEMANE

GOLDEN GATE

TO BETHANY

TO JOPPA, EMMAUS

WILSON'S ARCH

KIDRON VALLEY

JAFFA GATE

WESTERN WALL

HULDAH GATES

WATER GATE

GENNATH GATE

PINNACLE OF THE TEMPLE

TO BETHLEHEM, HEBRON

ROBINSON'S ARCH

PLAZA

CITADEL (PALACE OF HEROD)

DUNG GATE

ZION GATE

OPHEL

GIHON SPRING

HOUSE OF CAIAPHAS

TYROPOEON (CHEESEMAKERS) VALLEY

HEZEKIAH'S TUNNEL

UPPER ROOM

MOUNT OF OFFENCE

POOL

ROMAN STEPS

GATE OF THE ESSENES

POOL OF SILOAM

VALLEY OF HINNOM

AQUEDUCT

HACELDAMA

TO THE DEAD SEA

FOOTPRINTS OF JESUS

Part two

MIRACLES, PARABLES, CROSS – AND RESURRECTION

by W. L. Emmerson

First published in Great Britain by The Stanborough Press Ltd. 1956.

New edition 1986

ISBN 0-904748-27-8

Designed, printed and bound by

THE STANBOROUGH PRESS

GRANTHAM · LINCOLNSHIRE · ENGLAND

FOOTPRINTS OF JESUS

Contents

A view of Bethany, home of Mary, Martha and Lazarus, from a nineteenth century watercolour by David Roberts.

By permission of the Victoria and Albert Museum, London.

David Roberts R.A.

Bethany april 1839.

The shadow of the cross

On a number of occasions Jesus had hinted at the path of sorrow and suffering He had come to tread. When the disciples of John asked Him why His disciples did not fast, He replied that while the Bridegroom was with them, the 'children of the bridechamber' could only rejoice, but that one day He would be 'taken from them', and then they would have cause to fast and mourn.

Comparing Himself, in one of His discourses, to the 'Bread of life', He told the unbelieving Jews, 'Except ye eat the flesh of the Son of man, and drink his blood, ye have no life in you.'

To the ruler Nicodemus, Jesus declared that 'as Moses lifted up the serpent in the wilderness, even so must the Son of man be lifted up: that whosoever believeth in him should not perish, but have eternal life.'

All these intimations, however, had been couched in symbolic language which He had not explained to His disciples. Now, in this moment of high faith at Caesarea Philippi, Jesus began to tell them more plainly than ever before that 'He must go unto Jerusalem, and suffer many things of the elders and chief priests and scribes, and be killed.'

But, He went on to assure them, this would not mean the failure of His purpose. Rather would it be the prelude to triumph, for on 'the third day' He would rise victorious over sin and death to plead the merits of His sacrifice before His Father in heaven.

As Peter was foremost in bearing testimony to his belief in the Messiahship of Jesus, he was the first to express his horror at the path of humiliation which Jesus now revealed would be His lot. He had restrained himself with difficulty when Jesus submitted unresistingly to the scorn and opposition of the Pharisees and Sadducees, but he could not be party to allowing his Master's enemies to put Him to death.

Taking hold of Jesus in his anxiety to compel attention to his protest, Peter cried, 'Be it far from thee, Lord: this shall not be unto thee.'

The disciple's outburst was made out of deep love for Jesus and the honour of His cause, but it was misguided zeal and showed his lack of comprehension of the culminating purpose of Christ's first advent. While he recognized in Jesus the divine Son and the true Messiah, he still failed to

Looking from the Mount of Olives as early morning light bathes the Old City of Jerusalem.

It was this Jebusite city that David conquered and made into the capital of his kingdom about 1000 BC. Solomon built his magnificent temple here. Jeremiah lamented its sins and idolatry. Babylon and Rome razed its walls and temple, while Zechariah rebuilt and Herod contributed a stately temple, grand buildings and elegant walls.

To this ravaged yet immortal city Jesus came to preach, heal and die for its people and the world.

7

Jesus announced the agonizing yet victorious fulfilment of His work to His amazed disciples while they enjoyed a short respite at the remote but beautiful area around Caesarea Philippi.

declared that they 'must' be, if man's deliverance from the penalty of sin was to be accomplished.

By his impetuosity he actually allowed Satan to put words into his mouth to turn Jesus from His gracious purpose of redemption.

Detecting the voice of the tempter in Peter's outburst, Jesus turned quickly away saying, 'Get thee behind me, Satan: for thou art an offence unto me: for thou savourest not the things that be of God, but those that be of men.'

In these stern words Jesus did not identify Peter with Satan, but He showed him that, by allowing himself to become a mouthpiece for Satan, he had actually ranged himself with the great adversary in seeking to frustrate the divinely-ordained plan for the salvation of men.

The word 'offence' which Jesus chose to describe Peter was a most expressive one, for it was used of the trigger of a trap upon which the bait was placed. Peter had indeed allowed himself to become the bearer of Satan's most subtle temptation to deflect Jesus from His destined way. But from this experience, through the longsuffering of Jesus, Peter learned a profound lesson. And years later, in his letters to the churches, we find the aged apostle untiringly extolling the virtues of the 'precious blood of Christ'.

'Forasmuch as ye know', he wrote, 'that ye were not redeemed with corruptible things, as silver and gold, from your vain conversation, received by tradition from your fathers; but with the precious blood of Christ, as of a Lamb without blemish and without spot: who verily was foreordained before the foundation of the world, but was manifest in these last times for you.' What once was unthinkable now aroused his heartfelt gratitude and evoked his dearest love.

understand the relation between the 'sufferings of Christ' and the 'glory that should follow'.

By saying that these things should 'not be' he was directly contradicting Jesus who had

Having declared plainly to Peter and the other disciples that His death was essential to the fulfilment of His redemptive mission, Jesus went on to tell them that the 'cross' must precede the 'crown' in their experience also. 'If any man will come after me,' He solemnly declared, 'let him deny himself, and take up his cross, and follow me.'

Till now Jesus had not actually disclosed the awful end which awaited Him. Now they learned the worst, that He would die upon a cruel cross; and that if they loyally followed Him, they must be prepared for a like fate.

Crucifixion was the most terrible form of execution in ancient times. It had been practised by Egyptians, Babylonians, Persians, and Greeks, and under the Romans it was still a common form of punishment meted out to their enemies and for heinous civil offences. Countless Jewish rebels had suffered crucifixion within the memory of the disciples. Invariably it was preceded by scourging, and the victim was then compelled to bear his cross, or at least the upright or crossbeam, to the place of execution.

To accomplish man's redemption Jesus had willingly come to earth to suffer and to die 'even the death of the cross'. Could His disciples then do less than voluntarily take up their cross and follow in His steps?

But though they might be called upon to sacrifice their all in His cause – home, possessions, family and friends – and to suffer poverty, trial, persecution, and even death, Jesus assured them that the way of the cross would prove, as it would for Him a path to life and glory.

For paradoxical as it might seem, 'whosoever' should seek to save his life by forsaking Him and clinging to the world would ultimately 'lose it', while 'whosoever' would 'lose his life' for Christ's sake, would 'find it', eternally.

That self-seeking is self-losing while self-losing is self-finding will indeed be abundantly manifest when 'the Son of man shall come in the glory of His Father with his angels' to reward every man 'according to his work'. For in that day the glitter of earthly gain will be exposed as false and illusory, while the little crosses Christ's followers have borne will seem as nothing when they take from the hands of the Saviour the 'crown of glory' which will be the reward of the righteous.

When Jesus had ended His instruction on the challenge of discipleship He looked into the faces of His little band of followers. They were solemn and anxious and no one spoke. Even Peter was silent now. But Jesus saw that all except Judas had made their decision. They were ready to follow Him all the way to the cross if thereby they might be counted worthy to live with Him in His kingdom. And so, as He stood in their midst, He made them a striking promise: 'Verily I say unto you, There be some standing here, which shall not taste of death, till they see the Son of man coming in his kingdom.'

What did Jesus mean by this mysterious promise? He obviously did not mean that some would live to see His return in glory, for all have long since died.

Nor was He referring to His resurrection glory, for not some but all the disciples were witnesses of this.

No, the promise was fulfilled just over a week later on the Mount of Transfiguration when the three most intimate of Christ's disciples were granted a vision, in miniature, of their glorified Lord in order to establish their faith and the confidence of all who afterward should be called upon to follow Jesus along the way of the cross.

This chapter is based on Matthew 16:21-28; Mark 8:31-9:1; Luke 9:22-27.

Anticipations of glory

From the solitude of the hills around Caesarea Philippi, Jesus turned His steps again towards the lake towns of southern Galilee. The journey which was to end in Jerusalem and on Calvary had begun.

The minds of the disciples were confused by all that Jesus had told them, and their hearts were sad. Jesus had acknowledged the inspired testimony of Peter that He was truly the Messiah for whom Israel looked. Yet He had warned them that very soon He would be taken by His enemies, condemned, and put to death. It was all so different from their anticipations on the triumphant coming of Messiah. And so as they travelled southward they talked among themselves as to what it all meant. But they feared to question Jesus further lest He should reprove their slow understanding.

Just how long Jesus stayed in the region of Caesarea Philippi after the revelation concerning His future sufferings and death, or how long the little party took on their journey back to Galilee we are not told, but it was some six days after His momentous declaration that, as night was drawing on, Jesus announced to His companions that He was going up into a nearby mountain to pray and would take Peter, James, and John with Him.

His decision aroused no comment from the other disciples for Peter and the two sons of Zebedee had already, by their deeper understanding and clearer perception of His teaching, come to be regarded as Jesus' closest companions. They, of all the disciples, had been chosen to witness the raising of Jairus' daughter, and doubtless on other unrecorded occasions Jesus had taken them as His special companions during nights of prayer. At the last, too, they were to be nearest to Him in the darkness of Gethsemane. So bidding the other disciples make their way to a village for the night, Jesus led Peter, James, and John into the hills.

The location of the mountain which Jesus ascended has been the subject of considerable conjecture. Some have thought that it was one of the southern spurs of Mount Hermon, but the fact that they had already journeyed some considerable way would seem to preclude this. Moreover, when they met the disciples again the morning after, there was with them a large company of Jews, including some of the local rabbis, so that they must have left the more Gentile parts of of northern Galilee behind.

A tradition which goes back to the early centuries of the Christian era identifies the mountain as Mount Tabor, a few miles south of the Sea of Galilee on the edge of the Plain of Esdraelon. So strong was this tradition that the ruins of no fewer than three churches are to be found on the table-like summit of the mountain. This identification is, however, as unlikely as the other, for the record expressly states that they did not 'pass through Galilee' until the next day. It is also known, from the rock cisterns on the summit, that Tabor has always been an inhabited place, and in the days of Jesus a fortress crowned the hill. About AD 60, Josephus, governor of Galilee during the Jewish revolt, strengthened the walls in an endeavour to stem the advance of the Roman general, Vespasian, and the remains of his constructions are still to be seen. It is thus hardly likely that Jesus would have ascended Tabor in search of a quiet retreat for prayer.

We must, therefore, be content to leave unidentified the mountain where Jesus and His disciples spent the night, surmising that it was somewhere to the north of the Sea of Galilee, but not far removed from the Jewish cities beside the lake.

Standing 396 metres (1,300 feet) above the Plain of Jezreel on Mount Tabor is the Franciscan Basilica of the Transfiguration. It was built in 1921-3 on sixth-century Byzantine and later Crusader ruins. From this quiet and beautiful location a magnificent panorama of the surrounding countryside is to be seen.

Jesus and His disciples had been walking all day and by the time they reached the top of the mountain in the gathering darkness, they were all weary. The three joined Jesus in their evening devotions and then, wrapping themselves in their cloaks, they lay down on the grass. As it was summer they needed no protection from the elements and were soon fast asleep.

Jesus, however, remained awake and, moving a little way from the sleeping group, began to pray earnestly. First, He prayed for strength to tread the path of suffering which lay darkly before Him to the cross. Then He prayed, that, for a brief moment, there might be unveiled before the eyes of His three chosen disciples the glory He had had with His Father from eternity in the past and which would be His again when His mission was completed.

God accepted His self-dedication and answered His prayer. As Jesus rose from His knees the veil of humanity, which He took upon Himself when He came to tabernacle with men, was drawn aside and the glory of the eternal Son shone through. The darkness of the night was dispelled by a celestial

brightness which irradiated and transfigured the form of the Son of man.

The dazzling splendour awakened the
disciples and when their eyes became
accustomed to the unwonted brightness
they looked up in wonder at the radiant form
of Jesus. From the descriptions given to them
by the three disciples, Matthew records that
His appearance was as the sun, Mark
compares it to snow in its purity and
whiteness, while Luke declares that the
appearance of Jesus was like lightning. Even
His garments glowed and glistened.

Striking indeed is the similarity between
the description of the transfigured Jesus and
the inspired portrayals of Christ by Daniel
and John. But whereas they recorded only
visions of Christ's glory, the three disciples
on the Mount of Transfiguration actually
saw the glorified Jesus in person, for it is
specifically stated that the disciples awoke
to behold Him. They were not in a trance. It
was not a dream. They did not see a vision. It
was the Jesus they knew transfigured by the
heavenly radiance.

At His incarnation Jesus had 'emptied
himself' of His glory; the divine Son was
veiled in human flesh. In the transfiguration
the veil was taken away. Jesus was freed
from His human limitations and the glory of
the divine Son flashed through. It was the
miracle of the Incarnation in reverse.

If ever the disciples had doubted whether
Jesus was 'he that should come', they could
not doubt it now. Here was visible confirmation of what Peter had declared by
faith, that Jesus was the Son of the living
God.

No wonder that years later this apostle, in
one of his letters to the churches, confidently
declared that he had not deceived them with
'cunningly devised fables' about Jesus, for
he and his fellow disciples had been
'eye-witnesses of his majesty'.

*Eucalyptus trees beside newly-harvested fields
frame the 'dome' of Mount Tabor where, contrary
to modern opinion, tradition suggests Jesus was
transfigured.*

No wonder that John, who was with Peter
on 'the holy mount', declared in the opening
verses of his gospel, 'We beheld his glory,
the glory as of the only begotten of the
Father.'

And if James, the third witness of the
transfiguration, had not been the first of the
apostles to 'taste death' in the cause of
Christ, doubtless he would also have

recorded his abiding memory of that wonderful sight.

As the disciples gazed enraptured at the form of Jesus, they discerned two other figures of glorious appearance, one on either side, and engaging Him in earnest conversation. As they listened they heard the names of His companions. They were Moses and Elijah.

The presence of these two Old Testament worthies on this momentous occasion is taken by some to be a proof of the conscious existence of all the righteous dead. This conclusion, however, is quite erroneous.

The Bible consistently teaches that the righteous dead are not yet in heaven, neither are the wicked dead in purgatory or any fiery hell. The Scriptures clearly reveal that the dead are 'asleep', unconscious in the grave until the day Jesus returns, save for certain exceptional individuals, who, in the providence of God, have been permitted already to enter the glorious estate of heaven. Among these are Moses and Elijah.

Elijah, like one other Old Testament saint, Enoch, never died. Enoch walked with God so perfectly that the day came when he was translated without seeing death. He 'was

13

not; for God took him.' Elijah likewise was caught up in a 'chariot of fire' to the heavenly realm without dying.

Moses did die, and was buried by God Himself in the mountains on the other side of Jordan, but from this unknown grave he was called forth in a special resurrection as recorded in the epistle of Jude.

As a result of these unique circumstances, Moses and Elijah had already entered upon their heavenly service and could be commissioned by God to join Christ on the Mount of Transfiguration.

There were significant reasons for this divine commission. Moses was the instrument through whom God communicated the wonderful details of the sanctuary service, which vividly depicted the vicarious sacrifice of Christ, while Elijah was the greatest of the prophets who had proclaimed the coming of Messiah in glory. Elijah is also associated, in the last book of the Old Testament, with the warning message which was to herald Christ's second advent. 'Behold,' declared God through Malachi, 'I will send you Elijah the prophet before the coming of the great and dreadful day of the Lord.' John the Baptist announced the first advent of Christ in the 'spirit and power of Elias' and the message of mercy and warning which precedes His second coming again is often called the 'Elijah message'.

Who then could more appropriately come to Christ on the threshold of the completion of His earthly life than these two, whose witness was to be fulfilled in Him? If the angels 'desired' above all things to 'look into' the mystery of divine love in human redemption, how much more would Moses and Elijah be anxious to talk with Jesus concerning His atoning sacrifice.

Certainly no more fitting embassy could have come from heaven to bring Jesus the token of His acceptance with His Father and an assurance of the efficacy to His vicarious death.

The Bible uses a remarkable word for the subject of the conversation between Moses and Elijah and Jesus. While in our version it is rendered His 'decease', it is really His 'departure' or 'exodus'. The death of Jesus was not like the death of any other human being. Life was not taken from Him as it is from man. Jesus voluntarily departed out of life and accepted death on behalf of man. He willingly took 'the wages of sin' in order to free man from death's grip. Of His own will He entered the 'gates of hell' in order to open up a way through resurrection to new life for His redeemed. And who could better encourage Him in His predestined task than Moses and Elijah, for whom death was already conquered?

Peter was first to find words in the presence of the ineffable glory. 'It is good for us to be here,' he cried in ecstasy. It was indeed, for what had been faith until that moment suddenly became sight in the unveiled glory of the Christ. So thrilling an experience was it that Peter wanted to forget the sad world below and stay for ever in the glory of the mount.

Quickly he went on addressing Jesus: 'Let us make three tabernacles; one for thee, and one for Moses, and one for Elias.' It may be that, as the Feast of Tabernacles was not far away, he thought they could celebrate it there, but with his usual impetuosity, he did not consider what he was saying. For what he suggested could not be.

Jesus intended that the disciples should be strengthened by this foretaste of His triumph, but there was still work on earth for Himself and for them. He had to suffer and die and be raised from the dead. They had to go forth to proclaim a Christ crucified, risen, and coming again, that all might have the opportunity of sharing His glory. Only then could they be 'for ever' with their victorious Lord.

Jesus did not reply to Peter in word, but he received his answer as a luminous cloud of glory came down and blotted out the wondrous scene. As the disciples stood paralysed with fear, the voice of God spoke out of the cloud, 'This is my beloved Son, in whom I am well pleased; hear ye him.'

To Jesus the words were an assurance that God was pleased with the way in which He had carried out His earthly task.

From the top of Mount Tabor biblical scenes unfold before the imagination as you gaze towards Megiddo, Jezreel, Mt. Gilboa, Shunem, Endor and Nain.

To the disciples they were an added testimony to the identity of Jesus as Peter later wrote, 'For he received from the Father honour and glory, when there came such a voice to him from the excellent glory, This is my beloved Son, in whom I am well pleased. And this voice which came from heaven we heard, when we were with him in the holy mount.'

Falling upon their faces before the presence of God the disciples dared not lift their heads for fear until the voice of Jesus bade them gently, 'Arise and be not afraid.'

When they took their hands from their eyes the glory had faded, the heavenly visitors had vanished. Only the familiar figure of Jesus stood before them. They were disappointed that the blissful experience

had so soon passed away, but nothing could eclipse the assurance those moments brought to them. Gladly they would follow wheresoever He should lead.

By this time it was almost dawn and as the first light broke over the hills they descended the mountain track. As they walked Jesus counselled His disciples to say nothing of the events of the previous night 'until the Son of man be risen again from the dead'. They were not even to tell the other disciples. This command, strange as it may seem at first, underlines the purpose of the transfiguration. If the disciples had recounted their experience while Jesus was yet alive, they would not have been believed. The seemingly fantastic claim would only have exasperated the rulers of the Jews and increased their opposition to Him.

After the resurrection, however, it provided corroborative evidence of the miracle. The grave could not hold Him because He was the incarnate Son of God. And Peter and the other apostles effectively used the dramatic event of the transfiguration in their proclamation of the risen and glorified Son of God.

But the transfiguration was more than a witness that the Son of man was truly the Son of God; it was more than a manifestation of the heavenly glory He had set aside. It was also a preview of the future triumph of Christ at His second coming for His people.

Jesus had told His disciples at Caesarea Philippi that some of them would 'not taste of death' till they saw the Son of man 'coming in His kingdom', and Peter, referring to the transfiguration in his second epistle testifies that it proclaimed not only the 'power' but also the 'coming of our Lord Jesus Christ'.

The transfiguration was, in fact, a perfect miniature of His second coming.

In that glorious day Jesus will appear no longer in the 'form of a servant', but in all His majesty as the divine King. 'Then shall appear the sign of the Son of man in heaven,' declared Jesus on a later occasion, 'and they shall see the Son of man coming in the clouds of heaven with power and great glory.'

The two companions of Jesus in His transfiguration similarly portray in miniature the two classes of people who will be 'with him' in the day of His triumph.

Moses, who died on Mount Nebo and was raised by God, represents the 'dead in Christ' who will 'rise' to be gathered by the angels into the presence of Christ. Moses' garb of glory likewise fittingly portrays the 'body from heaven' with which they will rise and the 'white raiment' of righteousness with which they will be clothed.

Elijah, on the other hand, because he was caught up to God without seeing death, represents the living righteous who will be transfigured into the likeness of Christ at His coming.

Moses and Elijah witness also to the reality of the life of the redeemed. Identity will be preserved, recognition will be mutual, while all mental and physical disabilities will have vanished in the glory of the eternal world.

In only one respect the transfiguration could not portray the final triumph of Christ and His people. The transfiguration was the experience of a moment, a transient preview of the coming glory, but when 'the dead in Christ' rise and the living which 'remain' are 'caught up together with them in the clouds to meet the Lord in the air', the redeemed will not need, as Peter did, to beg to remain with Him in glory. They will be 'ever with the Lord'.

This chapter is based on Matthew 17:1-13; Mark 9:2-13; Luke 9:28-36.

16

The Feast of Tabernacles

The Feast of Tabernacles was now approaching when, for the third time in the Jewish year, from the fifteenth to the twenty-first day of Tisri (September-October), all who were able went up to Jerusalem to worship.

While perhaps not the best-attended, it was called by Josephus 'the holiest and greatest feast of the year', and its special importance was marked by the fact that representatives of all the twenty-four courses of priests came up to Jerusalem to take their turn of service.

The feast was given its name because, during their stay in Jerusalem, the visitors built booths of olive, palm, pine, and myrtle branches in the nearby fields and orchards and on balconies and house roofs in the city to commemorate God's providences during Israel's wilderness wanderings.

The fact that Jesus had not been up to any of the feasts in Jerusalem for eighteen months had been noticed with increasing concern by His brethren and so, as this closing feast of another year drew near, they decided to go over to Capernaum to urge Him to attend.

For one thing, they felt that His continued absence from the feasts would give the impression that He was indifferent to the national seasons of worship and give point to the criticism of the rabbis that He was undermining the law of Moses.

Furthermore, Jesus could never hope to be accepted as a spiritual leader of the nation if He remained in the obscurity of Galilee. Sooner or later He would have to show Himself in Jerusalem, the centre of the religious life of Israel, and the obvious time to do this was at the height of His popularity.

So they urged Jesus, 'Depart hence, and go into Judea. . . . If thou do these things, show thyself to the world.'

But Jesus had no intention of going to Jerusalem merely to satisfy His brethren.

Jesus was leaving the safety and success in Galilee to face hostility and certain death in Jerusalem.

They entirely misunderstood His mission. His purpose was not to be acclaimed King in Jerusalem, but to bear a final witness and to die there to accomplish man's redemption. Step by step He was moving towards the great climax of His earthly life, and when the hour came He would not flinch. But that time was not to be dictated by His brethren; it would be appointed by His Father.

So Jesus said to them, 'Go ye up unto this feast: I go not up yet; . . . for my time is not yet full come.'

Actually Jesus was fully intending to go up to the feast, but had He travelled with one of the caravans from Galilee, news of His approach would have gone before Him and He might have been prevented by His enemies from entering the city and completing His work.

When they arrived in Jerusalem they were

St. Anne's Church is one of the oldest and most beautiful in Jerusalem. It stands adjacent to the excavation of the Pools of Bethesda which can just be seen in the foreground. The church was built in 1100 by the Crusaders on the ruins of a Byzantine structure erected in the fifth century and destroyed by the Persians in 614. Tradition suggests that this site marks Mary's birthplace.

besieged on all sides, as Jesus had expected, by the excited demand, 'Where is he?' and when it was learned that He had not come up with the rest there was much discussion concerning Him. Some spoke up for Him saying, 'He is a good man'. Others declared, 'Nay; but he deceiveth the people.' But none dared speak openly against Him for fear of the Galilean pilgrims with whom He was a popular hero.

After the initial disappointment of not seeing Jesus, the multitudes gave themselves up to the full and joyous programme of the feast. At first light they were awakened by four triumphant blasts blown by appointed priests on the silver trumpets and all hastened to the temple to witness the striking ceremony which took place each day at dawn.

Just before the time of the morning sacrifice, a procession led by a priest and a choir of Levites went down to the Pool of Siloam carrying a golden vessel with a capacity of three logs or slightly under three pints. It was filled with water from the pool and then, lifted high, was borne ceremonially through the Water Gate, where the trumpets again sounded, and up to the Court of the Priests. Here, amid singing and rejoicing, it was poured into a silver bowl on the west side of the altar of burnt offering in commemoration of the water which flowed from the rock in the wilderness. At the same time a corresponding bowl on the other side of the altar received a wine offering, the two libations draining away through a channel in the

rock on which the altar stood.

If the position of the great altar was where the Dome of the Rock now rises in the ancient temple area, the cave below must have received these libations before they flowed away through the rock into the Kidron River.

Throughout the day the pilgrims thronged the temple courts carrying palm and myrtle branches in one hand and citrons, a melon-like fruit, in the other. At night the celebra-

The Church of the Dormition, a dominant landmark on Mount Zion. A feature of this elegant building is the circular mosaic floor depicting the apostles and symbolic descriptions of the Trinity.

A halo of gold as the sun sets over the Mount of Olives. This impressive backdrop of colour is seen from El-'Azariye (Bethany) on the Jericho road.

tions continued by the light of a giant candelabra fifty cubits high erected in the Court of Women, and supplemented by thousands of torches carried by the worshippers.

For four days this round of celebrations had gone on, when Jesus appeared and quietly and unostentatiously began to teach in the temple courts. In all probability He had taken the short cut through Samaria and so, although He started late, He reached Jerusalem not so very long after the regular caravans which had travelled by the Jordan Valley and Jericho.

Immediately Jesus was the centre of attraction. Many who had not heard Him before were spellbound by His gracious words and clear teaching. 'How knoweth this man letters, having never learned?' they asked. They knew He had never been in schools of Hillel or Shammai. Where then could He have gained His wonderful knowledge of the Scriptures?

The question gave Jesus the opportunity He wanted to declare the Source of His teaching. 'My doctrine is not mine,' He said, 'but his that sent me.'

'If any man will do his will,' Jesus went on, 'He shall know of the doctrine, whether it be of God, or whether I speak of myself.'

The apprehension of truth, Jesus plainly told His hearers is not dependent merely upon intellectual capacity, but upon moral desire. Readiness to obey opens the mind to understand the will of God, but pride and prejudice corrupt the heart and blind the mind to the comprehension of truth.

Annoyed at the suggestion that they did not really desire to do the will of God, some of those standing around made as if to contest the implication of Jesus' words, but Jesus continued, 'Did not Moses give you the law,' He asked pointedly, 'and yet none of you keepeth the law?' Time and again His enemies had claimed that they kept the law

while He broke it. Actually, however, the reverse was the case. Not only did they fail to keep the law, but they sought to kill Him who perfectly observed and fearlessly taught it.

More than once Jesus had effectively replied to their criticism that He was a Sabbath-breaker and now, by another illustration, He exposed the hollowness of their accusation.

'Moses . . . gave unto you circumcision,' He declared, yet 'ye on the Sabbath day circumcise a man.'

Now there could be no danger to the life of an Israelite if this symbolic rite were postponed until the following day if the 'eighth day', on which it normally was performed, happened to fall on the Sabbath. But the rabbis believed that the adoption of a soul into the holy nation of Israel was so important that the law of circumcision superseded even the law of the Sabbath.

Why then, Jesus asked, 'are ye angry at me, because I have made a man every whit whole on the Sabbath day?' 'Judge not according to the appearance,' He added, 'but judge righteous judgement.'

When the people heard Jesus openly rebuking the religious teachers of the Jews they could not understand why they took no action against Him.

'Do the rulers know indeed that this is the

very Christ?' some asked.

Others, however, ridiculed the idea that Jesus could be the Messiah. 'When Christ cometh, no man knoweth whence he is,' they said, 'Howbeit we know this man whence he is.'

Jesus listened awhile to the discussion; then He broke in. 'Ye both know me, and ye know whence I am: . . . but he that sent me, . . . ye know not.'

They might think they knew all about His earthly parentage, but they did not know the circumstances of His divine conception, nor did they truly know His heavenly Father.

'I know him,' Jesus went on: 'for I am from him, and he hath sent me.'

When they heard these words 'many of the people believed on him'. Others, however, were offended at His claim to be 'from God'. But again an unseen power prevented any from laying hands upon Him, 'because his hour was not yet come'.

By this time the Pharisees realized that if they did not do something quickly Jesus would gain the confidence of the people and their influence would be completely lost, so they summoned the officers of the guard who were responsible for order in the temple precincts and instructed them to arrest Jesus as a disturber of the peace of the sanctuary. Forcing their way through the crowd, the officers waited for Jesus to provide them

with some pretext on which to apprehend Him. Jesus discerned their intent and chidingly warned them that they would have to do their work quickly or He would escape out of their hands.

'Yet a little while am I with you,' He said to them, 'and then I go unto him that sent me. Ye shall seek me, and shall not find me: and where I am, thither ye cannot come.'

'What manner of saying is this?' the guards whispered among themselves. 'Whither will he go, that we shall not find him? will he go unto the dispersed among the Gentiles, and teach the Gentiles?'

They did not realize, nor did any who stood by, that six months later Jesus would be delivered for ever from their hands by His triumphant ascension to His Father in heaven.

Whatever He meant, however, the officers of the guard realized that they could bring no immediate charge of disturbing the peace against the quiet, dignified Teacher, and so for the time being they held their hand.

At last 'the great day of the feast' came when the celebrations reached their grand climax. Jesus was standing in one of the temple courts as, for the last time, the golden pitcher was carried in procession to the great altar. On this final day, however, the pitcher was empty to symbolize the still unfulfilled promises to the Jewish nation. The heart of

Jesus was saddened that none of the watching crowd recognized in Him the 'living Fountain', the true Source of the Water of Life for their thirsty souls. And so as the people parted to make way for the procession Jesus cried out, 'If any man thirst, let him come unto me and drink.'

'He that believeth on me,' He continued, as all eyes were turned upon Him, 'as the Scripture hath said,' out of his inner being 'shall flow rivers of living water', and he shall in his turn become a channel of life-giving grace to his fellow men.

'This,' the apostle John commented, as years later he recorded Jesus' words, 'he spake of the Spirit, which they that believe on him should receive.'

Again the people were divided by His startling words. 'Of a truth,' some said, 'this is the prophet,' meaning the one of whom Moses had spoken.

Others went further. 'This is the Christ,' they confidently declared.

'Shall Christ come out of Galilee?' others countered. 'Hath not the Scripture said, That Christ cometh of the seed of David, and out of the town of Bethlehem, where David was?'

As the excitement rose the temple guards decided that the moment had come when they could justifiably arrest Jesus for disturbing the ritual of the feast, but once again an unseen power held them back and 'no man laid hands on him'.

When they returned to the hall where the chief priests and Pharisees were gathered, the angry rulers demanded, 'Why have ye not brought him?'

In awed tones they replied, 'Never man spake like this man.'

Furious at the failure of their plan to secure His arrest the Pharisees sneeringly asked, 'Are ye also deceived? Have any of the rulers or of the Pharisees believed on him?' If those most qualified to decide on Jesus' orthodoxy all condemned Him, who were they to dispute this judgement? They had shown themselves no better than the ignorant rabble who would follow any sensational impostor.

Impatiently they dismissed the guards and began to debate among themselves as to how Jesus could be apprehended.

Among the group was Nicodemus, the Pharisee who had sought out Jesus by night two years before. Since that fateful interview, Nicodemus had followed the activities of Jesus and had come more and more to the conviction that He was indeed the Messiah. Now, though he still dared not declare himself openly, Nicodemus felt that he must do something to stop his fellow rulers from bringing the wrath of God upon them.

So he put to the council a point of order. 'Doth our law judge any man, before it hear him, and know what he doeth?' he asked.

The rulers knew perfectly well that they were going contrary to the law in condemning Jesus before He had had an opportunity to speak in His own defence, but they brushed the objection aside by accusing Nicodemus of being in league with Jesus.

'Art thou also of Galilee?' they sneered. 'Search, and look: for out of Galilee ariseth no prophet.' This of course was not true, for Jonah was of Gath-Hepher and Nahum was an Elkoshite. Even the great Elijah may have been born in Galilee.

Nicodemus did not reply, but his warning checked any precipitate action on the part of the council. They realized that as yet they had not the grounds to condemn Jesus. The meeting broke up 'and every man went unto his own house', while Jesus went to His leafy booth in a favourite olive grove on the Mount of Olives to rest beneath the stars.

This chapter is based on John 7:2-53.

Writing in the dust

The morning after the close of the Feast of Tabernacles Jesus was back again in the temple. It was still thronged with worshippers and when He sat down in His accustomed place to teach, a crowd quickly gathered. Jesus had not been speaking long when a number of scribes and Pharisees broke rudely into the circle of listeners, dragging among them a terror-stricken and dishevelled woman. Throwing her down on the ground at Jesus' feet they cried, in feigned indignation, 'Master, this woman was taken in adultery, in the very act.'

Without doubt the crowded conditions of the city, the makeshift accommodation anywhere and everywhere, and the excitement of the vintage feast provided ample opportunity for illicit associations among the less principled visitors to the feast, and probably by accident some of the priests had stumbled upon one such shameful scene. Apparently the guilty man had escaped unrecognized, for only the woman was apprehended.

In the law given by God to moses adultery was pronounced one of the most serious offences, undermining as it did the sacred family relationship instituted in Eden and on which the whole fabric of society depended. Hence it was decreed that this heinous sin was to be punished by the death of the offenders. 'So shalt thou put evil away from among you.'

Zion Gate in the south-west wall of the Old City of Jerusalem. It is so named because it gives access to Mount Zion from the City. Archaeological excavations show that the City of David (Zion) was located on the south-eastern hill, bounded by the Kidron Valley on the east and the Tyropoeon Valley to the west, rather than its traditional position.

The battle scars visible on this gate date from 1949 when the gate was the focal point for possession of the Jewish Quarter of the Old City.

So far, however, had Israel fallen from the high moral standard demanded of them as God's chosen people that the death penalty had long lapsed and the severest punishment in the days of Christ was to deprive the woman of her dowry and to give her a 'bill of divorcement'.

On any other occasion the rulers of the Jews would have allowed the husband of the immoral woman to appear before a properly constituted court, and on her guilt being established they would have pronounced their judgement. But as the rulers discussed this case among themselves, they saw here an opportunity to set a trap for Jesus.

Why not put the case to Him and ask His judgement in the light of the law of Moses? If He upheld the extreme penalty of the law they could claim that they were more merciful than Jesus. If He acquiesced in their weakening of the law they would be able to say that He had submitted to the ruling of the rabbis. While if the woman expressed penitence and Jesus counselled mercy He could be charged with undermining the morality of the nation.

Some have thought that the rulers may have conceived an even more dastardly plan, namely, that if Jesus pronounced sentence on the woman according to the law of Moses they might have carried out the sentence and then had a report conveyed to the Roman governor that Jesus had ordered an execution without first seeking ratification from the Roman authorities. This would certainly have resulted in His own immediate arrest and summary execution.

Whether this terrible scheme entered their minds we do not know but the plan of demanding judgement of Jesus certainly commended itself, and without bothering to find the husband, they hurried the humiliated woman to Him.

'Master,' they said to Him in pursuance of their plan, 'Moses in the law commanded us, that such should be stoned: but what sayest thou?'

Jesus did not fall into the trap. He knew that their addressing Him as 'Master' was insincere and intended as flattery in order to gain His favourable attention.

He knew also that there was no true devotion to the law of God in their hearts, for in countless ways they had altered and accommodated it to their own laxity and sin. Indeed, He read in their eyes guilty secrets which they had kept from their closest associates.

Righteously indignant at their hypocrisy, Jesus turned away from them, and, stooping down, began to write in the dust. At first the priests thought that He was seeking to evade the issue, and they repeated their demand. Slowly lifting His head, His eyes met theirs and He said solemnly, 'He that is without sin among you, let him first cast a stone at her.' Then He went on writing.

Leaning over they looked down upon the ground at what Jesus had traced and their faces blanched. For there open to the common gaze they read the hidden sins of their lives. They had brought this poor woman to be condemned in order to entrap Jesus, but instead they found themselves condemned before the judgement bar of Christ.

'Convicted by their own conscience,' their one anxiety now was to drop the whole case, and 'beginning at the eldest, even unto the last', they one by one turned and slunk away.

The crowd had drawn back from the embarrassing scene and in a few moments Jesus and the woman were alone. 'Woman,' said Jesus gently to her, 'where are those thine accusers? Hath no man condemned thee?'

'No man, Lord,' she tremblingly replied.

'Neither do I (or rather, shall I) condemn thee,' said Jesus, and placing His hand in

25

One of the delights of Jerusalem is a visit to the markets of the Old City, the souk, redolent of cinnamon, spices, shish kebab, leather, Turkish coffee, fresh bread and donkeys.
Here is a typical 'shop' dealing in religious souvenirs and other tourist mementos which are bought through the skill and enjoyment of bargaining.

forgiveness and blessing upon her head, He added, 'Go, and sin no more.'

In gratitude she threw herself at His feet assuring Him, between her sobs, that she would never sin in this way again. Well may we believe that the terrifying experience wrought true repentance in the woman's heart and that thereafter she lived a changed life.

This dramatic incident serves once again to reveal Christ's attitude to sinners and to sin. He did not in any way minimize the woman's guilt. He did not condone the sin. He called it by its right name. But Jesus also saw in the woman a victim of seduction, now truly repentant for her heinous offence, and He extended pardon and mercy to her.

For the callous and hypocritical rulers who cared nothing for her fate and were only too ready to use her downfall for their own evil ends, He had nothing but scorn and condemnation. They had asked that the sentence of the law be pronounced upon a poor sinner without regard to the mercy of God. By that law, therefore, without mercy they themselves should be judged.

The story reminds us, too, that though sin may be hidden successfully from the eyes of men, it is open to the eyes of Him who is able to read the thoughts and intents of the heart and is recorded in the books of heaven. One day those books will be opened and sinners will see written the things which they have sought to conceal as the scribes and Pharisees saw their sins written in the dust.

The Jewish rulers in the temple on this occasion were permitted to depart, but from the ultimate judgement of Christ there will be no escape.

How important it is, therefore, that we do not wait for Christ to uncover our sins, but that we send them 'before to judgement' that they may not in the final day rise to condemn us.

This chapter is based on John 8:1-11.

The Light of the World

At sunset on the first day of the Feast of Tabernacles the so-called 'Ceremony of Lights' took place. In preparation for this, two great golden candlesticks, each crowned with four bowl lamps, were erected in the Court of Women where the greatest crowds gathered. When darkness fell four lithe young priests ascended appropriately placed ladders carrying jars of oil and wicks made from priests' worn-out girdles. At a signal from below, the lamps were lighted and in a few moments the temple courts, all the rooftops of Jerusalem, and even the surrounding hills were lit up by the rising flames.

As the lamps flared up the multitude of worshippers in the courts below lit torches carried in their hands and, to the sound of the harps, cymbals, and trumpets, and the chanting of the 'Songs of degrees' by the Levite choir on the steps leading up to the Court of Israel, they sang and danced until long into the night.

As the ceremony of the golden pots of water from Siloam reminded the Jews of the provision of water in the wilderness, so the 'Ceremony of Lights' reminded them of the pillar of fire which illuminated the camp of Israel each night of their wilderness journeying.

Whether the ceremony was repeated each evening we do not know for certain, but the great candelabra certainly remained there during the feast, and it was as Jesus was teaching one morning beside the treasury chests in the Court of Women that He pointed to the great candlesticks and said, 'I

The souk has a mood of the East. Narrow shopping alleys with a jumble of wires, tin roofs, TV aerials and a wealth of merchandise which often drapes around your ears.

One interested glance and a vigorous sales campaign threatens to engulf the uninitiated.

am the light of the world; he that followeth me shall not walk in darkness, but shall have the light of life.'

Of all the titles by which Jesus described Himself during the course of His ministry none was more appropriate than this. For it was He who, in the beginning, spoke the creative words which flooded the new-made world with light, and it was through Him that the light of redemption had come to illumine the sin-darkened lives of men.

When the Pharisees in the crowd heard Jesus apply the Messianic prophecies of the coming of the divine 'Light' to Himself they were up in arms at once. 'Thy record is not true,' they cried in their blindness. According to the flesh He was indeed the Son of Mary, and the Carpenter of Nazareth, but if their minds had not been closed against Him they would have recognized that He was more than man, that He was, in fact, 'The Word made flesh'.

'I know whence I came, and whither I go', and 'my record is true', Jesus retorted, for in my 'witness of myself . . . I am not alone. . . . The Father that sent me (also) beareth witness of me.'

Had not an angel from heaven told Mary that the child that should be born of her would be 'the Son of God'?

Had not this same angel appeared to the shepherds, supported by multitudes of the heavenly host, to testify that the Babe of Bethlehem was none other than 'Christ the Lord'?

At His baptism did not a Voice from heaven testify to Jesus, 'Thou art my beloved son, in whom I am well pleased'?

And in the authority of His teaching and in the miracles that He had wrought the power of God had surely been constantly manifest.

But to the witness of the Father, the scribes and Pharisees and rulers of the Jews were wilfully blind. Therefore, said Jesus, 'Ye neither know me, nor my Father.' So 'I go my way, and ye shall seek me,' but 'whither I go, ye cannot come.' 'Ye . . . shall die in your sins.'

'Will he kill himself?' some of the Jews asked, completely failing to understand the import of His words.

Jesus brushed aside the foolish suggestion and told them plainly why they could not hope to follow Him. 'Ye are from beneath', He said; 'I am from above: ye are of this world; I am not of this world.'

Nonplussed at the plain and fearless witness of Jesus, the scribes and Pharisees could only lamely ask again who He was to make such claims. Jesus saw that it would serve no purpose to go again over all He had said to them, so He replied shortly, 'Even the same that I said unto you from the beginning.' But, He added, if they did not believe what He had already told them they would soon have the final evidence as to who He was, whence He came, and whither He was going, which they would not be able to gainsay.

'When ye have lifted up the Son of man,' He declared, 'then shall ye know that I am he.' If they refused to believe that He had lived by the power of God they would be compelled to recognize it in His death and resurrection.

Of course, none among His hearers, not even the disciples, realized the full import of this foreshadowing of His 'lifting up' upon the cross, but many who until now had held back from accepting Him were convicted by the authority of His words and 'believed on him'. To these He now turned. 'If ye continue in my word,' He said, 'then are ye my disciples indeed; and ye shall know the truth, and the truth shall make you free.'

Jesus knew that many of these new 'believers' still conceived of Him as the Messiah who would shortly deliver them from the Roman tyranny and restore their national

As soon as Jesus entered the temple He quickly became the centre of attraction and the target for the ridicule of the religious leaders.

independence. He knew too that when they discovered that He was not going to bring them national deliverance some would turn from Him and even demand His death. So He warned His followers that discipleship meant more than confessing Him in a moment of high emotion. Only if they 'continued' steadfast to the end would they be His true disciples.

The admonition is as necessary today as it was then, for all too often those who confess Christ in some great revival meeting or other occasion of spiritual fervour, fail to 'continue' when their faith is tested in the trying experiences of daily living. Again and again the Scriptures remind us that 'we are made partakers of Christ' only 'if we hold the beginning of our confidence steadfast unto the end.'

The unbelieving Jews had been listening with ever-growing anger as Jesus talked with those who had confessed belief in Him. When He spoke of the 'freedom through truth' which He offered they could contain themselves no longer, for the obvious implication was that the freedom which they claimed every morning when they prayed, 'Blessed be the Lord our God, King of the universe, who has made me a free man', was illusory.

'How sayest thou, ye shall be made free?' they demanded. 'We be Abraham's seed, and were never in bondage to any man.'

At once Jesus exposed their proud claim. They might be the physical descendants of Abraham but this did not confer any inalienable freedom upon them.

'Whosoever committeth sin,' He declared, 'is the servant of sin,' and in consequence he forfeits his right to a place in the house of the Father. Only the faithful Son 'abideth ever' in the house of His Father. Hence only if their status was changed from 'servants of sin' to 'sons of God' by His mediation could

Arab women have a tradition of wearing many bangles, beads and rings, so Jerusalem's markets are noted for the glitter of trinket stalls, which the tourists also find fascinating.

the freedom of the Father's house be restored to them.

Their own history should surely have convinced them that their freedom was dependent upon obedience to the commandments of God. Disobedience had time and again resulted in their being delivered into the hands of the enemies. In previous centuries they had been successively humiliated by bondage to Egypt, Assyria, Babylon, Persia, and Greece, and the occupation of their land by the Romans now made their claim to be free ludicrous.

Only 'if the son . . . shall make you free,' declared Jesus, shall ye 'be free indeed'.

'I know that according to the flesh you are

Abraham's seed,' Jesus said in effect, 'but by your actions you make it evident that you are alien to his house. If you had been Abraham's true children there could have been no enmity between you and me, the divine son. But now you seek to kill me.'

Further, Jesus pointed out, if they were truly the seed of Abraham they would 'do the works of Abraham'. Now Abraham was, above all things, obedient to the voice of God, for which reason he was called the 'father of all them that believe'. But they refused to listen to the Word of God when He declared it to them. 'My word hath no place in you.' Clearly then they were not Abraham's children.

Angered by the suggestion that they had forfeited their rights as the true seed of Abraham by giving their allegiance to sin, the Jews retorted, 'We be not born of fornication; we have one Father, even God.' Not only did they insist that they were true children of Abraham, but they claimed to be the true children of God as well.

But, replied Jesus, it was manifest that they were not children of God for the same reasons that they were not the true children of Abraham. 'If God were your Father,' He said, 'ye would love me; for I proceeded forth and came from God.' There could be no enmity between Him and them if they were all true children of Abraham, and there could be no enmity between them if they were the true sons of God.

Trying to turn this argument against Him the Jews replied that it was He, and not they, who was claiming falsely to be a true son of Abraham and of God. 'Thou art a Samaritan,' they said with reference to His physical ancestry, 'and hast a devil.'

Jesus took no notice of their counter-accusations, but reiterated what He had said before about the eternal consequences of their acceptance or rejection of Him. 'Verily, verily, I say unto you, If a man keep my saying, he shall never see death.'

'Now we know that thou hast a devil,' the Jews replied, seizing at a last straw to accuse Him. 'Art thou greater than our father Abraham, which is dead? and the prophets (who also) are dead?'

'Yes, I am,' Jesus said in effect for 'your father Abraham rejoiced to see my day: and he saw it, and was glad.'

'How can that be?' the Jews replied contemptuously. 'Thou art not yet fifty years old, and hast thou seen Abraham?'

'Verily, verily, I say unto you,' He said with solemn emphasis, 'Before Abraham was, I am.'

Often the Jews had heard Him claim God as His Father. Now in applying to Himself the divine title, 'I Am', He made the most astounding claim that had ever fallen upon human ears. He declared that He was none other than the Jehovah of the Old Testament who had called Abraham forth out of Ur of the Chaldees and revealed to him his high destiny as the father of the faithful people of God.

In the promises made to him, Abraham had seen 'afar off' the outworking of the plan of redemption. He had descried the better 'country' towards which his spiritual seed were bound, and had glimpsed the 'city, . . . whose Builder and Maker is God.' And he had 'rejoiced' as he saw the day of Christ's sacrifice and triumph.

To the unbelieving Jews this was the ultimate blasphemy and 'they took up stones to cast at him' from the piles lying around in the still unfinished temple. But once again, because His time was not yet come, Jesus escaped from them and, passing down one of the passages between the courts, He 'went out of the temple'.

This chapter is based on John 8:12-59.   31

Sight to the blind

It was not long after Jesus had declared Himself the 'Light of the world', as He taught in the temple, that He had an opportunity of demonstrating the truth of His words in a very practical way. One Sabbath day, as He was passing along a street leading to the temple, Jesus came upon a blind beggar. There was nothing unusual about this, as blind beggars were common enough in those days, and the busy lanes leading to the temple area were an obvious place to bring them into contact with the greatest number of people. This beggar, however, was particularly well known in the neighbourhood. For years he had loudly proclaimed to the passers-by that he had been born blind and craved, in consequence, their special sympathy.

Hearing the recital of his ills as they approached, the disciples began discussing among themselves how this affliction had come upon the poor man, and, of course, it was not long before they posed the question to Jesus. 'Master,' they asked, 'Who did sin, this man, or his parents, that he was born blind?'

Their question revealed the common attitude among the Jews towards physical affliction. On the basis of the warning in the Decalogue concerning the passing on of the consequences of sin from generation to generation, the Jews attributed all affliction to transgression, either on the part of the afflicted one, or in the lives of his parents, or even in his more remote forebears. 'There is no death,' declared the Talmud, 'without sin, and there is no suffering without iniquity.' And invariably, they believed, the punishment was appropriate to the sin committed.

The fact that the disciples thought the blind man might be responsible for his affliction even though he was born with it, reflects the fantastic teaching of the rabbis that sin might even be committed in the pre-natal state.

Actually, there was no reason for the Jews holding such limited views about responsibility for affliction, for in the book of Job it is made very clear that calamity may be Satan's malevolent work permitted by God, yet overruled by Him for the furtherance of His purposes and for the edification of men.

But Jesus did not, on this occasion, waste any time discussing Jewish misunderstandings about the cause of suffering. He was not concerned with tracing the affliction back to its source, but rather in making it an avenue of blessing to the poor sufferer and a means of glorifying God. So He answered, 'Neither hath this man sinned nor his parents: but (because of what he has suffered it is appropriate) that the works of God should be manifest in him.'

Both the man and his parents were sinners in common with all men, but their sin had nothing to do with the particular physical condition of the blind man. The cause, in fact, was irrelevant. To Jesus the poor man's condition was not a subject for theological diagnosis but for practical help.

'As long as I am in the world,' declared Jesus as He looked into the sightless eyes of the poor man, 'I am the Light of the world.' 'While it is day,' He added, 'I must work the works of him that sent me,' for 'the night cometh, when no man can work.'

Jesus was conscious that there was little time left for Him to go about 'doing good'. The 'day' of His earthly ministry was drawing to a close. While, therefore, the day of opportunity lasted, He must do the work for which His Father had sent Him. This was not to judge men with reference to their past, but

A blind man sits with his wares and personal possessions by the busy entrance to the Damascus Gate in Jerusalem.

32

Among the authentic biblical remains around Jerusalem is the Pool of Siloam. It dates from about 700 BC when King Hezekiah, realizing the danger of having a water supply outside the city walls, built a tunnel (right) 550 metres (600 yards) long, from the Gihon Spring (left) to the Pool of Siloam. The Gihon was the water source used by the Jebusites over 3,000 years ago during its earliest period known to archaeologists and has had a vital role in the city's history. One of the oldest Hebrew inscriptions ever found was recovered from the tunnel. It gave details of the moment when contact was made as the builders tunnelled from either end. Gihon was also the scene of the coronation of Solomon, King David's son. The waters of Gihon still flow through Hezekiah's tunnel and intrepid visitors, descending the entrance steps (left, inset) can still follow the course of this ancient piece of engineering skill.

to meet their need as He found them. So, approaching the pleading beggar, He moistened some clay from the ground with saliva and touched the poor blind eyes.

In the days of Jesus both clay and saliva were regarded as beneficial in eye complaints. Both Pliny and Suetonius mention them and Serenus Sammonicus specifically refers to the application of clay in the treatment of cataract. But we can hardly believe that the use of this procedure by Jesus was a recognition of any virtue in this primitive medicine.

The reason was doubtless twofold. On the one hand, Jesus wanted to arouse in the mind of the blind beggar a realization that somebody really cared for him, and to secure his co-operation in the restoration of his sight. On the other hand, Jesus intended by this miracle to take public issue with the rulers of the Jews. Hence He adopted a procedure which would involve prohibited Sabbath 'work' to which they would certainly object, namely the compounding of a remedy and its application when there was no immediate danger to life.

Jesus' act had the effect upon the blind man which He desired. Eagerly the man lifted his face towards Jesus and when He bade him, 'Go, wash in the pool of Siloam,' he rose unquestioningly to obey, though as yet no miracle had taken place.

Making his way down the Tyropoeon or Cheesemaker's Valley which descended

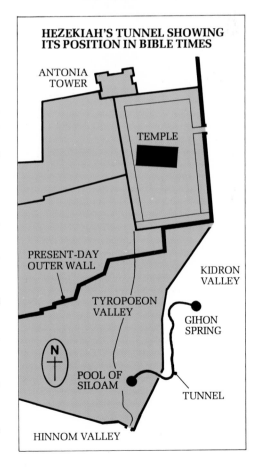

HEZEKIAH'S TUNNEL SHOWING ITS POSITION IN BIBLE TIMES

ANTONIA TOWER

TEMPLE

PRESENT-DAY OUTER WALL

KIDRON VALLEY

TYROPOEON VALLEY

GIHON SPRING

N

POOL OF SILOAM

TUNNEL

HINNOM VALLEY

between the horseshoe hills upon which Jerusalem stood, the beggar reached the pool just inside the city walls.

Feeling his way to the edge of the pool the blind beggar began to splash water over his face. As soon as the water touched his eyes the scales which covered them were detached and he saw clearly.

Transported with joy at the miracle, he jumped up and began to run back up the hill. As he neared his parents' home he was met by some of the neighbours. As they looked at the erstwhile blind beggar many could not believe their eyes. 'He is like him,' some said, but they could not believe that it really was the blind beggar they had known for so long. But the man, seeing their incredulity, cried out, 'I am he.'

At once the people crowded round and demanded, 'How were thine eyes opened?' 'A man that is called Jesus made clay, and anointed my eyes,' the man replied, 'and said unto me, Go to the pool of Siloam, and wash: and I went and washed, and I received sight.'

'Where is He?' they asked, anxious to see the Wonder-worker.

'I know not,' said the man, for, of course, he was still blind when he left Jesus and he did not see where his benefactor went.

So the neighbours took him along to the Pharisees, feeling that so notable an event should at once be reported to them. When the rulers of the Jews were told of the healing they were less interested in the blessing which had come to the man than in the fact that it had involved the violation of rabbinical Sabbath ordinances. Immediately, therefore, they called a meeting, probably of the minor Sanhedrin committee of twenty-three members, and before them the beggar was brought.

When the meeting was informed of what had happened a sharp division of opinion

developed among those present. Some said, 'This man is not of God, because he keepeth not the Sabbath day.' Others, however, perhaps including Nicodemus and Joseph of Arimathea, hesitated to condemn Jesus in this summary way. 'How can a man that is a sinner do such miracles?' they queried.

Unable to come to any unanimous conclusion on the matter they asked the man what impression he had gained of the one who had healed him. 'What sayest thou of him, that he hath opened thine eyes?'

The beggar was ready with his answer. In his mind there was no question but that Jesus must have worked the miracle by the power of God. 'He is a prophet,' the restored man declared confidently.

Annoyed that the beggar should dare to support Jesus against the authority of the Sanhedrin the rulers tried a new line of attack. They would minimize the miracle and argue that it was only ordinary medical skill and not supernatural power which Jesus has exercised. First, therefore, they sent for the man's parents to see if he was really as blind as he had been reported to be.

The manner in which the rulers' questions were asked put the man's parents on their guard. They knew the Pharisees disapproved of Jesus and had given notice that any who acknowledged His claims would be excommunicated from the synagogue, and they did not wish to get mixed up in any controversy about Him. They therefore confined their replies to the identification of their son and testimony as to his life-long affliction. 'We know that this is our son,' they said, 'and that he was born blind. But,' they went on warily, 'By what means he now seeth, we know not; or who hath opened his eyes, we know not: he is of age; ask him: he shall speak for himself.'

Satisfied that the parents were too fearful to support their son's story, the Pharisees

The Pool of Siloam, now called Berekhat ha Shiloah. Only a small part remains and bears little resemblance to the pool Jesus knew.

A church built over the pool in the fifth century was destroyed by the Persians in AD 614. Today a mosque marks the place where the blind man received his sight.

turned again to the restored man intending to frighten him also into a disavowal of Jesus. 'Give God the praise,' they urged: 'we know that this man is a sinner.'

But the beggar was not to be overawed by the weight of authority as his parents had been, nor was he impressed with their claim to superior knowledge in the face of what he knew had happened to him.

'Whether he be a sinner or no, I know not,' he replied: 'one thing I know, that, whereas I was blind, now I see.'

The Pharisees were taken aback by the man's unanswerable logic and could only demand again to know what Jesus had done that was so marvellous.

Emboldened by their evident embarrassment the man now waxed sarcastic. 'I have told you already, and ye did not hear,' he said. 'Wherefore would ye hear it again? Will ye also be his disciples?'

Angrily they turned on him for daring to suggest that they had any thoughts of countenancing Jesus as a prophet of God. 'Thou art his disciple,' they declared; 'but we are Moses' disciples. We know that God spake unto Moses; as for this fellow, we know not from whence he is.'

The man was now positively enjoying the argument and tauntingly replied, 'Why herein is a marvellous thing, that ye know not from whence he is, and yet he hath opened mine eyes.' They were supposed to be the religious leaders of the Jews, and here was a Man ministering to the suffering and needy in God's name and yet they professed that He was unknown to them!

'Since the world began,' he declared, 'was it not heard that any man opened the eyes of one that was born blind. If this man were not of God, he could do nothing.'

Such impertinence the Pharisees could not tolerate. The idea that an ignorant beggar should instruct them, the accredited religious leaders of the nation, was too much for them. Yet they could not counter his argument. They could only take refuge in abuse. 'Thou wast altogether born in sins, and dost thou teach us?' they replied angrily. 'And they cast him out'.

It was a courageous stand on the part of the healed beggar, for excommunication meant 37 social ostracism and the denial of all spiritual privileges. Probably the initial sentence was for thirty days with the threat that if he did not recant it might be extended to a life sentence, which would even deprive him of a religious burial at his death.

Shunned by his friends and even by his family for fear of being involved in his excommunication, the poor man must have felt his punishment keenly. But no sacrifice made for God ever passes unnoticed, and quickly Jesus sought him out to encourage and help.

'Dost thou believe on the Son of God?' Jesus asked him.

The man had recognized Jesus as a prophet, and thinking that He was now offering to introduce him to the One from whom He had received authority the man replied, 'Who is he, Lord, that I might believe on him?'

'Thou hast both seen him, and it is he that talketh with thee,' Jesus replied, as plainly and unequivocally as He had done to the Samaritan woman at the well of Jacob. Without hesitation the man replied, 'Lord, I believe,' and falling to the ground at Jesus' feet he worshipped Him.

That Jesus accepted this act of worship was confirmation of His divine claims. Had He been only a man He would have refused worship as Paul and Barnabas did in Lystra, and as the angel who appeared to John refused John's worship. The fact that He accepted divine honour corroborated His claim to be the Son of God.

Though Jesus rejoiced that His true nature was recognized by the restored beggar, He was grieved that the leaders of the Jews, who should have recognized Him, refused to do so. Half to Himself He said: 'For judgment I am come into this world, that they which see not might see; and that they which see might be made blind.'

Jesus had come to bring the blessings of salvation to those who were willing to receive Him, but inevitably those who rejected Him put themselves outside the sphere of His grace.

The Pharisees who were standing by sensed that Jesus' comment was a condemnation of their attitude to Him and they quickly retorted, 'Are we blind?'

'If ye were blind, ye should have no sin,' Jesus replied. 'But now ye say, We see; therefore your sin remaineth.'

No man is held responsible for failing to apprehend what he has not the capacity to see. But the Pharisees boasted of their spiritual discernment and so, on their own admission, were responsible for their judgements. This being so, they condemned themselves for refusing to recognize the long-foretold Messiah when He came.

Today there are many who similarly claim great enlightenment. They say 'We see' and 'We know', and yet they are willingly ignorant of all the evidence provided by the life, death, and resurrection of Christ, of the truth of the Gospel. They equally judge themselves unworthy of the mercies of God and condemn themselves to exclusion from His ultimate purpose.

Jesus spoke truly when He said that He judged no man. Men judge themselves by their acceptance or rejection of Him, and when He assumes the prerogative of judgement at the last day it will be merely to confirm the judgement which men have pronounced upon themselves by their attitude to Him.

If we deny Him in this life He cannot but deny us before the Father, but if we confess Him from our hearts and in our lives He will confess us before His Father and invite us to share His kingdom of light and life.

This chapter is based on John 9:1-41.

38

The Good Shepherd

Because the hilly character of many parts of Palestine makes agriculture difficult, sheep rearing has always been one of the chief occupations of the people. It was, therefore, a readily understood figure of speech to the children of Israel when God likened Himself to the Great Shepherd and described them as the sheep of His pasture, and their spiritual leaders as His undershepherds.

The comparison was indeed most apt, for just as the life of the shepherd in Bible lands is bound up with his flock as he leads them from pasture to pasture, and untiringly protects them day and night from the attacks of marauding animals, so God's supreme desire is to nourish and lead and protect His human flock until they are safely gathered into the fold of His eternal kingdom.

An Arab boy tends his sheep as they forage for food among tough, spikey plants in the desert-like conditions of the Jordan Valley near Jericho.

Describing the way in which God brought forth His people out of Egypt and guided them through the wilderness, David, himself from the sheepfold, said, 'Thou leddest thy people like a flock by the hand of Moses and Aaron.' And in the most beautiful psalm which he composed, the sweet singer of Israel tells of the divine Shepherd's individual care for one of His flock. 'The Lord is my Shepherd,' he declared; 'I shall not want.'

When Israel turned away from God in their iniquity, He described them as 'lost sheep'. 'Their shepherds have caused them to go astray,' He declared through Jeremiah, 'they have turned them away on the mountains: they have gone from mountain to hill, they have forgotten their resting place.'

But He assured them through Isaiah that if they would return to Him He would once again 'feed his flock like a shepherd: he shall gather the lambs with his arm, and carry

them in his bosom, and shall gently lead those that are with young.' And Ezekiel looked forward to the day when the sheep would be gathered again into one flock and God would 'set up one shepherd over them'.

These pictures of the divine Shepherd and His sheep from the Old Testament Jesus applied to Himself and His work in some of the most beautiful of His parables.

It must have been shortly after the healing of the blind beggar that Jesus told those who listened to Him in the temple that He was none other than the true Shepherd of Israel who had come to deliver them from the false shepherds who had so long being leading them astray.

'Verily, verily, I say unto you,' He began, 'he that entereth not by the door into the sheepfold, but climbeth up some other way, the same is a thief and a robber. But he that

Grazing sheep in the lunar-like Jordan Valley, where temperatures during the summer months reach 38-49℃ (100-120°F).

entereth in by the door is the Shepherd of the sheep. To him the porter openeth; and the sheep hear his voice: and he called his own sheep by name, and leadeth them out.'

Not only was Jesus by His life and teachings revealed as the true Shepherd while the rulers of Israel were condemned as false shepherds, but, Jesus added, His own true sheep would also be distinguished by their response to His call.

It was a common practice among the shepherds in Palestine to have a large sheepfold capable of holding all the flocks which grazed in one valley or upon one hillside. When night came the shepherds would lead their flocks to the common fold where they

41

would be enclosed for the night. This saved each shepherd going to the expense of building a fold for himself and it also enabled them to take turns in guarding the flocks during the night.

In the morning the shepherds entered the fold, and each with his own peculiar call would gather his flock. The sheep at once recognized their own shepherd's call and soon the sheep were divided and following their own shepherds to pasture for the day.

If one of the shepherds had tried to call the sheep of another, he would have been quite unable to do so, and if he sought to drive them into his flock they would run quickly away.

In the same way, said Jesus, when the true Shepherd 'putteth forth his own sheep, he goeth before them, and the sheep follow him: for they know his voice. And a stranger they will not follow, but will flee from him; for they know not the voice of strangers.'

Those, therefore, who listened to, and followed Him were thereby shown to be the sheep of God's flock, while those who turned from Him revealed that they did not belong to Him. This was clearly demonstrated in the response of the healed beggar to Jesus. The false shepherds had sought to lure him away after them, but he had heard the call of the true Shepherd and unhesitatingly followed Him.

'My sheep here my voice, and I know them, and they follow me,' Jesus said on another occasion. Just as plainly He told those who rejected His words, 'Ye believe not, because ye are not of my sheep, as I said unto you.'

Having revealed Himself as the true Shepherd to whom God's flock will respond and whom they will follow, Jesus told another parable in which He represented Himself not as the Shepherd, but as the Door of entrance into the fold of God.

'Verily, verily, I say unto you,' He explained, 'I am the door of the sheep.' This was in harmony with Jesus' description of Himself elsewhere as the 'Way' by which we have access to the fold of God.

Many, He said, had gone 'before', seeking to lead men after them and opening enticing doors for them to enter, but those had all been 'thieves and robbers' bent on destroying, and not preserving the lives of their victims. The scribes and Pharisees Jesus placed in this category.

But now, said Jesus, 'by me if any man enter in, he shall be saved, and shall go in and out, and find pasture,' the rich pasture of God's spiritual provisions and the quiet waters of God's peace.

'The thief,' He went on, 'cometh not, but for to steal, and to kill, and to destroy: I am come that they might have life, and that they might have it more abundantly.' Jesus' miracles of healing, and even of raising the dead, revealed His desire to bring abundant physical life to those who had lost it. His ministry to the souls of men showed His even greater concern to bring spiritual life to those who were dead in trespasses and sins. And beyond this life He held open the door to the perfect and never-ending life of His kingdom.

Into the fold of God there is one Door, and one only, and that door is Christ. The Door is wide enough to admit all who will enter. 'Him that cometh to me, I will in no wise cast out.' It is also strong enough to protect from every incursion of the enemy of souls. 'They shall never perish, neither shall any man pluck them out of my hand.'

In a third parable, as He sat and taught in the temple courts, Jesus returned to the theme of the true Shepherd, contrasting Himself this time with the hired shepherds whose interest in the flock was only for the wages which they received.

The underground water cistern (left) was constructed during the reign of Ahab in the ninth to eighth centuries BC, and is 16 metres (52 feet) in depth. It provided a constant water supply under siege conditions.

(Bottom left) An excavated four-room house from the same period.

Twelve kilometres (eight miles) north of Galilee stood the largest city in Canaan, Hazor. Dwarfing Jerusalem, it had a population of 35,000 when it fell to Joshua about 1500 BC. It was rebuilt by the Canaanite King Jabin. He and his commander Sisera met defeat twenty years later at the hands of Deborah and Barak the Israelites.

The city was levelled by the Assyrians in 732 BC but excavations in 1955 revealed the scale of this great city.

'He that is an hireling,' He said, 'and not the shepherd, whose own the sheep are not, seeth the wolf coming, and leaveth the sheep, and fleeth: and the wolf catcheth them, and scattereth the sheep. The hireling fleeth, because he is an hireling, and careth not for the sheep.'

The Jewish laws outlined quite specifically the limits of responsibility of the hired shepherd. If, for example, one wolf attacked the flock the shepherd was responsible for 43 driving it off. But if two or more wolves attacked the flock, or if the shepherd should be faced with a lion or a bear so that his own life was endangered, he was not regarded as negligent if he abandoned the flock to their fate in order to save his own life. He would be something more than a hireling if in such circumstances he jeopardized his life to save his sheep.

David showed himself to be a good shepherd indeed when he stood his ground against a lion and a bear to save his father's flock. And Jesus, as the greater Son of David, proved Himself the Good Shepherd when He was willing not only to come down into the world to share the perils of the wilderness and to grapple with man's spiritual enemies, but even to lay down His life for the sheep.

'I am the Good Shepherd,' He said; 'The Good Shepherd giveth his life for the sheep.'

Jesus was under no obligation to save mankind, for they had wilfully committed themselves to the care of the false shepherds. But voluntarily He came down from the courts of heaven, and faced the agony and shame of the cross in order to wrest God's sheep from the grip of the enemy of souls.

No wonder that Jesus was able to say, 'Therefore doth my Father love me.' For the love with which 'God so loved the world' was manifest in the supreme sacrifice of the Son.

As Jesus ended His parables of the Good Shepherd's love He reminded His Jewish hearers that they were by no means the only ones for whom the supreme sacrifice would be made. The exclusive Jews liked to think of themselves as the sole recipients of the grace and favour of God, and of the Gentiles as outcasts who were beyond the pale of God's kingdom. Jesus, however, warned them that they were in grave danger of being deprived of the heritage of Abraham, while those whom they regarded as outside the scope of

divine favour would inherit the blessings which they forfeited. 'Other sheep I have,' He told them plainly, 'which are not of this fold: them also I must bring, and they shall hear my voice; and there shall be one fold, and one Shepherd.'

The Jews had entirely misunderstood the purpose of God when they refused to share the privileges of the kingdom. The prophets had declared that Messiah was to be a light not only to Israel but also to the Gentiles that He might bring God's salvation 'unto the end of the earth'. In harmony with this Jesus had declared more than once that He was 'the Light of the world.' Now again, He reminded the self-centred Jews that He would gather His sheep from other folds than theirs. One day, when they had had their opportunity, the Gospel would go to the Gentiles and they would hear and answer His call.

When Jesus finished speaking, the people began to break up into groups and move away, discussing among themselves the challenging claims which He had made. Said many of them, 'He hath a devil, and is mad; why hear ye him?' But others said, 'These are not the words of him that hath a devil.' These alternatives, between which those who heard Jesus in the temple had to decide, are the alternatives with which Jesus still confronts men today. If the words of Jesus concerning Himself were false, then, indeed, He was an impostor. But if, like so many of those who saw and heard Jesus in the flesh, we are constrained to declare, 'These are not the words of Him that hath a devil,' nor can His works be credited to such a source, we must, with them, confess that the claims of Jesus are true. Then we too will answer the Good Shepherd's loving call and seek the peace and joy, the sustenance and protection of the strong fold of God.

This chapter is based on John 10:1-21.

44

The Good Samaritan

By the time Jesus had completed His tour of Samaria, the Feast of Dedication was drawing near. So, with His disciples, He descended the Jordan Valley, intending to take the main highway up through the wilderness of Judea to Jerusalem. Quite likely He stayed the night in Jericho. This was not the city captured by Joshua. Ever since the curse pronounced upon it the old town had lain buried under great mounds some miles to the north, while a new city has grown up astride the Jerusalem road much nearer to the hills.

It may have been in the evening after Jesus' arrival in Jericho that 'a certain lawyer' came to the house where He was lodging and begged leave to talk with Him. 'Master,' he began, 'what shall I do to inherit eternal life?'

The question seemed sincere enough, but actually it had been carefully prepared at the instigation of the priests and rulers to test the orthodoxy of Jesus. He immediately recognized this and replied, in the language of one teacher of the law to another, 'How readest thou?'

Without hesitation the lawyer answered with the verse of Scripture regularly recited by pious Jews every morning and evening in the Shema, or Jewish creed: 'Thou shalt love the Lord thy God with all thy heart, and with all thy soul, and with all thy strength, and with all thy mind; and thy neighbour as thyself.'

Detecting in his ready answer the self-satisfied complacency of a man who believed himself to be complying fully with the law's demands, Jesus said, 'Thou has *answered* right: this *do*, and thou shalt live.'

The intonation in Jesus' voice put the lawyer on the defensive. In common with the Jewish interpretation of his day this lawyer restricted his 'neighbours' to fellow Israelites. No Gentile could have any claim upon the love of a Jew. So he prepared himself for a theological dispute. 'Who is my neighbour?' he demanded of Jesus.

Jesus did not allow Himself to be drawn into an argument, but instead began to tell a story about the Jericho Road and the travellers who passed along it on their way to and from the capital.

'A certain man,' Jesus began, 'went down from Jerusalem to Jericho, and fell among thieves, which stripped him of his raiment,

The road from Jerusalem to Jericho where it descends below sea level.

A visit to the 'Inn of the Good Samaritan' guarantees business for a friendly old Arab and his camel.

and wounded him, and departed, leaving him half dead.'

Such tragedies were not infrequent on the wild road which descended steeply from the ridge of the Mount of Olives for some twenty-one miles through the barren wilderness of Judea to the Jordan plain. Indeed the caves in the parched brown hills had, from earliest times, not only been the haunt of religious hermits and ascetic communities but also of robbers waiting to hold up unwary travellers along the lonely road. In the days of Jesus it well merited its grim title, 'the ascent of blood'.

Continuing His story Jesus told how, 'by chance', while the wounded man lay dying by the roadside, 'there came down a certain priest that way'.

This, too, was an entirely likely occurrence, for Jericho was one of the priestly cities of Palestine and some 12,000 temple servants dwelt there. According to their rotas of duty they must constantly have been travelling between Jericho and Jerusalem, and the man Jesus cited was doubtless just returning home after a spell of duty in the temple.

That his sacred responsibilities had left little impress upon his sympathies for his fellow men, however, was evident as soon as he saw the mangled form. For, averting his gaze, he 'passed by on the other side'.

Probably the priest excused himself on the grounds that if the man was beyond hope, there was no sense in his exposing himself to ceremonial defilement by contamination with the dead. Moreover, if the robbers were still around he himself might share a like fate if he tarried long. So he hurried away from the scene of the attack.

Before very long a Levite came by. This man did have enough sympathy, or perhaps it was curiosity, to go over and look upon the wounded man, but he too decided that he could do nothing and 'passed by'.

Finally, 'a certain Samaritan, as he journeyed, came where he was'. This man had not been to Jerusalem to worship, but was most likely on a business trip to Perea.

When the Samaritan looked upon the poor man and saw that he was a Jew he might have reminded himself that the Jews had no dealings with the Samaritans. But this did not weigh with him as he beheld the poor man's distress. Nor did he think for a moment of his own danger from the robbers. Instead, 'he had compassion on him'.

Without hesitation he went down on his knees behind the wounded man. He poured onto his wounds an emollient and antiseptic ointment of 'oil and wine', such as is still used in Syria, and bound them up with strips torn from his turban or from one of his own garments.

When he had made the man as comfortable as he could, the Samaritan lifted him gently onto his own riding ass, and, walking alongside, he 'brought him to an inn', or rather 'the inn', some distance farther down the road.

Without doubt, this one inn on the wild mountain road stood upon the site of the modern 'Inn of the Good Samaritan', about half-way between Jerusalem and Jericho and which is still frequented by travellers on the old road. Its present walls date only from the time of the Crusaders, who used it as a fort, but in the courtyard are fragments of ancient walls and rock cisterns which show that an earlier building stood on this spot in the first century of the Christian era.

All the evening after their arrival at the inn the kind Samaritan merchant personally tended the wounded man. 'On the morrow', when it was necessary for him to continue his journey, he gave the innkeeper two 'pence' or denarii and bade him care for the man until he was well enough to leave. As his gift was equal to two days' wages of a peasant he doubtless felt that this would be adequate, but in case it was not, he assured the innkeeper, 'Whatsoever thou spendest more, when I come again, I will repay thee.'

There Jesus ended His story and turning to the lawyer who had been listening intently, He asked, 'Which now of these three, thinkest thou, was neighbour unto him that fell among the thieves?'

The lawyer realized that there was only one answer to Jesus' question, but he could not bring himself to say that a Samaritan had proved himself more of a neighbour than his own co-religionists. So he evasively replied, 'He that showed mercy on him.'

Jesus did not press for a more precise answer, but, bidding the lawyer, 'Go, and do thou likewise,' He left him to ponder the lesson of the parable and went His way.

In this parable of the Good Samaritan, Jesus once again exposed the hypocritical religion of the Jewish leaders. The Old Testament, which they professed to expound, clearly taught that the 'stranger' was entitled to the same consideration as a fellow Israelite. There was therefore no justification for their narrow nationalistic interpretation of the term 'neighbour'. If they truly loved God they would show it by service to their fellow men, Jew or Gentile. Their love would have been as wide as God's.

Besides pointing the contrast between true religion and the hypocritical profession of the Pharisees, the parable of the Good Samaritan was yet another wonderful portrayal of the character and mission of Jesus. The man robbed and left for dead well typified the victims of Satan's malice. God had appointed the spiritual leaders of Israel to minister His consolation and salvation to such, but, like the priest and the Levite, they 'passed by on the other side'. Because of their failure, Jesus came down to earth to bind up the wounds that sin had made. And on the cross He bore the whole cost of man's restoration to spiritual life and health.

Jesus is the Good Shepherd. He is also the Good Samaritan.

This chapter is based on Luke 10:25-37.

In the home of Mary and Martha

The morning following His conversation with the lawyer of Jericho, Jesus set out for Jerusalem along the road which had provided the setting for His parable of the Good Samaritan. Instead, however, of going right on into the city, He stopped in the little village of Bethany on the eastern slopes of the Mount of Olives, about two miles short of Jerusalem, for there lived Lazarus, a loyal friend and disciple, and his two sisters, Martha and Mary.

Just when these folk became His followers we are not told, but they must have known Him well for Jesus found the same welcome in their home whenever He visited Jerusalem as He had found in the home of Peter in Capernaum.

There is, of course, no real evidence that the spot now pointed out as the home of Lazarus is correctly identified, but as one looks at the modern village spread out over the slopes of the mountain and surrounded by fields and groves of olives and figs, one can readily see how convenient and delightful a retreat Jesus found it after the tumult and confusion of Jerusalem just over the crest of the hill.

Lazarus was either a widower or unmarried and shared the home with his two sisters. Martha, the elder, and perhaps herself a widow, evidently took the lead in the management of the home, for the record states that she received Jesus into 'her house'. The family seem to have been in good circumstances and were able to provide Jesus with every comfort during His visits. Lazarus was doubtless an influential man in the community.

The striking difference in temperament between the two sisters became apparent as soon as Jesus arrived. Practical Martha immediately began bustling around preparing a royal repast for Jesus. But for Mary the visit was a spiritual privilege of which she must take the fullest advantage. Oblivious of the fact that all the burden of hospitality was falling on her sister, she seated herself at Jesus' feet and was soon deep in converse with Him.

In his account of the visit Luke does not explain the reason for Mary's profound devotion to Jesus, but gathering together several strands from the other Gospel writers we begin to see what Mary owed to Him.

There is good reason to believe that Mary of Bethany was identical with Mary of Magdala out of whom Jesus cast seven devils during one of His missionary tours in

One thing is needful; and Mary
hath chosen that good part.
LUKE 10/42

To-day as in the past, the Love of Jesus
seeks a refuge, where He is lovingly
expected and where He can rest.
He finds our hearts are filled with distractions
—people, work, our own interests—
He longs for us to empty our hearts and
lovingly receive Him.

Eins ist not —
Maria hat das gute Teil erwählt.
LUKAS 10/42

Jesu Liebe sucht heute wie einst ein Bethanien,
eine Herberge, wo man Ihn liebend erwartet

A tablet on a wall in Bethany offers a poignant comment on the hospitality of Lazarus, Mary and Martha. Written in English and German, these tablets are found at sites connected with the life and ministry of Jesus.

Galilee. It would appear that in her earlier years Mary had been led into sin so deeply that for shame, she left home and went to live with friends or relatives in Magdala on the shores of the Sea of Galilee. So low did she sink that she actually became devil possessed.

Visiting Magdala, Jesus found her and, arousing repentance in her heart, He cleansed her from the demon possession which had overtaken her in the depths of her sin.

Restored and changed beyond recognition. Mary returned home to be received with joy by her brother and sister. When, therefore, Jesus came to visit their home it is little wonder that Mary, even at the cost of Martha's displeasure, could not tear herself away from the presence of her Deliverer.

On the road from Jerusalem to Jericho stands the Muslim village of el-'Azariye, biblical Bethany. In the vicinity of the olive grove and the Greek Orthodox Church (foreground) the ruins of ancient Bethany have been excavated.

At first Martha was content to busy herself with the domestic duties, while her younger sister talked with Jesus; but after a time, when Mary showed no signs of coming to help, she began to feel hurt and annoyed that all the work was left to her. At last she could contain her resentment no longer and as she passed by on some domestic errand, she said to Jesus, 'Lord, dost thou not care that my sister hath left me to serve alone? bid her therefore that she help me.'

Though Martha's complaint was primarily against Mary and that Jesus should appeal to her sense of fairness, the suggestion that He did not 'care' was a veiled criticism of Him for allowing Mary to sit there idly while she did the work. But Jesus passed over the implied accusation and gently replied, 'Martha, Martha, thou art careful and troubled about many things.'

Jesus appreciated more than He could say the love she had for Him, which she showed by doing everything possible to make Him welcome. But He tried to show her it was not necessary to go to such trouble. His needs were simple and He would have enjoyed a dish of the simplest food if it had given Him more opportunity to talk with her about spiritual things. For energy and hospitality Martha left nothing to be desired. She was a perfect hostess, but in Jesus' eyes, she lacked 'one thing', and that was the deep spiritual love in the heart of her sister which kept her close beside Him.

'Mary,' He said, 'hath chosen that good part, which shall not be taken away from her.'

We are not told how Martha took the gentle rebuke. Perhaps it was not until Jesus was taken away from them that she realized why He was so anxious to talk with them and with Lazarus. But we may be sure that she sensed the deep earnestness of His appeal. On future occasions doubtless she concerned herself less with the house and her cooking, and gave Him opportunity to minister to her spiritual needs.

How grateful we should be for this intimate little glimpse into the hospitable home of Bethany, for it has a message for many a busy Martha today. We have reason to be profoundly thankful to those untiring souls whose greatest happiness is in making their homes places of welcome and hospitality to all who enter. But like Martha of old, it is possible for them to so wear themselves out in ministry that they are too tired to sit at the feet of Jesus in personal devotion and meditation. And in this there is grave spiritual loss.

No one has a right to make such demands upon the willing ministrations of our Marthas that they have no time to make provision for their own soul's good. And the busy Marthas should realize, too, that ministry to the needs of others must never be allowed to crowd out personal communion with God. Many, like Martha, find it easier to minister than to meditate. Their bent is for the active rather than the contemplative life, but neither is sufficient without the other. The active life of service needs constantly to be fortified and sustained by seasons of quiet communion with God.

Nor does this lesson need to be learned only by the Marthas who minister to the material welfare of their fellow beings; it needs to be learned by the Peters and Johns who minister the living Bread to the souls of men. If Jesus needed constantly to renew His spiritual strength for ministry to the multitudes by spending much time in communion with His Father, how much more necessary is it for His servants to sit at His feet if they are to gain and sustain the spiritual strength to work for Him.

This chapter is based on Luke 10:38-42.

The lost sheep found

In His parable of the great supper, Jesus told the guests in the Pharisee's house plainly that because they despised the Gospel invitation, it would be extended to others who would appreciate it. As they left the house they had an immediate demonstration of what Jesus had said when there 'drew near unto him all the publicans and sinners for to hear him.'

Seeking to disparage the popularity of Jesus and justify their own self-righteous exclusiveness, 'the Pharisees and scribes murmured, saying, This man receiveth sinners, and eateth with them.' In saying this they inferred that Jesus appealed to the publicans and sinners because He was of their sort, while their sense of holiness kept them from associating with unrighteous men. The truth, however, was just the opposite. Jesus mixed with sinners not because He was a sinner, or because He condoned sin, but because He had compassion upon sinners and sought to rescue them from the consequences of their sins. The exclusiveness of the Pharisees, on the other hand, was not an evidence of superior holiness, but of the selfish lovelessness of their lives and the hypocrisy of their profession.

Turning to His critics Jesus answered them with three of His best known parables, the lost sheep, the lost coin, and the lost or prodigal son.

Sheep and lambs content in the security of the fold in a desolate, hostile area near Heshbon in Jordan.

These parables were not just repetitions of the same lesson, but each emphasized a particular aspect of man's lost condition and the way back to God.

'What man of you, having an hundred sheep,' Jesus began, speaking not only to the scribes and Pharisees, but to the crowd which had gathered round, 'if he lose one of them, doth not leave the ninety and nine in the wilderness, and go after that which is lost, until he find it?'

In choosing this illustration Jesus knew that it would appeal to the listening crowd of Pereans, for the uplands on the other side of the lower Jordan valley contained rich grazing lands which supported large flocks of sheep. Back in Old Testament times, when Perea was part of the kingdom of Moab, it was particularly mentioned that the king of Moab was a 'sheep-master', and doubtless there were many shepherds among those who listened to Jesus. A hundred sheep was a typical Perean flock, just about the largest number that one shepherd could adequately care for.

The incident which Jesus related was no uncommon occurrence, for despite the shepherd's watchful care, every now and

The shepherd is a prominent biblical figure, which is understandable considering how important sheep farming was to the Jewish economy. The sheep was considered to be a stupid, timid, defenceless animal, characteristics that provided an apt symbol for sinful man, while God was symbolized as the devoted, protective, providing shepherd.

then a sheep would wander away, following patches of luscious herbage up some remote wadi, and become lost. Missing the bleating of the other sheep it would look up from feeding, only to discover that the rest of the flock were not in sight. Not knowing which way to go it might easily run farther and

farther away, and perhaps in its panic fall over a precipice or into some gully, where it would lie wounded and helpless and lost.

When evening came, however, the shepherd would number his flock as he drove them into the safety of the fold for the night, and discover that one was missing.

The shepherd of Palestine loved his sheep. He had a name for every one and the thought that one had strayed away and perhaps at that moment was lying wounded and help-less at the mercy of the wild beasts of the hills, would drive all thought of rest and refreshment from his mind. Even though only one sheep was lost it mattered to the shepherd. He must go out into the hills again and find it.

Leaving the rest of the flock in the care of one of his boys the shepherd sets off to scour the hillside. He knows the wild gullies up which a sheep might stray, and in the gather-ing darkness he picks his way across the stony slopes.

Soon in the distance he hears the faint bleat of the missing sheep. He makes his way down the steep declivity in the direction of the cry, pushing his way through brambles and thorn bushes until at last he sees the sheep lying where it has slipped and fallen. Perhaps it is only shaken, but maybe it has a broken leg or an even worse injury.

He has no words of scolding or anger for the sheep when he reaches it. He is only too happy to have found it before it was attacked by some beast of prey.

Nor does he begin to drive it back up the hillside. Tenderly he lifts it and sets it across his own strong shoulders just as Jesus told in His parable. 'And when he hath found it, he layeth it on his shoulders, rejoicing.'

Struggling up the steep hillside he makes his way back over the ridge to the sheepfold and home. If the sheep is uninjured he puts it with the other sheep in the fold. If it is hurt

53

he gently lays it down in a quiet corner, bathes its bruises, and sets the broken bone. Then he goes back to his home in the village, calls together his neighbours, and says, 'Rejoice with me; for I have found my sheep which was lost.'

More than once Jesus had called Himself the 'Good Shepherd' and in this story He again declares His love for His spiritual flock. It provides a vivid picture of how Israel had become lost in the wilderness of sin and how multitudes today are alienated from the fold of God.

All through their history Satan had sought to tempt Israel away from the care of the Great Shepherd by the allurements of the heathen nations around. How well he had succeeded in his evil design Isaiah revealed when he said of his people, 'All we like sheep have gone astray; we have turned every one to his own way.' And in His day Jesus described the Jews as the 'lost sheep of the house of Israel'.

The spiritual leaders of Israel should have been alert to recover the straying sheep, but all too often they showed themselves to be mere hirelings, interested only in their own comfort, and leaving their flock as 'sheep without a shepherd'.

Through Ezekiel, God described the faithless shepherds when He said of them: 'Woe be to the shepherds of Israel that do feed themselves! should not the shepherds feed the flocks?

'Ye eat the fat, and ye clothe you with the wool, ye kill them that are fed: but ye feed not the flock. The diseased have ye not strengthened, neither have ye healed that which was sick, neither have ye bound up that which was broken, neither have ye brought again that which was driven away, neither have ye sought that which was lost.

'And they were scattered, because there is no shepherd: and they became meat to all the beasts of the field, when they were scattered. My sheep wandered through all the mountains, and upon every high hill: yea, my flock was scattered upon all the face of the earth, and none did search or seek after them.'

It was because the unfaithful shepherds had left the sheep to their fate that Jesus, the Good Shepherd, came down from heaven into the dark and dangerous world to seek and find the lost.

In contrast with the false and faithless shepherds of Israel, Ezekiel describes prophetically the ministry of the Good Shepherd: 'For thus saith the Lord God; Behold, I, even I, will both search my sheep, and seek them out. As a shepherd seeketh out his flock in the day that he is among his sheep that are scattered; so will I seek out my sheep, and will deliver them out of all places where they have been scattered in the cloudy and dark day.'

'I will seek that which was lost, and bring again that which was driven away, and will bind up that which was broken, and will strengthen that which was sick.'

'And they shall no more be a prey to the heathen, neither shall the beast of the land devour them; but they shall dwell safely, and none shall make them afraid.'

While the parable applied in the first place to the lost sheep of the house of Israel it is, of course, equally true of lost mankind in all ages, for Jesus came not only to Israel, but to seek lost humanity. Indeed the parable may properly be viewed against the background of the whole universe of God, for, so far as we know, our earth is the one world of all the myriads which God created which has been marred by sin. Our earth is the one 'lost world' which Jesus came to seek and to save. And if there had been only one soul in this one world Jesus would have come in search of that one!

The parable makes very plain that it was

Tents of the nomadic Bedouin dot the sometimes harsh landscape. They have roamed Palestine's hills for centuries, raising sheep and goats for food, clothing and shelter. Small strips of land are cultivated where water is available.

solely due to the initiative of the faithful shepherd that the sheep was saved. It was lost by its own foolishness and stupidity, and if the shepherd had not gone out in search of it, it could never have found its own way back. It would have wandered hopelessly until it died of exposure, or was torn to pieces by marauding animals.

So also the soul that is lost in the wilderness of sin, through leaving the side of the Great Shepherd of the sheep, is impotent to find his own way back. It is only through the initiative of the divine Shepherd that his return to the safety of the fold of God is made possible. 'We love him because he first loved us.' It is not we who take the initiative in the search for God, but He who in His love and mercy sets out in search of 'that which was lost'.

This lesson of the parable stands out in direct contrast to the teaching of the rabbis. They declared that the sinner must first repent before God would condescend to extend His mercy to him. But Jesus taught, as the apostle Paul explained on another occasion, that it is 'the goodness of God' that 'leadeth thee to repentance'.

How far the divine initiative was prepared to go in seeking lost sinners was supremely seen when the Good Shepherd Himself went down even into the valley of the shadow of death in order that He might recover His lost sheep.

The work of the Good Shepherd was not finished when His earthly life came to an end. He is still seeking personally and through His under-shepherds His 'other sheep' who are lost in the wilderness of paganism and materialism. And today there is 'joy in heaven' over every lost sheep that He brings back to the fold.

Greater even than the 'joy of salvation' which comes to the sinner who finds the peace and shelter of the fold of God is the joy of the Saviour who 'shall see of the travail of his soul, and shall be satisfied' and of the Father Himself as He rejoices with singing over the redeemed.

When Jesus said that the 'joy in heaven over one sinner that repenteth' was 'more than over ninety and nine just persons, which need no repentance', He was not, of course, intending to suggest that restored sinners claim more of heaven's benediction and favour than those whose loyalty to God has never faltered, for that would make sin seem desirable. What He meant was that above the constant joy of heaven in the loyalty of God's faithful people is a special paean of praise as each long-lost sinner is brought back to the warmth and fellowship of the fold of God.

Perhaps there was also something of the ironical in the concluding words of Jesus, for certainly there was more joy in heaven over a publican or a sinner who returned to God than over the ninety and nine Pharisees who thought themselves 'just persons' standing in no need of repentance, but who were actually far from Him.

This chapter is based on Luke 15:1-7.

The lost coin

The menfolk in Jesus' audience had listened with rapt attention to the parable of the lost sheep. For the second illustration of His ministry to lost mankind, Jesus chose a domestic scene which would appeal to the women in the crowd. 'Either what woman having ten pieces of silver, if she lose one piece, doth not light a candle, and sweep the house, and seek diligently till she find it? And when she hath found it, she calleth her friends and her neighbours together, saying, Rejoice with me; for I have found the piece which I had lost.'

In Bible times the houses of the peasants usually consisted of one windowless room which was lighted, in the daytime, only by the open door. So if any small object was dropped by accident on the dusty earth floor, it would be no easy task to find it.

The woman in the parable, like all the married women of her time, wore upon her forehead an ornament called a 'samedi' or frontlet which, in her case, contained ten coins or drachma, received either as a present on her betrothal, or handed down as an heirloom from her mother. As she was busy about her work in the house one of the coins became loose and fell off, rolling away into the dust of the floor.

The lost coin had little intrinsic value, the ten drachma altogether being worth not more than about fifty pence. But each coin had a very great sentimental value. The woman was, therefore, much perturbed by her loss and could not rest until she had recovered the missing coin.

Lighting one of the little earthenware saucer lamps used to illuminate the humble home at night the woman took a brush and began systematically to sweep every part of the floor. At last she saw in a dark corner a silvery glint and, with a cry of delight, she bent down and picked up the half-covered coin.

Quickly she produced needle and thread and sewed it back into position on her frontlet. Then she called her friends from the nearby houses, and as they came running across to her door she cried, 'Rejoice with me; for I have found the piece which I had lost.'

The women who were listening smiled at one another as Jesus came to the happy ending of His story, for they knew that if they had lost one of their dowry coins they would have been just as worried, and equally delighted when they found it again.

When Jesus added, 'Likewise, I say unto you, there is joy in the presence of the angels of God over one sinner that repenteth,' they saw that, like the story of the lost sheep, it revealed the love of the seeking Saviour and the joy in heaven when lost souls are reclaimed for the kingdom of God.

Some features of this second parable were, of course, identical with that of the first.

Both the sheep and the coin were lost in the darkness, one on a dark mountainside and the other in a dark room, each suggesting the sorry plight of the sinner alienated from the love of God. Both also were diligently sought for, one by the faithful shepherd and the other by the diligent wife, and in each case the story ended with the finding of the lost and a joyful celebration.

There are, however, features peculiar to the parable of the lost coin which give special point to this second story.

If the sheep, with its proneness to wander, is a fit symbol of human folly and sin, the coin suggests the worth of a soul in the eyes of God. Jesus was willing to come down into this dark world to recover us from the dust, and clean up our tarnished lives so that we may once again 'show forth' His glory.

Again, it is to be noted that the sheep in the first parable lost itself by foolishly running from one attractive patch of herbage to another and failing to keep the shepherd in sight. The coin, on the other hand, could not in any way be held responsible for being lost. In like manner, there are souls who have known the fellowship of the flock of God, but have lost their way by foolishly following after the allurements of the world instead of keeping their eyes on Christ. There are also innumerable others who are not conscious of being lost because they have never known the love and fellowship of God.

In Jesus' day the lost sheep, perhaps, most strikingly portrayed the condition of apostate Israel, while the lost coin fitly represented the Gentiles who were ignorant of God's care. Jesus loved both. He sought after the 'lost sheep of the house of Israel' and He was equally anxious to recover the lost among the Gentiles.

A final contrast suggests itself. The lost sheep strayed far from the shepherd before it was recovered, but the coin was lost near at hand in the house where the woman lived.

A typical first-century dwelling house (above) unearthed and reconstructed at Chorazin, situated 3 km (2 miles) north of Galilee. On this site of a town condemned by Jesus for its resistance to His teaching, are the remains of an elaborate black basalt synagogue (below) destroyed in the second century. A sculptured frieze (left) is typical of the craftsmanship of its builders.

So while there are those who wander away and are lost, there may be also in our own homes, wives, husbands, children who are just as surely alienated from God and need to be sought for and recovered.

But whether Jew or Gentile, far away or near at hand, all who are lost are equally loved by God and the objects of diligent search by the seeking Saviour. And all arouse equal joy among the angels of heaven when they are gathered again into the safety and peace of the kingdom of God.

This chapter is based on Luke 15:8-10.

The prodigal's return

Jesus had contrasted His ministry to the lost with the hypocritical exclusiveness of the Pharisees in the parables of the lost sheep and the lost coin. Now He tells a third story which has been aptly called the king of parables, for it is probably the best known and best loved of all – the parable of the prodigal son.

The story itself provides a wonderful picture of parental love, while its spiritual application vividly depicts the follies of sin and the compassion of a forgiving God whose arms are ever open to receive the repentant sinner again to Himself.

The great difference between this parable and the two earlier ones is that in them the emphasis is on the seeking Saviour; in this it is on the returning sinner.

'A certain man,' began Jesus, 'had two sons: and the younger of them said to his father, Father, give me the portion of goods that falleth to me. And he divided unto them his living.'

The father of this Jewish family was a prosperous farmer who, in harmony with the practice of those days, had brought up his two boys to help him run his farm. The older boy was evidently perfectly happy at home and had no other desire than to work with his father while he lived, and then carry on the farm in partnership with his brother. The younger boy, however, was an adventurous youth and the thought of living all his life around his boyhood home appalled him. He had probably heard from friends who had been abroad of their thrilling life in Damascus or Alexandria, in Athens or Rome, and he longed to travel.

When he talked to his father about this desire, his father told him that there were

Believing Israel to be the 'promised land', it is ironic that the Jewish centre of worship, the historic temple area, is now an Islamic shrine. The present El Aksa mosque was built in AD 1034 after several previous structures were destroyed by earthquakes. It is Islam's holiest place after Mecca and Medina, and is erected over the area where King Solomon placed his magnificent palace just south of the temple. The Crusaders captured Jerusalem in 1099 and converted this mosque into their headquarters.

Near the main entrance are found the tombs of the murderers of Thomas à Becket, Archbishop of Canterbury. Saladin rededicated El Aksa to Islam (1187) and, followed by Suleiman and others, added to its structure.

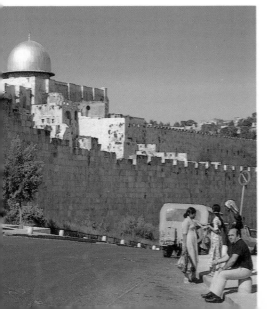

temptations and dangers as well as attractions in the big cities and he would be well advised to wait at least until he was older before going off on his own. But the boy was restless and impatient. He was not a child any longer, he declared, and was well able to look after himself.

Now there was nothing really wrong in the boy's desire to see the world and carve out for himself a career according to his tastes. All over the Roman Empire in those days there were Jewish colonies established by young men fired with the spirit of enterprise and adventure. The trouble with this young man was that he did not appreciate all the love and care which had been bestowed upon him from his earliest years, and he chafed at the restrains of home which were

59

for his good. He felt that his life had been dull and prosaic and restricted by comparison with the stories he had heard of the gaiety of city life. It was not so much a spirit of enterprise that fired his ambition, as that he wanted to do as he liked and have a 'good time'. Through a distorted sense of values he was ready to give up the solid blessings of home for the gaudy lights and garish pleasures of the sinful cities.

When the father saw that his headstrong boy would never be satisfied till he had tasted the free life of the world outside, he made no further attempt to dissuade him. He sought to counsel the boy from his years of experience but he recognized that ultimately his son was responsible for his own life and he must be permitted free choice in the use he made of it.

So when his son asked that he might be given his portion of the family inheritance to meet the expenses of his journey he put no obstacle in his way. He would have been perfectly within his rights to refuse to divide his inheritance during his lifetime, for it doubtless involved selling some of his land or stock. But, wise father that he was, he believed that there comes a time when parental authority ends and individual responsibility begins. So, having gained his elder son's grudging consent, he divided his fortune, giving one-third to the younger son and deeding the remaining two-thirds, according to Mosaic law, to the older boy who would have to care for his mother and unmarried sisters if his father should die before them.

A few days after the legal arrangements had been made, the younger son 'gathered all together, and took his journey into a far country'. He may have travelled by the Great North Road to Damascus or beyond, or he may have gone by the great southern highway or Way of the Sea into Egypt. He may

even have taken ship for Greece or Italy. His main idea was to get right away from home so that he would be free to do as he pleased.

Wherever it was that his choice took him it was very soon evident that his father's fears were justified, for instead of settling down to a useful career, he began to live riotously on the money he had brought with him. He sought the company of associates as wild as himself, who led him further into profligacy and sin. And in the pagan environment of this far country he not only forgot all the good counsel his father had given him, but he forgot his father's God as well.

Doubtless he told himself that when he had had his fling he would take up a steady career, but he found so many friends to help him spend his money that before he realized it his resources had dwindled to nothing.

Being of a generous nature he naturally thought his friends would help him in his difficulty, but he quickly discovered how false they were. In his poverty they all left him and 'no man gave unto him'. Such is the friendship that money brings! To add to these misfortunes 'there arose a mighty famine in that land' and soon 'he began to be in want'.

Because the famine had rendered so many of the people of the land unemployed it was impossible to get a job adequate to support himself and at last, in desperation, he pleaded with a citizen of the country to employ him as a swineherd in return for the barest famine rations. He could not have fallen lower. Even among the pagans the swineherd was regarded as beyond the pale of society, and to a Jew it was the ultimate degradation. Declared the Talmud, 'Cursed is the man who raises swine.' Yet even though he had so degraded himself, he was still unable to get enough to eat, and to allay the pangs of hunger he actually contemplated eating the carob pods fed to the pigs. It

The carob or locust tree is native to the Mediterranean coasts, where its long pods are commonly used for feeding domestic animals. They are rich in sugar and protein, and were food for John the Baptist and a possible means of survival for the prodigal son.

was an abstemious diet for John the Baptist to subsist on carob beans, but even he did not descend to eating the pods, which were only suitable for animal fodder.

Whether in His story, Jesus intended any reference to the Jewish saying that 'when Israel is reduced to the carob tree they become repentant', we cannot say, but it was as the young prodigal fingered the carob husks, while his filthy herd wallowed around in the mire, that he 'came to himself'. He began to ponder the steps that had brought him to his present plight. All his illusions were now gone and he realized what a fool he had been. Back at home his father's 'hired servants' had 'enough and to spare'. Yet 'I perish with hunger', he said bitterly. He was not even a hired servant. He was a slave to circumstances.

Once he had thought of home as drab and confining. Now it seemed to him like heaven itself. But how could he expect to be received back again after the shameless way he had treated his parents? Certainly he

deserved to be disowned by them for ever.

But then a thought came to him. If he could no longer hope to be a son, he would be infinitely better off as one of his father's servants than as he was now.

'I will arise and go to my father,' he decided, 'and will say unto him, Father, I have sinned against heaven, and before thee, and am no more worthy to be called thy son: make me as one of thy hired servants.'

So saying he arose and, telling his employer that he was going back to his own country, he set off, begging his way from city to city along the road.

All the time that the young man had been away he had never written home, but he had been constantly in his parents' thoughts. As the shepherd grieved for his lost sheep and the woman for her lost coin, the devoted father yearned for the return of his lost son. Time and again he would go onto the roof of his house and gaze along the white thread of road which vanished over the hill, wondering if he would ever see his boy again.

One day he stood looking, almost vacantly, along the road when he noticed a familiar form approaching. The youth was still far away. He looked tattered and unkempt and he staggered along as if he were weak and sick, but there was no mistak- 61

ing the figure. It was his young son coming back. Not stopping even to tell the family, he descended the outer steps leading to the courtyard and ran out into the road.

The returning boy, as he plodded along the road, strained his eyes to catch a glimpse of someone he knew, and when he saw his aged father come out onto the road and begin to run towards him his heart pounded within him. He quickened his steps, framing his confession as he drew near.

As they met the boy was about to fall in contrition to the ground, but his father flung his arms around him in a fond embrace and kissed him again and again. The ragged travel-stained garments and the thin, drawn face of the boy told their tragic story only too well, but this only heightened the joy of the old man as, with tears in his eyes, he clung to his long-lost son.

Gently releasing himself from his father's arms the boy began his prepared confession, 'Father,' he said, 'I have sinned against

After winter's cold and rain, spring warmth and sunshine brings a profusion of flowers.

heaven, and in thy sight, and am no more worthy to be called thy son.'

But he got no farther. Love needed to hear no more. Calling to the servants who had followed him down the road, the father bade them, 'Bring forth the best robe, and put it on him; and put a ring on his hand, and shoes on his feet.' And as father and son walked arm in arm towards the house the servants hurried off to do as they were bidden.

The now happy father asked no questions about how his boy had been reduced to this terrible plight. He did not scold him for going away. It was sufficient that he had come back. He only wanted to begin again where their lives as father and son had been broken off.

Whether the returned prodigal ever told his father that he had intended asking if he could be a servant in his household we do not know, but the clothes which the servants brought made it evident that no such thought ever crossed their master's mind.

The robe was a rich stola such as would be worn by the son of a wealthy father. And as his poor rags were replaced by it the boy knew that he was coming back as a true son again.

When sandals were put on his bruised and naked feet he realized that he was leaving his bare-footed servitude behind for ever.

And when his father himself put a ring on his finger he knew that he was being received back into favour and high regard. It was unbelievable but true.

And this was only the beginning of his welcome home. 'Bring hither the fatted calf,' the father ordered, 'and kill it; and let us eat and be merry: for this my son was dead and is alive again; he was lost and is found.'

Without delay the feast was prepared and soon father and son, with a few guests hastily called, were reclining before a generous repast. With the long-lost son in the

seat of honour 'they began to be merry'. The prodigal's restoration was complete!

Simply as a portrayal of parental love the story of the prodigal's return is most heart-moving, but beyond that it is full of spiritual meaning. The attitude of the loving and wise father to his restless son strikingly exemplifies the relation between God's sovereign authority and man's free will. The father could have refused his son the money to leave home because he knew that his son would waste it and get himself into trouble. But if he had taken a strong line, his son would have remained at home in subservience to his authority rather than from love for his father. Ever after he would have cherished a sense of injustice.

In the same way God could have prevented our first parents from transgressing in Eden. He could have prevented Satan's rebellion in heaven. But if God had compelled obedience on the part of Satan and Eve, angels and men would thereafter have served Him from fear rather than from love.

In the picture of the father allowing his son to do what he liked with the resources made available to him we see God deliberately limiting His own authority and even permitting the prostitution of His gifts in order to allow man the exercise of free choice and to teach him the bitter consequences of disobedience.

But just as the devoted father was deeply grieved at the ingratitude of his son, so God was grieved 'at his heart' at the defection of our first parents and by every wayward sinner who has followed in their steps. 'How shall I give thee up?' is the cry of our loving heavenly Father for His estranged children.

The picture of the young prodigal reveals the fearful fascination of the 'pleasures of sin' and the impotence of man to release himself from their ever-tightening grip. In the utter degradation to which the young

63

man sank we see the dire consequences of despising the counsel of God. Sin does indeed lead men 'far' from God, and sooner or later all its fair fruits turn bitter as gall. Far from achieving freedom and release, sin's victims find themselves reduced to the most abject slavery.

But the parable also shows that however far the sinner is separated from the heavenly Father's house there is always the opportunity of return for the soul that casts itself upon the forgiving love of God.

In the bitterness of calamity the young man 'came to himself' and to a true sense of values as have countless others who have travelled the same road. And like the prodigal they too have determined to go back 'home'.

It would, however, be a mistake to argue that, because the boy made the decision to go back home, this parable teaches that the sinner takes the first step towards his salvation. It was actually the remembrance of his father's patience and love that led the boy to decide to go home, and with us, as Paul says, it is the 'goodness of God' that leads us to repentance. The motivating force in the salvation of men is the seeking love of God. We love God, 'because he first loved us.'

The poor prodigal was perfectly right when he considered himself utterly unworthy of his former status in the family of his father. Nor has the sinner any valid claim on the heavenly Father's forgiveness and favour. But the parable vividly shows that though the sinner has no claim upon the mercy of God, divine Love is only waiting to bestow grace abounding upon the returning sinner. The father running to embrace his wayward boy in his arms most beautifully portrays the eagerness of God to receive the penitent sinner back into His arms of love.

On our lips as we come to Christ is the confession, 'I have sinned . . . and am not worthy.' But just as the father broke in upon his son's confession with an assurance of forgiveness full and free, so we are assured that 'if we confess our sins, he is faithful and just to forgive us our sins, and to cleanse us from all unrighteousness.' Like the prodigal back from a far country we who 'were far off are made nigh by the blood of Christ.'

There is a deep significance in the clothing with which the joyful father reclothed the tattered figure of his son.

The prophet Isaiah describes the garments of the sinner as 'filthy rags' while the garments of righteousness which we receive in exchange are pictured as 'fine linen, clean and white.'

In several places in Scripture mortal man is commanded to remove his shoes in the presence of the majesty of God. To receive shoes from God then is to be welcomed into His presence.

The conferment of a ring by a monarch was a sign of honour and authority, as when King Ahasuerus gave a signet ring to Mordecai and Pharaoh to Joseph. To receive a ring from God is to be raised to a place of honour in His kingdom.

As the father made a feast for his son, so Christ will invite all His redeemed people to sit down to eat and drink with Him in His kingdom. 'Come, eat of my bread, and drink of the wine which I have mingled,' God will say. 'My soul,' says the Psalmist in eager anticipation of the feast, 'Shall be satisfied as with marrow and fatness.'

Lastly, the joyous announcement which the father made concerning his son, 'For this my son was dead, and is alive again; he was lost and is found,' will be gloriously true of every redeemed soul in the kingdom of God. For, as the apostle Paul declares, 'The wages of sin is death; but the gift of God is eternal life through Jesus Christ our Lord.'

This chapter is based on Luke 15:11-24.

Lazarus, come forth!

While Jesus was teaching in Perea a messenger arrived from Mary and Martha of Bethany with the news that their brother Lazarus was very ill. 'Lord, behold, he whom thou lovest is sick.' The wording of the message reveals the deep affection of Jesus for this family, and they for Him. We do not know how long He had known them, but it is quite possible that they were converts from His early ministry in Judea. There was always a welcome for Jesus in Bethany whenever He was in the vicinity of Jerusalem, and in their distress at their brother's illness Mary and Martha turned immediately to Jesus for help.

The Franciscan Church of the Custody. This modern building is part of a long history of churches in Bethany dating back to the fourth century. Its design is symbolic of the resurrection, having no windows gives it a 'closed in' feeling, but light floods in from above through the oculus in the dome.

Following so soon after Jesus' parable of the rich man and Lazarus, some have connected the two men, but of course there was no connection whatever. The Lazarus of the parable was a poor beggar while Lazarus of Bethany was a highly respected and probably a reasonably well-to-do man. It may be, however, that Jesus chose the name of the beggar in the knowledge of what was to transpire, for the miracle was indeed a striking sequel to the parable.

In their message to Jesus the sisters did not actually ask Him to come to Bethany to heal Lazarus. They knew the fierce enmity of the rulers of the Jews towards Him and had no desire to place His life in peril. They realized that it would be just as easy for Him to speak the healing word where He was and so they simply told Jesus of their brother's illness, leaving the decision with Him as to what He should do.

What reply Jesus sent to Bethany is not

recorded, but to His disciples He said, 'This sickness is not unto death, but for the glory of God, that the Son of God might be glorified thereby.' Jesus knew, of course, that Lazarus would die. What He meant was that death would not retain its hold on Lazarus, that a great miracle would be wrought which would bring glory to God and to His Son. So instead of restoring him to health there and then or setting off immediately to Judea, He sent the messenger back and proceeded with His ministry for two whole days.

Knowing the affection which Jesus had for Lazarus and his sisters, the disciples must have wondered at His failure to respond to their call. At the same time they were relieved, for they feared that His life would be in danger if He ventured again so near to Jerusalem.

Their relief, however, was short-lived, for after two days Jesus said to His disciples, 'Let us go into Judea again.' At once the disciples began to remonstrate with Him. 'Master,' they said, 'the Jews of late sought to stone Thee; and goest thou thither again?'

In reply Jesus answered, 'Are there not twelve hours in the day? If any man walk in the day, he stumbleth not, because he seeth the light of this world. But if a man walk in the night, he stumbleth, because there is no light in him.'

'I have been given a day by God in which to fulfil my mission,' He said in other words, 'and as long as my day lasts and I do my Father's will, no harm can come to me.'

Here is a principle in which every Christian may find encouragement. We each have our allotted 'day' in which to do God's service, and if we walk in the light which He sheds upon our pathway not only will the burden be 'light', but by His providence we will be kept safe whatever the circumstances that may surround us.

66   Explaining to His disciples what He was

The Byzantine remains of the side-chapel of the second church on this site in Bethany. The first was destroyed by extensive earthquakes in the fifth and sixth centuries.

going to do Jesus said, 'Our friend Lazarus sleepeth; but I go, that I may awake him out of sleep.'

Jesus' reference to Lazarus being asleep seemed to the disciples a reason why Jesus should not expose Himself to danger, and so they again pressed their argument that He should not go. If Lazarus was sleeping he must be improving and doubtless would soon be well again.

Seeing that His disciples misunderstood His words, Jesus now declared plainly, and without metaphor, 'Lazarus is dead.'

When Jesus visited the home of Jairus He perplexed those who had come to mourn the little girl's death by saying, 'She is not dead, but sleepeth.' And once again He used the same metaphor concerning Lazarus to emphasize the hope which He had to bring to the bereaved.

'The wages of sin,' the Bible declares, 'is death,' and through sin all men are subject to death, which, apart from some miracle of grace, must be for ever. But God through Christ has made provision whereby men may be recovered from the power of death to life again. In Christ, therefore, death has become a 'sleep' from which the one asleep may awake to life again.

The fact is borne out by the word Jesus chose to describe the 'sleep' of death. He did not use the physiological term 'hupnos', but 'koimesis' which means 'repose'. Thus His intention was to emphasize that while the phenomenon of death is real, the dead are now only 'resting' from their labours, and that in God's good time and by the summons of Jesus they will be aroused from their sleep.

In demonstration of His power to raise the dead from their 'sleep' Jesus had restored the widow's son of Nain, He had called Jairus' daughter back from the sleep of death, and now He was about to show that Lazarus too was only 'sleeping'.

When the disciples saw that Jesus was determined to go to Bethany, Thomas, who was also called Didymus because he was a twin, said to his fellow disciples, 'Let us also go, that we may die with him.' His courageous appeal provides an interesting sidelight on the character of Thomas. He may have found theological problems rather difficult to comprehend and he may have been rather pessimistic by nature, but these in no way affected his unswerving loyalty to Jesus.

The journey of some twenty-five miles from Perea to Bethany could have been accomplished in one long day, but as Jesus was not hurrying and probably ministered on the way, it took two. So if Lazarus had died just about the time the messenger found Jesus, he would have been dead as the record states, four days by the time Jesus and His disciples reached Bethany.

When Martha heard that the 'Master' was coming up the mountain road, she went to meet Him, leaving Mary sitting disconsolately at home receiving the condolences of friends.

Finding Jesus just outside the village, Martha impulsively burst out, 'Lord, if thou hadst been here, my brother had not died. But I know,' she added, 'that even now, whatsoever thou wilt ask of God, God will give it thee.'

She knew of the raising of the widow's son of Nain and Jairus' daughter from the dead and she was sure that Jesus could raise Lazarus if He so willed. Gently Jesus replied, 'Thy brother shall rise again.'

Thinking at first that Jesus was comforting her with the hope of the general resurrection of the righteous she said, somewhat disappointed, 'I know that he shall rise in the resurrection of the last day,' but she had hoped that He would be ready to work an immediate miracle on behalf of the dead Lazarus.

Jesus' next words made her heart beat fast. 'I am the Resurrection and the Life,' He said, 'He that believeth in me, though he were dead, yet shall he live. And whosoever liveth and believeth in me shall never die. Believest thou this?'

'Yea, Lord,' Martha replied quickly. 'I believe that thou art the Christ, the Son of God which should come into the world.'

Sure now that Jesus was going to raise her dead brother to life, Martha needed no second bidding when He bade her go and bring Mary. Slipping quietly into the house so as not to excite the mourners, she whispered to Mary, 'The Master is come, and calleth for thee.' Immediately Mary rose and followed her into the street.

When the mourners saw Mary leave they thought that she was going to the grave to mourn, and in sympathy they followed at a distance. But Mary and Martha hurried to the spot where Jesus was waiting.

As soon as Mary saw Him she fell weeping at His feet, and from her lips came the same agonized cry that Martha had uttered, 'Lord, if thou hadst been here, my brother had not died.'

Jesus was deeply affected by Mary's tears. 'Where have ye laid him?' He asked the Jews who had come with Mary. 'Lord, come and see,' they said, and as He turned to follow them, He wept.

'Behold how he loved him,' the mourners said to one another. But it was not alone His sympathy with the distraught sisters that caused Him to weep. In the grief that had come to His dear friends, Jesus saw the sorrow that bereavement had brought to millions from the beginning of time.

Some of the hostile rabbis, however, sneered at the tender emotion Jesus showed. If He was as sorry for the bereaved family as He seemed to be, and if all the stories they had heard about His miracle-working power were true, why had He not prevented the tragedy? 'Could not this man, which opened the eyes of the blind, have caused that even this man should not have died?'

By this time Jesus had arrived at the rock tomb where Lazarus was buried. Since the days of Origen in the third century of the Christian era, it has been identified with a rock-hewn sepulchre in the ancient cemetery to the south-east of the village. It is entered through a vestibule, probably a natural cave some nine feet square, just large enough to receive the bier and the immediate mourners. In the floor of this antechamber a slab-covered aperture leads down into the actual tomb chamber about six feet square, cut out of the soft chalky rock.

Death is swallowed up in victory. O death, where is thy sting? O grave, where is thy victory?
— 1.CORINTHIANS 15/54 + 55

The glory of God shall be seen by those who put their faith in Jesus in times of greatest distress and hopelessness; they are certain that He is greater than any distress, even greater than death itself.

Der Tod ist verschlungen in den Sieg. Tod, wo ist dein Stachel? Hölle, wo ist dein Sieg? 1. KORINTHER 15/54 + 55

Herrlichkeiten Gottes sollen jene sehen, die in grösster Not und Ausweglosigkeit Jesus

Like all other traditional Bible sites it has been lined with marble and transformed into a chapel so that the ledge on which the body lay has gone, but without a doubt it was originally a tomb, and if not the actual sepulchre of Lazarus it could not have been very far away.

In one respect the tomb corresponds exactly with the Bible account. The description says that a stone 'lay upon it', that is, it covered a vertical descent into the tomb chamber in contrast with the tomb of Jesus in which the stone was 'rolled' horizontally in front of the entrance.

'Take ye away the stone,' Jesus ordered when the party reached the tomb. Forgetting for the moment the hope that Jesus had put in her heart, Martha was appalled at the thought of exposing the body of her dead brother to the common gaze, for he had been dead four days and by now the corpse would have begun to decay.

The repeated emphasis in the story on the four days which had elapsed is significant. Without doubt Jesus had deliberately waited as long as this because, in current Jewish thinking, this was the day beyond which

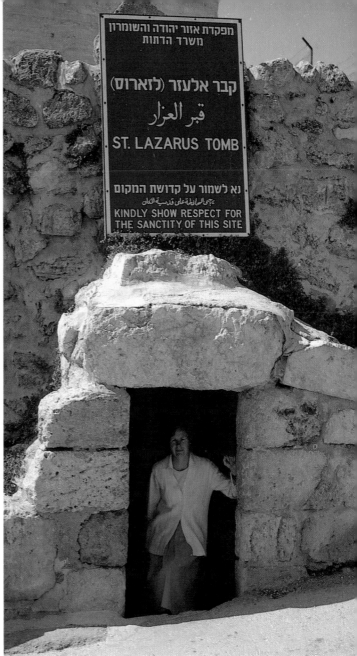

restoration was impossible. For the first three days after death relatives would visit a tomb to view the body hoping that the condition might only be a coma. At the end of the third day, all hope was given up and the tomb was closed with a heavy stone. If Jesus had raised Lazarus during the first three days His enemies could have asserted that there had been no miracle, but when the conventional three days had passed and the tomb had been sealed, this argument was completely excluded. The signs and odours of decomposition would force the Jews to admit that Lazarus was dead.

Gently Jesus recalled Martha to her faith in Him. 'Said I not unto thee, that, if thou wouldest believe, thou shouldest see the glory of God?' Recovering her composure Martha stood aside and allowed the men around to lift the stone from the opening in the floor of the outer chamber.

Standing before the gaping aperture Jesus raised His eyes to heaven and said, 'Father, I thank thee that thou hast heard me.' He spoke

The tomb of Lazarus in Bethany, a traditional pilgrim site handed down by the early Jerusalem church. It has seen changes over the years, principally to the entrance which, since the sixteenth century, faces north instead of east.

these words aloud so that those standing around might witness the communion that He had at all times with God.

The critical Jews had been asking why, if He was all He professed to be, He had not prevented the death of Lazarus. Jesus' words were intended to show them that He and His Father were one in their purpose for Lazarus and that when the moment came, the power of God for his recovery, even from the dead, 69 would be revealed.

Then bending forward and speaking into the yawning mouth of the cave He cried, in a voice of authority which will one day awake all the dead from their dusty beds, 'Lazarus, come forth.'

There was a sound of shuffling in the dark depths of the tomb and a moment later a figure, bound hand and foot in grave clothes and with his face encircled by a napkin, staggered up the steps. Evidently his legs had been bound separately in Egyptian fashion or he would not have been able to walk at all.

'Loose him, and let him go,' Jesus commanded, and as the Jews sprang forward to divest Lazarus of the restricting clothes, they were amazed to see him standing before them, not feeble and emaciated, but erect, fresh of complexion, and perfectly well.

While this was not the first time that Jesus had raised the dead, it was certainly the most spectacular miracle of resurrection. The raising of Jairus' daughter followed quickly upon her death, and had been witnessed only by her parents and three of the disciples. More saw the raising of the widow's son of Nain, but they were inhabitants of a very obscure little village. But Bethany was an important place on a main road within a couple of miles of the capital, a large number of influential people from Jerusalem were present, and Jesus had waited until the death of Lazarus was beyond all question before He performed the miracle. It was the crowning evidence of His divine power.

It was conclusive evidence too of the 'sleep' of death. If the 'soul' of Lazarus had departed from his body at death he would surely have brought back to his earthly life some remembrance of his brief sojourn in paradise, but he had absolutely nothing to say. Clearly, he had not been to heaven or to purgatory or anywhere else. He had been 'asleep', and of the interval between his falling asleep in death and awaking in resurrection he knew nothing. And such will be the experience of all who now sleep the unconscious sleep of death. Whether the interval be four days or four centuries or four milleniums it will be unremembered when they are awakened by the call of Jesus on the resurrection morn.

The reactions of the people to the miracle were again various. 'Many of the Jews' who had come to comfort the two sisters 'believed' in Jesus as a result of the miracle. But others hurried to the Pharisees, alarmed at the excitement aroused by the miracle-worker from Galilee.

It was impossible to call all the seventy-one members of the Sanhedrin together at short notice, but the chief priests and Pharisees immediately gathered as many as they could to decide what was to be done.

'What do we?' they debated among themselves, 'for this man doeth many miracles.' While Jesus confined His teaching and miracles to Galilee it was not so serious, but now He had come back to Judea and was drawing the multitudes after Him, they would have to act quickly if a popular uprising in His favour was to be averted.

'If we let him thus alone,' they argued, 'all men will believe on him,' and the Roman authorities, imagining that He was starting a rebellion, would 'come and take away both our place and nation.' On the other hand, they did not know how to silence Jesus without turning the animosity of the people against themselves.

The chairman of the council was the high priest, Caiaphas, a Sadducee and the son-in-law of Annas, who some years before had been deposed from the office of high priest by Valerius Gratus, but who had succeeded in keeping the high priesthood in the family. Impatient at the inconclusiveness of the

As the morning light dispels the gloom and fear of night's darkness, so the promise, 'I am the resurrection and the life', brings hope over the grave.

discussion he called the meeting to order.

'Ye know nothing at all,' he declared, 'nor consider that it is expedient for us, that one man should die for the people, and that the whole nation perish not.'

Caiaphas saw that there was only one way out of the dilemma. Charges must be framed against Jesus which would secure His condemnation and execution by the Romans. The choice was between one man dying or a whole nation being sacrificed. The obvious answer was that Jesus must die.

Little did Caiaphas realize, as he expounded his evil plan that his words were an unconscious prophecy. 'He prophesied' truly, the record says, 'that Jesus should die for that nation; and not for that nation only, but that also He should gather together in one the children of God that were scattered abroad.'

But the death of Jesus would not accomplish the purpose Caiaphas intended. While the merits of Jesus' sacrifice would bring salvation to those who received it, the rejection of Jesus' sacrifice would bring salvation to those who received it, the rejection of Jesus by the great majority of the people would make certain the national disaster which Caiaphas sought to avoid.

But the time for the great sacrifice had not yet come. Jesus' 'day' of labour was not yet ended. His 'hour' had not come. There was still work for Him to do. So, when he learned of the decision against Him, He 'walked no more openly among the Jews', but retired to the edge of the wilderness near the city of Ephraim.

Here for two weeks Jesus found a quiet retreat where in communion with God He prepared Himself for the final ordeal, and day by day instructed His disciples against the time, not far distant now, when He would be taken from them.

This chapter is based on John 11:1-57.

Sunrise over the Sea of Galilee.

How God's kingdom will come

As Jesus journeyed down the Jordan Valley on His way to the Passover in Jerusalem, He was accosted by some of His priestly enemies, who sarcastically demanded to know when 'the kingdom of God', which He had been preaching for more than three years, was going to come. In spite of all that Jesus had said about His mission these Jews still clung to the popular belief that Messiah would appear as a warrior-king, another Maccabeus, a greater David, to liberate them from the Roman yoke and usher in the kingdom of God. So they said to Jesus, in effect, 'If You are the Messiah, as You claim to be, when are You going to deliver Israel and ascend Your throne? If You do not act soon we will be justified in declaring You an impostor, a deceiver, a false Messiah.'

The taunt provided Jesus with yet another opportunity to show these supposedly learned Jews how completely they had misunderstood the prophecies of Messiah and to set forth in more detail than ever before the course of events leading up to the establishment of His kingdom.

The kingdom of God that He had been announcing, Jesus explained, was not a temporal kingdom to which anyone could point and say, 'Lo here! or, lo there!' It had not been heralded with any 'outward show', but even now it was 'in the midst' of them. It was 'all around' them. It was 'within' the hearts of those who were willing to receive it.

The kingdom Jesus proclaimed was not only the future kingdom of glory, but the present kingdom of grace. Though it may have no external glory it is a real kingdom which men may enter by entering into fellowship with Jesus, its King.

It has, as Paul explained further on another occasion, a real throne, 'the throne of grace' to which souls may come and 'find grace to help in time of need'. Upon its subjects is conferred a heavenly 'citizenship', and to them it is granted now, by faith, to 'sit together in heavenly places in Christ'. It was to bring this kingdom near to men that the Son of man had 'first' to 'suffer many things' and be 'rejected' and die.

One day, in God's good time, Jesus warned His enemies and assured His followers, the Son of man would appear in His glory and in His kingdom. 'For as the lightning, that lighteneth out of the one part under heaven, shineth unto the other part under heaven; so shall the Son of man be in his day.' But the suffering Servant must precede the conquering King. The cross must come before the crown.

To the longing children of the kingdom the time of waiting between the 'sufferings' and the 'glory that should follow' might seem long. It would call for patient faith, and they would need to be on their guard aginst those who would give false alarms, saying, 'Lo, here is Christ, or there.' But when the time came, if they were vigilant and watchful, they would have unmistakable evidence of His approach. They would know beyond the possibility of doubt that His coming was at hand.

Sad to say, however, in that day the great majority would not be waiting and watching for His coming. Men would be as blind to the signs of His second advent as they were to His first coming. Indeed, declared Jesus, the world will be 'as it was in the days of Noe.' As in the days before the Flood an unheeding world will be absorbed in sensual pleasure and greedy acquisition and vice, and His second advent will be as shattering a surprise as when the Flood descended upon the antediluvian world and 'destroyed them all'.

The world in the days of the Son of man, Jesus further declared, will be in the same condition as the sinful inhabitants of Sodom when God 'rained fire and brimstone from heaven', and as suddenly and as completely will the wicked be blotted out and vanish in a final catastrophe of judgement.

But in that day a precious remnant will be watching and waiting for the coming of the King, and there will be a dramatic separation between those who are ready to meet Him and those who are unprepared.

Vividly Jesus described the scene. 'I tell you, in that night there shall be two men in one bed; the one shall be taken, and the other shall be left. Two women shall be grinding together; the one shall be taken, and the other left. Two men shall be in the field; the one shall be taken, and the other left.'

Whether the 'taken' are the saints who are gathered into the kingdom and the others are those who are 'left' out, or whether the 'taken' are the ones who are carried away in the judgement and the 'left' those who are surrounded by divine protection, is immaterial. The important point is that the righteous and the wicked will be separated for good or ill, for ever.

And what will be the characteristics of those who are received and those who are rejected in that day? Jesus gave two distinctive marks of His faithful people.

They will be those who are so eager to join

Lion's Gate, so named after the carvings on either side of the gateway. It is also called St. Stephen's Gate due to the ancient tradition that Stephen was martyred nearby.

Dung Gate on the south side of Jerusalem that served as access to the Valley of Hinnom for the disposal of the city's refuse.

their Lord that the things of the world will have completely lost their hold upon them. If they are 'upon the housetop' when the call comes, they will have no desire to go down into the house to gather their earthly possessions before going out to meet the King. If they are 'in the field', they will make haste to escape from the doomed world into the divine protection. They will not be like 'Lot's wife' who, when judgement threatened, 'looked back' and was engulfed in the city's destruction. Earth's hold upon them will be so slight that at the sign of the coming King they will leave all and go forth to meet Him.

73

Again, said Jesus, those who qualify for a place in the kingdom of glory will be those who are so eager for their heavenly reward that they·will be willing to surrender their earthly life in martyrdom if need be rather than fail God in the final crisis. Christ will be more to them than life itself. Those who prize life and the things of life above loyalty to God will have their full reward in this world and perish in its fall. But 'whosoever shall lose his life' in the cause of Christ will assure its continuance in the everlasting kingdom of God.

Amazed at Jesus' startling portrayal of the drama of His coming the disciples asked Him, 'Where, Lord', will those go who are denied a place in the kingdom? What will become of them when the faithful people of God are gathered in?

'And He said unto them, Wheresoever the

Jesus, there will be no place for the rejectors of His mercy and grace to hide from the righteous wrath of God. 'Where the slain are' the vultures of destruction are inevitably to be found; equally surely will decisive and inescapable judgement overtake a spiritually corrupt and sinful world.

It was a grim answer to the wicked rulers of the Jews who had unwarily asked when and how the kingdom of God would come, and its solemn warning must have struck home to many hearts as Jesus passed on His way.

What will that day mean to you? Will it be a day of happy realization or a day of terror and judgement?

Whether you are 'taken' into the kingdom of glory or 'left' out in that day will depend upon whether you have been received into, or are still outside, His kingdom of grace.

Will you not, then, while there is time, heed the appeal of the apostle Peter and 'make your calling and election sure'?

This chapter is based on Luke 17:20-37.

The road north out of Jerusalem passed through the Damascus Gate, now the most ornate of the city's gates. The present structure, built by Suleiman about AD 1540 stands on the site of two previous gates built by Herod and Hadrian. The first arch of the Roman gate (right) can be seen below street level to the left of the main entrance (above).

body is, thither will the eagles (or vultures) be gathered together.' In that day, declared

The Pharisee and the publican

When it became known that Jesus was among the company of people travelling to the Passover, many sought Him. Some desired healing, others spiritual counsel. Besides these, of course, there were always the Pharisees hovering around, trying to entangle Him in argument. As a further warning to these self-righteous Jews, Jesus related another parable.

'Two men,' He said, 'went up into the tem-ple to pray; the one a Pharisee, and the other a publican.'

They were not alone, of course, as they wended their way from the lower city up to the sanctuary on the highest hill of Zion. It was doubtless the time of morning or evening prayer and Jesus picked out these two men from the crowd as they passed through the great gates into the temple.

The Pharisee, Jesus noted, ostentatiously

took up a position where everyone could see him and, adjusting his prayer robe about him, he began, in a loud and affected voice, to pray.

It was evident, however, from his manner that he was not praying to God, but talking 'with himself'. He had not come to seek God, but to give God the opportunity to look at him. His thoughts were directed not to a contemplation of the divine glory, but upon his own virtues. He came not in self-abasement and with a sense of need, but in complete self-satisfaction. His prayer revealed the measure of the man.

'God, I thank thee,' he began, but his seeming gratitude was only a mockery of self-congratulation. He really meant that God ought to be thankful that He had so devout a follower.

'I thank thee,' he went on, 'that I am not as other men are, extortioners, unjust, adulterers, or even as this publican.' The common herd were dishonest; he was scrupulously honest. They were sinners; he was meticulously righteous. They were immoral; he was a model of propriety. The publican who followed him into the temple revealed the depths of degradation to which a Jew could sink, while he was a paragon of virtue, the epitome of all that was highest and best in Israel.

To prove his claim, he instanced to God two examples of his scrupulous righteousness.

'I fast twice in the week.' The law of Moses prescribed only one fast day in the year, namely, on the Day of Atonement; but in order to show how righteous they were, the Pharisees had multiplied fasts until there were two every week, on Mondays and Thursdays.

Furthermore, said the Pharisee, 'I give tithes of all that I possess.' The law of Moses required the faithful Israelite to tithe the increase of his corn, wine, and oil, and also of his herds. But in this, too, the Pharisees went to extremes, tithing even their 'mint, and anise, and cummin', the minutest of garden herbs. In all this the Pharisee was pointing out to God that whereas others might observe only the minimal letter of the law he went far beyond the law's requirements.

But what was missing from his prayer was even more significant than what he put into it. There was no confession of sin, for he felt he had none to confess. He did not offer any petition for pardon, for he had no sense of guilt. He made no plea for help, for he was conscious of no need of any kind.

In actual fact, however, the Pharisee represented everything God hated. He was proud, self-righteous, self-sufficient, utterly conceited. His ostentatious external righteousness was an abomination because his heart was proud. How different was the character of the publican to whom Jesus now turned.

'The publican, standing afar off, would not lift so much as his eyes unto heaven, but smote upon his breast, saying, God be merciful to me a sinner.'

He did not ostentatiously take up a position where everyone would see him. In his shame he stood apart in the shadows. He was oblivious of the other worshippers. He wanted to be alone with God.

The publican did not begin by inviting God to take note of his virtues. He was so conscious of his sinfulness in the presence of a holy God that he stood with downcast eyes and smote his breast in deep contrition. He felt like the Psalmist when he said, 'Mine iniquities have taken hold upon me, so that I am not able to look up.'

When he spoke there poured from his heart an agonizing plea for mercy and forgiveness. Literally, he said, 'God be merciful

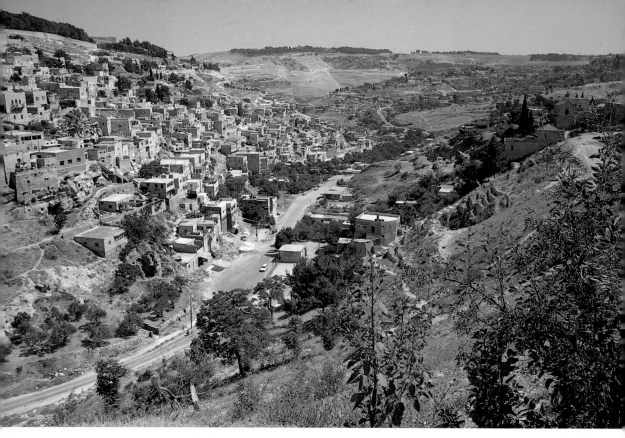

The Kidron Valley looking south from the Old City of Jerusalem. The Arab village of Silwan on the left is built on the Mount of Offence, where King Solomon worshipped the false gods of his wives. The hill on the right is the Ophel where the original city stood when captured by King David. Excavations on this site (below) have revealed part of the walls of the ancient city of Yara Salem.

to me *the* sinner.' Like the apostle Paul he regarded himself as 'chief' of 'sinners'.

No wonder Jesus, concluding His dramatic description of the two men in prayer, declared with emphasis, 'I tell you, this man,' the publican, 'went down to his house justified rather than the other.' On another occasion Jesus gave a similar verdict when He declared that 'the publicans and the harlots' would go into the kingdom before the proud, self-satisfied, and complacent Pharisees and those like them.

The sin of the Pharisees stemmed from the same root as Satan's first transgression, 'thine heart was lifted up'. Paul put his finger upon it when in one of his epistles he accused the Pharisees of 'going about to establish their own righteousness' while neglecting 'the righteousness of God' which is ours by grace and through faith in Christ.

For, Jesus added, 'Everyone that exalteth himself shall be abased; and he that humbleth himself shall be exalted.'

The doors of grace will always be barred against the proud and self-righteous, but to the humble and contrite heart the floodgates of divine mercy and forgiveness are ever open.

This chapter is based on Luke 18:9-14.

Blessing the children

It was just after Jesus' discussion with the Pharisees about marriage and His subsequent talk with His disciples, that an opportunity presented itself to reveal His deep interest in the fruits of this sacred human relationship. As He journeyed along toward Jericho there were brought to Jesus 'little children, that he should put his hands on them, and pray'.

It was the custom in those days for mothers to present their children in the synagogue at about the age of a year, or in the remoter places to ask a blessing from any rabbi who happened to be passing through their village. Jesus, of course, was recognized by the common people as a notable rabbi and naturally parents were eager for His special blessing.

The disciples, however, felt it their duty to protect Jesus from these continual delays and so they 'rebuked' the mothers, and bade them not to trouble Him.

But Jesus was 'much displeased' by their unkindness and said reprovingly, 'Suffer little children, and forbid them not, to come unto me: for of such is the kingdom of heaven.' And He laid His hands upon the older ones who clustered round and took the youngest 'in his arms' and 'blessed them'.

By this act Jesus fulfilled yet another Messianic prophecy, for did not Isaiah declare of Him, 'He shall feed his flock like a shepherd: he shall gather the lambs with his arm, and carry them in his bosom, and shall gently lead those that are with young'?

Jesus had shown, in His teaching on the marital relationship, its beneficent purpose in character training, and now, as He blessed the children, He pointed out some of the profound lessons to be learned from them.

By stopping to talk with the mothers and draw their little ones into His embrace He showed that the young are as precious in His sight as those of mature years. His reproof to the disciples is a standing rebuke to the Church that fails to realize the paramount importance of the children in its midst.

It was to emphasize the place of chil-

A Jewish boy takes part in a Bar Mitzvah ceremony at the Western Wall in Jerusalem. This occurs on his thirteenth birthday at his 'coming of age' when he is considered able to fulfil the requirements of the Law.

Inquisitive Jewish schoolboys size up the photographer, while (below) little Arab boys in Jerusalem are entrusted with the safe conveyance of thirty eggs!

dren in the family of God that just before Jesus left His disciples to return to heaven, He instructed Peter not only to 'Feed my sheep,' but also to 'Feed my lambs'.

In the Old Testament the aged preacher bade the young, 'Remember now thy Creator in the days of thy youth' and in the New Testament the aged Paul, writing to the young minister Timothy, had a special word of commendation for his mother Eunice, and grandmother Lois, for the godly training that had laid the foundation for his life of dedicated service. In the home, the school, and the Church it is the solemn responsibility of the followers

of the Great Teacher to assure their little ones of God's tender love for them and to inculcate into their young minds the sterling principles of goodness and truth. Tragic indeed will be the judgement which will fall upon those who hinder the coming of the children to the waiting arms of God.

As representatives of the Lord, the patriarchs blessed their children and their grandchildren, and the priests pronounced a benediction upon the children who were presented in the temple or synagogue. As Jesus laid His hands upon those who were brought to Him and prayed for them He showed that the blessing of God was the supreme good which could come into their little lives. And though He may no longer walk among men as He did in the long ago, He is still just as ready to receive the children who are brought by godly parents for His blessing.

There is, however, confusion in the minds of many parents as to just how they should present their children to the Lord. Some have been led to believe that God's blessing is received through the baptism of infants in their earliest years, but infant baptism is actually a misapplication of a divinely-given ordinance and a misunderstanding of the nature of the Church of God.

It is true that when national Israel were the chosen people of God, children were admitted into the holy nation from birth as a hereditary right by the ordinance of circumcision. By reason of this Moses could say to the assembled Israelites: 'Ye stand this day all of you before the Lord your God; your captains of your tribes, your elders, and your officers, with all the men of Israel, *your little ones*, your wives.' It is equally true that baptism is the corresponding rite of entrance into the Chris-

tian Church. But it does not therefore follow that infant baptism is a biblical ordinance.

In contrast with the hereditary right of the Israelite to be reckoned among the people of God, entrance into the New Testament Church, or spiritual Israel, is only

on personal profession of faith. In consequence, the only true baptism is 'believer's baptism', administered to those who have come to years of discretion.

Jesus did not baptize the children who were brought to Him, nor did He instruct His disciples to do so. But He did dedicate them to God by taking them in His arms and invoking the blessing of the Lord upon them. In like manner believing parents may present their children today in the Church of God, with the assurance that He will enfold them in His bosom until the time of personal decision.

As Jesus received the mothers and drew their children one by one to Him, He taught His disciples yet another profound and beautiful lesson. 'Verily, I say unto you,' He said, 'Whosoever shall not receive the kingdom of God as a little child, he shall not enter therein.'

It was the mothers' faith in the first place which brought the children to Jesus, but as they stretched out their hands to receive His kindly embrace, they beautifully portrayed the attitude of the true child of God.

Their spontaneous reaching out after Jesus well illustrates the sinner's sense of need as he casts himself in confidence and trust upon God.

The resting of the little ones in the arms of Jesus reveals the supreme satisfaction of the contrite sinner in the Father's forgiving love.

Their upturned faces as He laid His hands on them and blessed them portrays the humble, teachable spirit of the child of God as he receives the seeds of truth and righteousness into his heart.

Then as the happy mothers and their children waved good-bye as Jesus went on His way we glimpse, on the one hand, the joy of the Lord in His 'beloved' and the

Children from India, Africa, Korea, Thailand and from all nations are equally precious to Jesus, especially the poor, the abused, unloved and discarded.

grateful praise and devotion which should continually well up in the hearts of His children for all the blessings received at His hands.

We may be sure that those mothers returned to their homes strengthened to meet the demands and burdens of their daily lives by the knowledge of Jesus' interest and care, and we may well believe that many of these children, when they came to mature years, gave themselves personally to God and to life-long service for Him.

To dedicate our little ones to God from the earliest years and bring them up in 'the nurture and admonition of the Lord' is indeed to lay the surest foundation for a life of obedience and faith.

This chapter is based on Matthew 19:13-15; Mark 10:13-16; Luke 18:15-17.

The great refusal

Jesus had not gone far along the village road after the blessing of the children, when a richly apparelled young man, probably in his early thirties, came running up. Pushing his way among the disciples he prostrated himself at the feet of Jesus and burst out, 'Good Master, what good thing shall I do, that I may have eternal life?'

We are not told who the young man was. He may have been a district magistrate or a ruler of the local synagogue. Without doubt, he was well known for his wealth and piety and the people following Jesus gazed in amazement at the sight, for the Pharisees had often expressed their disapproval of Jesus by the contemptuous question, 'Have any of the rulers or of the Pharisees believed?'

That the young man came running may give a hint of the struggle of mind which he had had before approaching Jesus. At first he may have allowed Jesus to pass without speaking to Him. Then as he saw Jesus disappearing down the street he realized that if he did not speak to Him now he might never have another chance. So he swallowed his pride, ran after Jesus, and fell at His feet in reverence and humility.

How often this is repeated in the lives of proud sinners when Jesus is passing by in their experience, perhaps through a tract or magazine given to them, or an invitation to a Gospel meeting. In their pride, for a time they hold back. They cannot bring themselves to admit their spiritual need. Some delay too long and the opportunity passes, perhaps for ever. But happy are those who, like this young man, run to the Saviour while He is still to be found.

In addressing Jesus as 'Rabbi' or 'Master' the young ruler recognized Him as a distinguished teacher, just as Nicodemus had done, and by calling Jesus 'Good Master', he admitted that Jesus was unique among all the eminent rabbis he had met. But he did not accept Him as the divine Son and Messiah. Jesus sought, therefore, first of all to bring him face to face with the vital question as to whom he was addressing.

'Why callest thou me good?' Jesus asked him, seeing that 'there is none good but one, that is, God?'

'You know well enough,' Jesus said in effect, 'that in the writings of the elders God is described as "he that is good and bestows good". If you see in me one whom you are constrained to call good, should you not ask yourself whether I may not be both good and God?'

Without pressing the thought further Jesus turned to the question which the young man had asked Him. He could have pointed out to him that eternal life is not, as the Pharisees fondly imagined, to be earned by doing anything, however good, but that it is 'whosoever believeth in him', who will not 'perish, but have everlasting life'. That was what Jesus told the ruler Nicodemus when he came to Him in similar circumstances. The reason He did not turn the conversation in this direction now was because the young man was not ready to face the challenge of believing in Jesus. As a devout Pharisee he believed that 'good works' were the qualification for entrance into the kingdom of heaven, and he believed himself quite capable of meeting God's requirements if they were made clear to him. He wanted to know what he should do to qualify for eternal life. So Jesus dealt with him at the level of experience where his question placed him, and plainly set before him the standard of obedience to which he must attain to obtain eternal life for himself.

A street in the Christian quarter in Old Jerusalem looking similar to the streets Jesus would have walked.

'If thou wilt enter into life,' He said, 'keep the commandments.'

But Jesus' answer did not satisfy the young man. He knew quite well what the Psalmist had declared of the commandments of the Lord: 'By them is thy servant warned; and in keeping of them there is great reward.' He was familiar, too, with the counsel the wise Solomon had given: 'My son, forget not my law; but let thine heart keep my commandments: for length of days, and long life, and peace, shall they add to thee.'

What he expected from Jesus was a fuller elaboration of his duty. He knew that there were various schools of thought among the rabbis regarding the spiritual duties of chief importance and he was anxious for Jesus' counsel on what he ought to concentrate upon in order to gain eternal life. So he asked again, 'Which?'

In reply Jesus recited to him several of the commandments of the moral law, 'Thou shalt do no murder, Thou shalt not commit adultery, Thou shalt not steal, Thou shalt not bear false witness, Honour thy father and thy mother,' and by way of summarizing the rest, 'Thou shalt love thy neighbour as thyself'. Instead of discussing the minutiae of the rabbinical tradition Jesus drew his attention to the 'weightier matters' of the law, which the Pharisees habitually overlooked. Further, He deliberately limited His recital to the second table of the Decalogue, describing man's duty to his fellow-man, for reasons which were soon to appear.

With a gesture of impatience that Jesus should have cited such obvious commandments, the young man replied, 'All these things have I kept from my youth up: what lack I yet?'

In saying this the young man was not intending to be conceited or boastful. He had been brought up with a deep sense of his responsibility to God, and not only did he feel that he had scrupulously kept all the commandments of the moral code, but all the elaborations of the oral tradition as well. In the eyes of those who knew him he was a man of irreproachable character and eminent piety, and he was offended that Jesus should think it necessary to remind him of such elementary duties.

Jesus looked intently at the young man. The record actually says that He looked 'into' him. He saw that he sincerely desired the approval of God. He knew the struggle he had had to humble himself in public and He 'loved' him because he had overcome his pharisaic prejudice and had taken the first step of faith. Jesus 'loved' him as He loves every soul who comes in his ignorance and sin to Him. It was also in 'love' that He spoke the words that at a

85

blow shattered the young ruler's self-righteousness and left him broken and without hope save in the grace of God.

'One thing thou lackest,' Jesus said slowly and deliberately. 'If thou wilt be perfect, go and sell that thou hast, and give to the poor, and thou shalt have treasure in heaven: and come and follow me.'

The young man was crestfallen and a look of alarm clouded his fresh features. He had always considered himself a generous man. The treasurer of the synagogue knew that he had always paid a faithful tithe and the local community looked up to him as a noble benefactor. Yet Jesus knew that all he had given had been out of his abundance. His generosity had never cost him anything. It had involved no sacrifice. When Jesus suggested a liberality which would really hurt, He uncovered the fatal flaw in the young man's character which not even he, let alone his contemporaries, had suspected.

For the first time he realized that there had been no real merit in anything he had done. In a moment he saw all his boasted virtue dissolve into nothingness. All his works had been 'dead' works. They had gained him the approval of men, but not of God. He was shaken to realize that even on the level of his responsibility to his fellow men he was weighed in the balances and found wanting. He did not love his fellow men enough to give till it hurt, and he did not love God sufficiently to surrender all for Him.

He had come to Jesus feeling that he was but a step from the kingdom. Now he realized that that step was across the great gulf between calculated obedience for the accumulation of merit, and selfless obedience springing from love.

As he stood before Jesus he saw that the vital question was not *which* commandments he had still to keep to attain to 'perfection', but *how*, in his own strength, he could keep any of the commandments of God.

If, as a result of this disclosure, he had been willing to give up once and for all the attempt to establish his 'own righteousness', and had come to Christ with humble and contrite heart, he could have exchanged the 'filthy rags' of his

pharisaic profession for the true 'righteousness which is of God by faith'. Through the operation of the Spirit of God, as Jesus told that other Pharisee, Nicodemus, he could have been 'born again' and become a 'new creature' in Christ Jesus. Then he would have been able to say with the apostle Paul, 'The life which I now live in the flesh I live by the faith of the Son of God, who loved me, and gave himself for me.' And in the power of the indwelling Christ, the 'righteousness of the law' would have been perfectly fulfilled in his life not as a 'merit' to *earn* salvation, but as a *result* of his saving relationship with Christ. Only in this way could he attain to the perfection which would qualify him for 'eternal life'.

As the young ruler stood, with head bowed and silent, Jesus saw the struggle that was going on in his heart. He knew what He could do with that strong young life if he would give himself wholly to God. But he could not make the decision for him. The young man must make the surrender himself.

A few moments passed and the young ruler's shoulders began to heave with an uncontrollable grief. But it was not a sorrow that was leading him to repentance. It was an angry sorrow that the price Jesus asked was too high for him to pay. He was too proud to start all over again by 'believing' and he was not prepared to exchange his 'great possessions' for the heavenly 'treasure'.

Without looking again at Jesus he turned and walked swiftly away. He might have become a great apostle for God and his name might have lived for ever in the Lord's book of remembrance, but he refused the offer of grace and walked away into oblivion, a tragic example of all proud sinners who 'neglect so great salvation'.

The disciples had followed the interview with deep interest, thinking what an acquisition this young ruler would have been to their company. As he passed beyond earshot they looked in questioning disappointment at Jesus.

'How hardly shall they that have riches enter into the kingdom of God!' Jesus commented shortly. Then seeing the look of bewilderment upon their faces He enlarged on what He had said.

'Children,' He declared, 'how hard it is for them that trust in riches to enter into the kingdom of God!' 'It is easier for a camel to go through the eye of a needle, than for a rich man to enter into the kingdom of God.'

By this Jesus did not intend to suggest that wealth is something evil in itself, and that it must inevitably alienate its possessors from God. Abraham was rich, yet he was called the 'friend of God'. Joanna and the other women were also rich and used their possessions in the cause of Christ. Jesus meant that those who 'trust in riches' will thereby exclude themselves from the kingdom of God. The trouble about riches is that all too often their acquisition leaves no time to worship the God who gives 'power to get wealth'. As the rich add house to house and field to field the craving for more drives all thoughts of God from their lives. The possession of riches satisfies their minds with material goods and they come to believe that there are no greater riches. So they develop a false sense of self-sufficiency and security, from which they are not disabused until too late when God says, 'This night thy soul shall be required of thee.'

In His striking illustration Jesus showed that the way to the kingdom is too narrow to go through hugging earthly possessions. Expositors differ as to whether He was referring to the impossibility of a camel going through one of the small side entrances in the ancient gateways, or to the impossibility of a rough rope [kamilos] passing through the eye of a bone or metal needle, but His meaning in either case was clear. The kingdom can be entered only by the soul that is prepared to cast away every earthly attachment. The disciples took this step when they 'forsook all' to follow Jesus. The young man refused to let go his 'great possessions' and found himself turned back at the very gate of the kingdom.

Disappointed and perplexed by the loss of so promising a convert the question came involuntarily to the lips of the disciples, 'Who then can be saved?'

'With men,' Jesus replied, 'this is impossible; but with God all things are possible.'

The truth is that there is no hope for either rich or poor if they imagine that they can earn salvation by their own efforts. No sinner can ever lift himself out of the pit into which he has fallen. But if men will avail themselves of God's free provision of grace there is none whom He will reject, none that He cannot save.

The fundamental requisite for acceptance with God is that we forsake 'all' self-righteous merit and approach Him in poverty of soul, relying solely upon the riches of His grace.

As Jesus declared in His Sermon on the Mount, it is the 'poor in spirit' to whom the kingdom of God is given, it is those who are empty of all merit and who 'hunger and thirst after righteousness' who will be filled.

This chapter is based on Matthew 19:16-30; Mark 10:17-31; Luke 18:18-30.

The reward of grace

As the disciples pondered the departure of the rich young ruler and Jesus' declaration that the heavenly 'treasure' was for those only who were prepared to forsake all for Him, they began to speculate as to what their reward would be on this basis. So heated did they become in discussing their respective claims that at last they decided to submit the matter to Jesus.

As usual Peter was the spokesman. 'Behold,' he said, joining Jesus as they walked, 'we have forsaken all, and followed thee; what shall we have therefore?'

In the tone of Peter's question Jesus was quick to detect a note of spiritual pride in respect of his own sacrifice to the cause of Christ, but He did not at once reprove him.

First, Jesus assured the disciples that the offer He had made to the young ruler was as valid for them as for him. For all who would break every fetter which bound them to the world there would be 'treasure in heaven', before which the treasures of earth would pale into insignificance.

'Verily I say unto you,' declared Jesus, 'that ye which have followed me, in the regeneration when the Son of man shall sit in the throne of his glory, ye also shall sit upon twelve thrones, judging the twelve tribes of Israel.'

Moreover, He went on, 'there is no man that hath left house, or brethren, or sisters, or father, or mother, or wife, or children, or lands, for my sake, and the gospel's, but he shall receive an hundredfold now in this time, houses, and brethren, and sisters, and mothers, and children, and lands, with persecutions; and in the world to come eternal life.'

Because the young ruler was not willing to give up the position of earthly influence to which he had attained he forfeited the place of leadership which might have been his in the Church of God on earth, as well as a place in the kingdom of God. The disciples, on the other hand, who had surrendered every earthly ambition and advantage would have their reward with Christ in His kingdom. When earthly kings and governors had been cast down, they would reign as kings and priests in heaven.

The young man refused to give up the baubles of earthly riches at the call of Christ. In consequence, he had his reward in full on the earth. The disciples who had given up all material advantages to follow Christ, however, were assured that God would give them 'an hundredfold' more, as well as eternal life, in the earth made new.

Besides the promise of an abundant recompense in the kingdom, Jesus promised the disciples also a rich reward 'now in this time'. What did He mean by this? It is true that Job's suffering was rewarded by his receiving 'twice as much' as he had before, while he still lived, and there have doubtless been many other occasions when God has seen fit to bestow rich material blessings on His servants. Multitudes, however, through the ages, have had to suffer the loss of all earthly possessions because of their loyalty to Christ, so that the 'hundredfold' was not primarily to be in material blessings.

What Jesus really meant was that though His people might have to sacrifice their temporal possessions and even their kith and kin according to the flesh for Him, they would be rewarded even in this life with manifold spiritual riches. Though suffering the 'loss' of earthly things, they would have the 'great gain' of godliness, together with new spiritual relationships with God and with their brethren and sisters in the faith, which would far outweigh this world's goods and associations.

The full blessing of God would, of

course, be tempered in this life by the 'persecutions' they would have to endure, but, as the apostle Paul triumphantly declared, 'The sufferings of this present time are not worthy to be compared' with the enduring substance and the 'eternal weight of glory' that shall be hereafter.

In the heavenly kingdom, added Jesus, there will be a complete reversal of fortunes as seen in this present world. The 'first shall be last; and the last first'. Those who in this life feel themselves secure in their position and possessions will find themselves deprived of everything, while those who have given up all for Christ will be rewarded beyond their dreams. The rich and influential of earth will find themselves thrust into outer darkness, while the humble and the deprived will be given authority and wealth in the kingdom of heaven.

Having thus assured the disciples that the rewards of grace would be more than abundant, Jesus had some serious counsel for Peter and the other disciples about the spirit which had prompted their question.

Truly, they had forsaken 'all' to follow Him and they would have their reward, but it was wrong of them to think that this reward would be in proportion to what they had given up for Him.

Judas had doubtless implanted this idea in their minds, for when he joined himself to the disciples it was with the shrewd expectation of a handsome reward in wealth, position, and dignity when Jesus became King. Peter and the others had not followed Him primarily for such mercenary ends, but in harbouring the thought that their reward would bear a definite relation to their sacrifice, they were making a 'merit' of self-renunciation which was as offensive to God as the Pharisees' expectation of reward in proportion to

their good works.

Jesus will indeed fulfil all the 'great and precious promises' of the Gospel and it is perfectly proper that we, like Moses, should have regard to the 'recompense of the reward'. But at the same time it is important that we recognize that the reward will be solely of grace and not of debt, that it will be a gift received by faith and not in proportion to works or even to our sacrifices or labours for God.

To impress this all-important lesson Jesus told His disciples the parable of the labourers. 'The kingdom of heaven,' He began, 'is like unto a man that is an householder, which went out early in the morning to hire labourers into his vineyard.'

At vintage time many more workers were needed in the vineyards than were employed regularly through the year and so the vine cultivators had to engage casual labour to gather in the harvest. The market place was the labour exchange of those days, as it still is in many oriental cities today, and so this particular man went there soon after dawn, probably about six o'clock, to hire the extra help he needed. With each of the men who was willing to work he agreed on a payment of one 'penny', that is a Roman silver denarius or Greek drachma. This was the usual wage for a day labourer. Incidentally, it was also the daily wage of a soldier who was conscripted from agricultural labour for service with the army.

When arrangements had been made with the men they were sent into the vineyard to work.

Apparently, the owner of the vineyard was not able to engage all the workers he needed at his first call, and so at 'about the third hour', or nine o'clock, he went again into the market place 'and saw others standing idle'. To them he offered employment, but without specifying the particular pay they would receive. 'Go ye also into the vineyard,' he said, 'and whatsoever is right I will give you.' A number agreed to these terms 'and they went their way'.

At the sixth and ninth hours, that is at noon and three o'clock in the afternoon, the owner of the vineyard repeated his visit and engaged still more men.

At the eleventh hour, only an hour before sunset, there was still a great deal of the harvest yet to be gathered in, so for the last time the owner of the vineyard went into the market place. Finding some still 'standing idle' he 'saith unto them, Why stand ye here all the day idle?' They replied, 'Because no man hath hired us.' Much to their surprise at so late an hour, the man said, 'Go ye also into the vineyard; and whatsoever is right, that shall ye receive.' Some of these men may have been too lazy to accept work earlier in the day, but the majority had probably been seeking work elsewhere in vain and had come to the market place just in time for this last call. Only too glad to earn something to buy food for their families,

Israel is still a land of vineyards. Here delicious seedless grapes are harvested near Bet Zera just south of the Sea of Galilee.

they responded with alacrity and worked hard till sunset.

As the disciples listened to the story they began to wonder how it would end. Presumably the labourers in the vineyard would be rewarded in proportion to the time they had worked. This, in fact, was what the rabbinical regulations prescribed.

Judge their surprise, therefore, when Jesus said, 'When even was come, the lord of of the vineyard saith unto his steward, Call the labourers, and give them their hire, beginning from the last unto the first.'

This was unusual to say the least, for those who had worked longest were surely entitled to be paid first so that they could get away and buy food for the evening meal.

91

They were still more surprised when Jesus went on, 'And when they came that were hired about the eleventh hour, they received every man a penny.' This was the wage agreed upon as fair and just for a full day's labour, and here were the eleventh-hour men getting paid first and receiving a whole day's pay.

Thinking that this was an evidence of the generosity of the lord of the vineyard the disciples waited to see how much more those who had worked longest would receive.

The labourers in the story who had worked since dawn also 'supposed that they should have received more', but when they were summoned 'they likewise received every man a penny'.

At once these workers murmured against the good man saying, 'These last have wrought but one hour, and thou hast made them equal unto us which have borne the burden and heat of the day.'

The disciples looked at one another and nodded as much as to say that they entirely agreed with the protest. But the owner replied to the spokesman, 'Friend, I do thee no wrong: didst thou not agree with me for a penny? Take that thine is, and go thy way: I will give unto this last even as unto thee. Is it not lawful for me to do what I will with mine own? Is thine eye evil (or jealous), because I am good?'

Their objection was indeed unworthy of them. The workers who had only served part of the day had families to feed just as those who had been fortunate enough to get a whole day's employment. The owner of the vineyard generously took this into consideration and rewarded them with enough to feed their families. But because he had done this there was no reason why he should dip further into his profits to give a bonus to those who had simply re-

Solomon's Pools, south of Bethlehem, were built during the reign of Herod the Great to supply water for Jerusalem and the fortress of Herodion. The three reservoirs have a combined capacity of 160,000 cubic metres, quite an undertaking for the period. The conduits that conveyed the water to Jerusalem can still be seen.

ceived a fair day's pay for a fair day's work.

As the disciples thought over the story they realized that the lord of the vineyard was a very wise man. Unfortunately, as later events showed, they failed for a long time fully to see the spiritual implications of the parable.

In this familiar market scene Jesus was portraying the call of God, the divine householder, to men to become His disciples and to aid Him in gathering the Gospel fruit from the vineyard of the world. The 'day' represents each life's opportunity of labour. The 'penny' is the spiritual reward of those who agree to work as 'labourers together with God' until 'the night cometh'. God is the Owner of the vineyard and Christ is the Steward who dispenses the rewards of grace.

As most of the disciples were young men when they came to Christ they gave practically the whole of their life's 'day' to the cause of Christ, like the men who were engaged at dawn. John, for example, was probably not more than thirty when he was called and he was actually the last of the disciples to die at an age probably approaching a hundred years. Paul could

not have been very old when Christ appeared to him on the Damascus Road and Timothy received a knowledge of Christ 'as a child' from his mother and grandmother. These early disciples laboured long and hard in the Lord's cause and gave a full 'day' of service before they laid down their burden. So also have countless others who have given their hearts to God in the strength of their youth.

Those called at the third, sixth, and ninth hours represent those who have not given their lives to Christ until more mature years, perhaps because they failed to recognize the spiritual opportunity offered, or because they did not hear the call till later life. But when the call did come they dedicated the rest of their 'day' to Him for faithful labour.

The ones called at the 'eleventh hour' represent those who, in the latest years of their lives, accept Christ and give Him the feeble strength of their declining years. Even those, like the penitent thief on the cross, who respond at death's door will not fail to receive their reward, though their service is only a dying witness to the forgiving grace of God.

In the work of the world, there may be an argument for differential rewards, but this method of calculation is quite inapplicable in reference to the rewards of the kingdom.

In the first place, as Jesus pointed out on another occasion, we are all at best, 'unprofitable servants'. There is nothing we can do, however long or hard we labour, whatever talents we contribute, or means we sacrifice, to earn the rewards of the kingdom. None can demand the 'penny' as his on 'merit' and none can put forth the claim that his reward should be greater than that of any other. In any case it is quite impossible to determine the intensity of love or the extent of devotion of a soul who responds to the call of God by years of discipleship, or any other measure, for one may crowd more energy of faith into a year than another into a lifetime. One might need greater grace to tear away from the evil practices of years than another whose lot was cast in pleasanter places.

None, therefore, can claim that his devotion or service is greater than that of another, for whatever we are and in whatever way we have been privileged to serve, we must all say with Paul, 'By the grace of God I am what I am.'

Furthermore, as the 'penny', in its spiritual sense, represents the blessings of the kingdom, the reward must be the same for all. There will be no special privileges for some which are denied to others, so that the 'penny' cannot be added to or detracted from. If we are granted an entrance into the kingdom all the privileges of salvation will be ours, at whatever stage in our lives we have responded to the call of God, or whatever the burdens we have borne for the Lord. And when we get to the kingdom none will complain that someone else has got in more easily than him. All will account their reward far beyond their deserts and give glory to the Lord for His mercy and grace.

Besides this individual application of the parable there is another which was needed to make clear to the still-prejudiced disciples that the Gentiles were to share equally with believers from God's ancient people in the privileges of the Gospel. Those called at the dawn of day may be taken to represent the first Christians called from among the Jews at the beginning of the 'day of salvation'. In the earliest days of the apostolic church, represented by the 'third hour', the majority of the converts were still from the Jewish synagogues throughout the Roman empire. But as the 'day' of salvation wore on the Gospel began to go to the Gentiles. In His parable Jesus showed that when this time came, God would make no distinction between those whose lineage went back to the patriarchs and prophets and those who formerly were Greeks or barbarians, aliens from the commonwealth of Israel.

That this lesson was very much needed, is indicated by Paul's reference, in his epistle to the Thessalonians, to those who forbade him to 'speak to the Gentiles that they might be saved'.

So in this parable Jesus sought to teach the disciples that the Gospel rewards would not be based upon any 'merit' either of sacrifice or labour, nor upon any privilege of birth. The Gospel call knows no ethnic boundaries and in the heavenly kingdom there will be no class distinction or racial prejudice. Whether from east or west, north or south, all who respond will be fellow-heirs, and will equally partake of the riches of the inheritance of the saints.

All will be there through the free grace of God, appropriated by faith, and from every heart will arise the confession which Wesley put so beautifully into the words of his hymn:

Two wonders I confess,
The wonder of His glorious love,
And mine own worthlessness.

This chapter is based on Matthew 20:1-16.

94

Zacchaeus entertains Jesus

From the tropical jungle through which the muddy Jordan flowed, a winding road ascended through a parched, treeless region to the fertile plain which extended to the foothills of the wilderness of Judea. On this plain, watered by the Fountain of Elisha and other abundant springs, stood the Herodian city of Jericho. A mile or so to the north and nearer to the hills lay the scattered ruins of the Jericho destroyed by Joshua.

In the days of Jesus, Jericho was one of the most beautiful cities in all Palestine. All around, spreading across the lush plain, were date palm groves, balsam and rose gardens, rich orchards of almond, citron, cherry, pomegranate, and orange.

Looking north from the site of Jericho where the parched Jordan valley meets the foothills of the wilderness of Judea.

Beyond were fields of wheat and maize which ripened earlier than anywhere else in Palestine and sometimes produced a double harvest.

Lying astride the main road from the Jordan ford to Jerusalem, Jericho was also an important caravan city. Along this highway came traders and travellers from the tetrarchy of Galilee and Perea, from the Nabataean kingdom to the south, and from Arabia and beyond. And at the time of the Jewish feasts the road was thronged with pilgrims going up to Jerusalem to worship.

Because of its position on the main caravan route across the lower Jordan, Jericho was one of the most important customs posts in Judea. Indeed, as a revenue collecting centre it occupied a position corresponding precisely with that of Capernaum in the north. Customs duty was

imposed there on all goods coming in from Herod's territory in Galilee and Perea and beyond, and it was doubtless also the financial centre for the rich farms and estates of the surrounding plain.

The chief commissioner of the tax office in Jericho was a Jew named Zacchaeus. Just what his reputation was we do not know, but it probably completely belied his name, which ironically meant 'pure'.

Like all the Jewish tax gatherers working for the Herods or the Roman government, Zacchaeus had enriched himself by extorting from merchants and the local population far more than he was required to pay to his employers, and for his rapacity and disloyalty to his own nation he was without doubt hated by his fellow countrymen.

But, like the erstwhile tax gatherer Matthew-Levi, Zacchaeus was not without his better feelings. Though rich, he was unsatisfied in heart. He may have been influenced first by the preaching of John the Baptist, who had urged the publicans in his audience to 'exact no more' than was due to them, and probably he had also listened to Jesus on a number of occasions when He was passing through Jericho. He may even have learned how Matthew-Levi had become one of Christ's disciples. At any rate, what he had heard had aroused in him a desire to reform his life, and already he had begun to make amends where he could to those whom he had defrauded.

When he learned that Jesus was in Jericho again with the Passover pilgrims, Zacchaeus determined that he must hear Him, and if possible speak to Him. So, leaving his desk, he joined the noisy crowds which thronged after Jesus.

Unfortunately, Zacchaeus was of very short stature and though he ran hither and thither among the multitude he could not get within sight or earshot of Jesus. Being a

Ask a friendly Jericho Arab and he will assure you that this is 'the' tree climbed by Zacchaeus. The tree was probably a Sycamore Fig, not to be confused with the European Sycamore.

resourceful little man a bright idea soon came to him. He would slip ahead of the crowds and get up into one of the Egyptian fig or sycamore trees which bordered the road on the outskirts of the town. This would be easy enough as the roots of these trees arched out from the trunk above the ground and provided convenient steps up which he could readily ascend to one of the lower branches. In such a position he would have a good view of Jesus as He passed by.

No one took any notice of the rich publican as he hurried off, for quite likely other people also were intent on finding a good position, and no sooner was he ensconced in a convenient tree than Jesus came walking slowly along. As He passed right under where Zacchaeus was sitting the little publican was amazed to see Him suddenly stop and look straight up into his face. Then He spoke. 'Zacchaeus,' said Jesus, 'make haste, and come down; for today I must abide at thy house.'

Zacchaeus was so surprised and excited that he almost fell out of the tree in his eagerness to obey Jesus. It was a mystery to him how Jesus knew his name, and it was unbelievable that He should offer to enter the house of a despised tax-gatherer. But he was only too glad to have such a wonderful opportunity, and quickly he led Jesus to his palatial home.

Quite likely Zacchaeus lived some little distance out of Jericho on his own farm or estate, and so in going there Jesus did not need to retrace His steps. In the home of Zacchaeus He would be able to take His midday meal and rest much more comfortably than by the dusty roadside.

That Jesus should offer to enter the home of a publican aroused consternation and murmurings among some of the local inhabitants, especially the proud priests, who took it as an insult that He should prefer such company to theirs.

At any other time Zacchaeus might have been angered by their criticisms, but so touched was he by the kindness of Jesus that he determined there and then to make public confession of his past misdeeds, and of his resolve to make more than full restitution for all the injustice he had done. 'Behold, Lord,' he declared in the hearing of his enemies, 'the half of my goods I [will] give to the poor; and if I have taken anything from any man by false accusation, I [will] restore him fourfold.'

Those who knew Zacchaeus must have been staggered at the promise he so publicly made. Normally the law of Moses required only the addition of a fifth when restitution was voluntarily made for dishonesty. When a matter came before the courts, a fine of double might be imposed; but only in the case of the most deliberate

and felonious fraud was four times the amount exacted. And here was Zacchaeus voluntarily imposing upon himself the extreme penalty of the law.

What a contrast this revealed between the rich publican and the young ruler who had come to Jesus not many days before. The publican was willing to surrender all to win Christ. The ruler clung to his riches and lost the precious word of salvation.

In recognition of his confession and promise of restitution, Jesus immediately responded, 'This day is salvation come to this house', and for the benefit of the priests in the crowd He added, 'Forasmuch as he also is a son of Abraham'.

As a servant of Rome and a traitor to his country Zacchaeus had, in the estimation of the strict Jews, forfeited his birthright; but Jesus acknowledged him to be a truer 'son of Abraham' than they, for the essential qualification for kinship with Abraham was not so much descent according to the flesh, but faith in God and in His Son, and this Zacchaeus certainly had. As Paul, on an-

Jericho, advertised as the world's oldest city, has had the claim confirmed by several archaeological digs. Excavations have revealed Jericho through many periods including the city destroyed by Joshua.

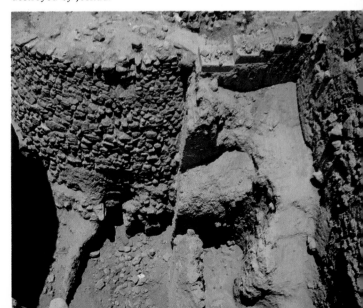

The monastery of Quarantal perched on a rockface of the wilderness of Judea near Jericho. It commemorates the forty-day fast and temptations that Jesus endured.

other occasion, said, 'He is not a Jew which is one outwardly; . . . but he is a Jew which is one inwardly.' The true children of Abraham are not the children of the flesh, but the children of faith. That is why Abraham is called 'the father of the faithful'.

In Zacchaeus' experience is revealed the true relation of faith and works in the life of the believers. The Pharisee in the temple ostentatiously told God all the good works he was in the habit of doing, in the expectation of receiving due recognition from God. But such works were rejected as valueless because he was 'going about to establish his own righteousness'. Zacchaeus came to Jesus acknowledging his sin and by faith alone found salvation. Then, as the new power of grace came into operation in his life, it manifested itself in works of faith which Jesus at once commended.

The works of Zacchaeus were not carried out with a view to claiming credit for his actions, but were the result of the faith gen-erated in his heart by the power of Jesus. The Pharisees' works were, in the sight of God, 'dead works', but the works of Zacchaeus were the fruit of his new relationship with Jesus and with God.

Faith in Christ does not render works unnecessary as some have thought, for James truly says, 'Faith without works is dead', but the works of the true child of God are the result of the outworking of faith, and not a basis for earning salvation.

That Jesus during His brief sojourn in Jericho should have stopped to heal poor Bartimaeus and his companion, and then brought salvation to the home of the rich publican Zacchaeus, emphasized again the universality of His ministry. Truly He said as He left the home of Zacchaeus, 'The Son of man is come to seek and to save that which was lost'. It does not matter to Jesus whether the seeking soul is rich or poor, learned or ignorant, Jew or Gentile. It matters only that he realizes his need of Jesus, and none who seek Him in faith will He ever turn empty away.

This chapter is based on Luke 19:1-10.

At Simon's feast

As Sabbath, the eighth of Nisan, six days before the Passover, drew on, Jesus reached Bethany. The pilgrims who had no relatives or friends in the neighbourhood of Jerusalem set up camp for themselves on the nearby slopes of the Mount of Olives, but for Jesus there was always a comfortable room in the house of Mary and Martha and Lazarus.

On this occasion He was especially welcome, for when He had come two months earlier it was to a house of sorrow. Now, through the miracle Jesus wrought, Lazarus was alive and well and helping in the preparation to receive Jesus.

During the Sabbath, though great crowds gathered to see Jesus, He did not engage in any public ministry. Most of the day He spent in meditation and prayer, preparing Himself for the supreme ordeal which awaited Him.

In the evening after the Sabbath, however, Jesus did accept an invitation to dine with Simon the Pharisee, who also lived in Bethany, and whom Jesus had healed of leprosy. Through this miracle Simon had become a friend of Jesus, though he was not yet persuaded that He was the Messiah. When he heard that Jesus was staying in the village he naturally invited Him to a meal. As he knew Lazarus, Mary, and Martha, he invited them, too, as well as the disciples. He also took the opportunity to ask some of his Pharisee friends, who had criticized his friendship with Jesus, so that they might meet Him on more intimate terms than in His public ministry.

When it was known that Jesus was at Simon's house a great concourse of people made their way there in the hope of seeing and hearing Him, and also to get a glimpse of Lazarus whose restoration to life was the sensation of the district.

As the guests took their places at the table Jesus was, of course, given the seat of honour. Simon sat on His right hand and most likely Lazarus was placed on His left.

As usual, Martha had offered to help with the meal, but Mary stood by the door watching Jesus as He talked with His host and the other guests. Perhaps as Martha passed she chided her sister again for not helping. Little did she realize, however, the memorable part that Mary was to play on this occasion.

The meal had been proceeding for some little time when Mary moved towards the head of the table, drawing from her bosom as she went a small long-necked alabaster cosmetic vase full of spikenard or pure oil of nard, one of the most precious perfumes of the ancient East. It was an essence, something like myrrh, derived from the roots and blossoms of a fragrant herb which grew in the mountains of Syria and high up in the Himalayas of India. The Indian nard, because of its rarity and the long distance it was brought, was the most expensive. Only the rich could afford to buy it for cosmetic purposes or to perfume special sacrifices.

Unnoticed by the feasting guests, Mary reached the divan where Jesus reclined on His left elbow with His feet, from which He had removed His sandals at the beginning of the meal, extended backward away from the table. Quietly breaking the long neck of the vase Mary proceeded to pour some of the ointment upon the head of Jesus and the rest upon His feet. Then, laying aside the empty vessel, she knelt to kiss His feet in token of her deep love and devotion. As tears of uncontrollable emotion fell upon Jesus' feet she loosed the braid which held up her long hair and began to wipe them with the beautiful tresses. Soon the exquisite perfume was spreading across the room, alerting the whole company to Mary's loving deed.

When the guests recovered from their amazement, a babel of discussion broke out as to the propriety of her act. Judas, who was sitting near Jesus, leaned over and remonstrated with Him for permitting such 'waste'. 'Why was not this ointment sold for three hundred pence,' he said, 'and given to the poor?' If she was wealthy enough to buy such expensive ointment, she could surely have used her money better in the giving of alms.

As the disciples, to whom three hundred pence was a small fortune, listened to the conversation, they nodded approval of what seemed to them a very proper citicism. It was not, however, thrift or any special love for the poor which led Judas to speak as he did. His plea was only a cover for his secret covetousness. He would have liked the three hundred pence to have been deposited in the common purse, which was in his keeping, so that he could have helped himself to it. For, unknown to the disciples who held him in high esteem for his business acumen, 'he was a thief'.

This revelation concerning Judas may lead some to wonder why Jesus ever allowed him to become the purse-bearer. The probability is that it was the disciples who chose Judas, as the most business-minded among them, and Jesus could not have questioned their choice without indicating that He distrusted him. So He allowed Judas to accept this responsibility

Part of the western wall of the Old City of Jerusalem. Behind the Jaffa Gate (on the left) the Citadel is located. This was the site of Herod's great palace with its three massive, defensive towers, Phasael, Hippicus and Mariamne. Phasael still partly stands and is called David's tower.

as a test of his desire to overcome his besetting sin.

Distressed at Judas' accusation of extravagance and waste, Mary arose hastily to leave the room, but Jesus motioned her to remain. He had read the mind of Judas and could have exposed him before the disciples, but in His longsuffering patience He did not. Instead, He said quietly, 'The poor always ye have with you: but me ye have not always.'

There would be plenty of opportunities in the future for self-denial and benevolence towards the poor, but what Mary had done in His honour was something for which there would not be opportunity much longer. Her action was not a misdirected 'waste', but eminently timely.

In Jesus' reply to Judas there is sound counsel for us today on avenues of Christian benevolence. Sometimes gifts for the beautifying of the house of God or the enhancement of its worship are subject to the same criticism as was levelled against Mary. In such cases the answer of Jesus is equally relevant. The poor stand in as great need of the help of the Church as in Jesus' day and should be generously treated, but it is not waste or extravagance to give gifts for the ennobling and beautifying of God's sanctuary. He is deserving of our best gifts, and it is entirely proper that we should worship Him in the beauty of holiness, provided that we have due regard also for the needy and suffering. Both objects should have their proper

place in the hearts of God's people.

But Jesus had more to say to Judas. 'Why trouble ye the woman?' He went on, 'for she hath wrought a good work upon me.' 'Against the day of my burying hath she kept this,' and now 'she is come aforehand to anoint my body to the burying.'

Of all the followers of Jesus, only Mary had taken seriously His many references to His approaching death; and feeling that no sacrifice for Him would be too great, she had purchased and set aside this precious ointment. In that sad day, of which He spoke, she could at least show the love she bore Him by perfuming His dead body as a last token of respect.

But now there was so much excited talk about Jesus proclaiming Himself King that she did not know what to do. If He was going to be King she wanted to be the first to honour Him with the oil of anointing. So she decided to take the bottle with her to Simon's house, and as she watched Him the impulse came overwhelmingly upon her to use the ointment there and then.

Jesus read all this in Mary's heart, and in His words of reproof to Judas He told her that He recognized and accepted her great love. At His birth He had received a gift of myrrh, and now again just before His death Mary had given Him a similar gift symbolic of His suffering and death on behalf of a sinful race. The fragrant memory of her deed He would carry with Him to the cross.

More than that, He added, 'Wheresoever this Gospel shall be preached throughout the whole world, this also that she hath done shall be spoken of for a memorial of her.' Far from being a 'waste', the perfume of her self-sacrifice would spread through the world to inspire countless souls to similar self-surrender and dedication.

If Judas was indignant at Mary's 'waste', Simon was embarrassed by the incident. He well knew the reason for Mary's weeping, and the fact that Jesus accepted her gift without any reference to her past life perplexed him.

'This man,' he said to himself, 'if he were a [lit. "the"] prophet, would have known who and what manner of woman this is that toucheth him: for she is a sinner.' Jesus answering the unspoken thought, leaned across to the Pharisee, and said, 'I have somewhat to say unto thee.'

'Master, say on,' Simon responded immediately. 'There was a certain creditor [or money lender] which had two debtors', Jesus began: 'the one owed five hundred pence [about £18], and the other fifty [about £2]. And when they had nothing to pay, he frankly forgave them both. Tell me therefore, which of them will love him most?

Wondering what Jesus was implying, Simon answered cautiously, 'I suppose that he, to whom he forgave most.'

'Thou hast rightly judged,' Jesus replied, and pointing to Mary He said to the Pharisee, 'Seest thou this woman? I entered into thine house, thou gavest me no water for my feet: but she hath washed my feet with tears, and wiped them with the hairs of her head. Thou gavest me no kiss; but this woman since the time I came in hath not ceased to kiss my feet. My head with oil thou didst not anoint: but this woman hath anointed [not only my head but also] my feet with ointment. Wherefore I say unto thee, her sins, which are many, are forgiven; for she loved much: but to whom little is forgiven, the same loveth little.'

Out of his mouth Simon had condemned himself for his ingratitude just as Nathan caused David to pronounce judgement on himself for his sin. Simon's healing had not been followed by a reformation of character, and his gratitude for physical restoration was nothing like the profound experience that had come to Mary. Consequently, when Jesus came to Simon's house he was more consumed by pride at the honour he was doing Jesus than conscious of the gratitude he should have had towards Him.

Between Simon and Mary it was very clear who loved Jesus more and who had the deeper consciousness of sins forgiven. Turning to Mary, Jesus said tenderly, 'Thy sins are forgiven.'

We are not told how Simon reacted to the reproof, but we would like to think that this time he experienced a real conversion and gave himself unreservedly to Christ. His priestly friends, however, seized on Jesus' assurance to Mary and said among themselves, Who is this that forgiveth sins also?' Here was further evidence which they must remember in order to accuse Jesus.

But Jesus took no notice of the whispered criticisms, and as Mary turned to go He said assuringly to her, 'Thy faith hath saved thee; go in peace.'

This chapter is based on Matthew 26:6-13; Luke 7:36-50; Mark 14:3-9; John 12:1-9.

The betrayal plot

When Jesus retired to Perea after the raising of Lazarus, the chief priests issued an injunction 'that if any one knew where he were, he should show it, that they might take him'.

Doubtless it was in response to this order that the priests who had seen Jesus at Simon's house hurried over the Mount of Olives to Jerusalem with the report that He was in Bethany and that crowds were flocking to see Him. They went straight to the palace of Caiaphas near the temple, and when the high priest heard the news he at once convened a meeting of all the available members of the Sanhedrin. The fact that Nicodemus and Joseph of Arimathea were not there suggests that they were not told because of their known sympathies with Jesus.

At their last meeting Caiaphas had told the Sanhedrin that Jesus must be dealt with summarily before He started a popular rising and brought upon them the wrath of the Romans. The latest news from Bethany convinced them that there was now no time to lose. Jesus was coming to the feast, and already excitement was rising. They must apprehend Him without delay and Lazarus must die also, for as long as he was alive he would be an incontrovertible witness to the power of Jesus.

The one difficulty was that they dared not arrest Jesus openly during the feast. There would be too many people around whom He had helped, and His fellow Galileans would certainly rise up in His defence. They were regretfully coming to the conclusion that it would be better to wait till after the Passover crowds had departed, when their discussions were interrupted by the announcement of a visitor. As they turned to see who it was, Judas entered the room. He had followed

the priests out of Simon's house furious at the reproof of Jesus, and hearing them say that they were going to the high priest in Jerusalem, he had followed, determined now to do what he had been contemplating for a long time, namely, to force Jesus to declare Himself or finally break with Him.

When Judas first joined the disciple band he had hoped that Jesus would quickly proclaim Himself the Messiah, expel the Roman usurpers, and set up His kingdom. In it he counted on getting a good position for himself. But ever since Jesus refused the kingship after the feeding of the five thousand he had become more and more impatient of His slowness to manifest Himself.

When, soon after they crossed the Jordan on their way to the Passover, Jesus had once again begun to warn the disciples of His approaching sufferings and death, Judas decided that there was no longer any purpose in staying by Him, and the sooner he got out of this embarrassing association the safer it would be

for him. He now only wanted an excuse to sever his connection.

His opportunity came with the reproof Jesus administered at Simon's feast. Judas finally surrendered himself to the promptings of the evil one and was impelled irresistibly on to the supreme treachery. Says the record, 'Then entered Satan into Judas, surnamed Iscariot'.

Well may we be warned by the tragic experience of Judas. Satan is ever lying in wait to 'enter into' unwary souls to beguile them into sin. Biding a favourable opportunity, he entered into Eve and led her to commit the first transgression. He entered into Ananias and caused him to lie to Peter and the Holy Ghost. His spirit is constantly working in 'the children of disobedience', driving them mercilessly to destruction. But we need not be ignorant of his devices. If, in the strength of the Lord, we 'resist the devil', as James tells us, he will 'flee' from us defeated. Judas did not resist the Devil. He yielded to his promptings again and again in petty pilfering, words of criticism, and acts of dis-

loyalty against Jesus, until at last he passed completely into his power.

As soon as the priests who had seen Judas at Simon's house recognized him, they introduced him to the others. Asked why he, a disciple of Jesus, had come to them, Judas explained that he had become

In the central southern area of the Old City of Jerusalem, overlooking the Temple Mount is the Jewish Quarter. The war in 1948 left this area in ruins but has been rebuilt in an elegant yet traditional style. Seen as part of the new (above) is the Hurva, meaning a ruin, of the Bet Yaakov Synagogue.

increasingly sceptical of His claims and had decided to dissociate himself from Jesus. Indeed, he said, he was now prepared to help them to secure His arrest and condemnation.

When the Sanhedrin heard this 'they were glad'. The help of Judas altered the whole situation. It would not now be necessary to wait until after the feast, for he knew the movements of Jesus and could lead them to Him when the multitudes were not around. So they gladly 'covenanted to give him money' to commit this treacherous act.

Judas readily accepted their offer. He had followed Jesus in the hope of a tangible reward for his services. Now he had decided to change sides, he might as well make as much out of it as he could.

But if Judas thought he was going to receive a handsome reward for his treachery, he was mistaken, for the rulers were as mean as himself. In the estimation of the chief priests Jesus was an impostor and the price for apprehending Him should be no more than the price of a slave. So 'they covenanted with him for thirty pieces of silver', or shekels, from the temple treasury.

How truly the apostle wrote when he declared that He who was 'equal with God' took upon Himself the 'form of a slave', for the price set upon His head was precisely that of a slave. And in agreeing to accept this payment, Judas fulfilled two other prophecies concerning His betrayal. David had declared that his greater Son would be betrayed by His 'own familiar friend' and Judas was, as the Record significantly says, 'one of the twelve'. Now he fulfilled the word of Zechariah who, by inspiration, declared, 'So they weighed for my price thirty pieces of silver.' What a price Judas received in exchange for his

soul!

Whether he imagined that Jesus would not allow Himself to be taken we can never know. It may be that as a last resort he intended to try to force Jesus' hand and compel Him to reveal His power. Then he could go back to Him and say that he did it with the best of intentions in his desire for the coming of the kingdom. The fact that he committed suicide when his plan went awry, would suggest that he never foresaw that such a tragedy would happen.

When the terms of the betrayal had been fixed the priests raised the question as to when Judas would deliver Jesus into their hands. It must not be on 'the feast day', they told him, 'lest there be an uproar of the people'. Judas agreed and proposed that he should bring them to Jesus in the Garden of Gethsemane where He was wont to go by night with His disciples to pray. This entirely satisfied the priestly plotters and they arranged to meet Judas again two days before the feast, to finalize on the plan.

Little did they realize as they dispersed that their altered plans would synchronize with still another prophecy 'which must needs be' fulfilled. For now His arrest and condemnation would bring about His death at precisely the time of the sacrifice of the paschal lamb. Antitype would meet type at the high moment of the Passover feast, and the most fateful prophecy of all Scripture would be fulfilled to the letter and on time.

Meanwhile Judas hurried back to Bethany to rejoin the disciples before they had time to suspect the terrible deed he was about to commit.

This chapter is based on Matthew 26:1-5, 14-16; Mark 14:1, 2, 10, 11; Luke 22:1-6; John 12:10,11.

Thy King cometh

After the feast in Simon's house, Jesus returned to the home of His friends Mary, Martha, and Lazarus, and the next morning He rose early to go to Jerusalem. It was now the ninth of the Hebrew month Nisan and the Passover crowds were multiplying daily. On the morrow the Passover lambs would be selected in preparation for the climax of the feast on the fourteenth of the month.

On previous occasions when Jesus went up to the temple, He had walked unobtrusively among the crowds to the place where He usually taught, but on this occasion He acted quite differently. The time

The traditional setting of Bethphage on the eastern slopes of the Mount of Olives. The little church that marks this site (right) stands over a mediaeval painted rock depicting the events leading to Jesus' kingly entry into Jerusalem. It is purported to be the actual rock that Jesus used to mount the colt.

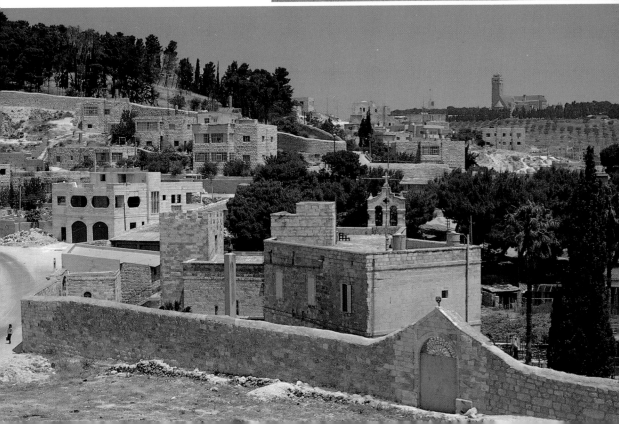

had almost come in the outworking purpose of His earthly life for His redemptive ministry to culminate on the cross of Calvary. But before He paid the supreme sacrifice it was necessary that He, whom John had described at the 'Lamb of God', should be conclusively identified with the Messiah-King of Israel. So, when the disciples joined Him at the house of Lazarus, He bade two of them, possibly Peter and John, go on a special errand for Him to the nearby village of Bethphage.

The location of this place is not now precisely known, but from its name, which means, 'the house of unripe figs', it must have stood among the fig orchards which covered the upper slopes of the Mount of Olives, somewhere to the north-west of Bethany. A twelfth century pilgrim placed it about a mile up the slope between Bethany and the summit of the mountain, and there is still to be found on this spot the ruins of an ancient church and the so-called Stele of Bethphage, on the four sides of which are pictured the momentous events enacted here and in Bethany.

'Go your way into the village over against you,' Jesus bade the disciples, and 'as soon as ye be entered into it . . . ye shall find an ass tied, and a colt with her: . . . whereon never man sat; . . . Loose them, and bring them unto me. And if any man say unto you, Why do ye this? say that the Lord hath need of him; and straightway he will send him hither.'

Obediently the disciples went to the village and just as Jesus had said, they found an ass and its colt tethered outside the gate of a house which stood at the junction of the main road into the village and a side road. This was most unusual, for the owners of such animals would normally tie them up in the inner courtyard

for safety and convenience.

At once the disciples knew that these were the animals Jesus meant and they began to loose the colt. As they did so the owner of the animals came out and said, 'Why loose ye the colt?' As they had been told, the disciples replied, 'The Lord hath need of him.' And without further demur the owner let them lead the colt away with the mother trotting along behind.

Reading this remarkable story it is natural to wonder whether the owner of the animals knew Jesus and whether even a prior arrangement had been made with him. Of this we cannot be sure, but the fact that when the disciples said, 'The Lord hath need of him,' the man seemed to know at once who the 'Lord' was, suggests that he may have been one of Jesus' followers. In this case he would be only too happy to be of service to his Master. So just as Jesus at His birth was laid in a borrowed cradle, one of His last journeys to Jerusalem was taken upon a borrowed mount. He who owns all things could rightfully have claimed anything He wanted, but always He found His greatest joy in asking and receiving the willing help of the lowliest of His followers.

When they got back to Bethany, the disciples, for lack of trappings of royal purple which were their Master's due, took off their own outer garments, and placed them on the back of the colt. On them Jesus took His seat and the little party set off on the road to Jerusalem.

There had been much discussion, both among the rulers of the Jews and the people, as to whether Jesus would show Himself at this feast of the Passover; and so, when the crowds of pilgrims who were streaming into Bethany saw the cavalcade moving off towards the city, they began excitedly to acclaim Him.

Doubtless, the majority of the crowd were Galileans who had followed Jesus up the road from Jericho, and it was a source of great satisfaction to them that they could acclaim the great Prophet as a fellow countryman. Many were men and women whom Jesus had healed of crippling diseases and who for the first time for years were able to come up to Jerusalem for the feast. Among them, too, were healed lepers who never imagined that they would be able to mingle freely with the Passover crowds again.

To us it seems almost unbelievable that such sincere and joyous acclamations could be turned in but a few days to bitter cries of 'Crucify him'. Nor need we suppose that these rejoicing crowds ever turned against their Benefactor and Friend. It is much more likely that their acclaiming voices were drowned at the last by the Jewish rabble of Jerusalem, who held no brief for the Galilean, and were easily inflamed by the jealous priests into demanding His condemnation and death.

Some of the crowd now ran ahead of Jesus and spread their garments in the road for the colt to pass over, while others picked up palm fronds and small leafy branches lying in the fields, and strewed them in the way or waved them at His approach.

By these acts the people showed clearly how they regarded Jesus, for this was the oriental way of paying homage to kings and men of high estate. When Jehu was called to the kingship of Israel, the people 'hasted and took every man his garment, and put it under him on the top of the stairs . . . saying, Jehu is king.'

In Israel, palm branches were a symbol of joy and victory, and in the Revelation the saints are pictured as marching in

Some of the crowd now shouting 'Hosannah to the King', were soon to be shouting 'Crucify'.

triumph to the heavenly Zion with palms in their hands.

Only a little while before, the Pharisees had threatened that any who acclaimed Jesus as the Messiah would be put out of the synagogue, but this was forgotten in the excitement of the hour. Led by the disciples, who in spite of what Jesus had said about His sufferings and death, were sure He was about to proclaim Himself David's greater Son, the crowds began to

109

chant in ecstasy the words of two of the Messianic victory psalms: 'Hosanna to the Son of David: Blessed is he that cometh in the name of the Lord. . . . Blessed is the king of Israel that cometh in the name of the Lord. . . . Hosanna in the highest.'

While the people did not realize it, and even the disciples did not at the time connect these events with Messianic prophecy, all this was a fulfilment to the very letter of what Zechariah had foretold before. 'Fear not, daughter of Zion,' he wrote, 'behold, thy king cometh, sitting on an ass's colt.'

The Jews had always believed that when Messiah appeared it would be with a great show of kingly might, but Zechariah had clearly told them to look for Him at His first appearance not upon a war horse in pomp and magnificence, but upon the gentle colt of an ass in token of His mission of salvation and peace.

The colt of an ass may seem a very insignificant, even incongruous, mount for Jesus on this occasion, but in the East asses of noble breeding and stately appearance were commonly used by persons of high estate on peaceful missions in contrast to the horses and chariots of military occasions. It was therefore entirely appropriate that such an animal should be used by the King-Messiah to symbolize His mission of redemptive grace.

The fact that the colt had never been ridden before likewise linked the One it bore with the unblemished sacrificial animals of the sanctuary services 'upon which never came yoke'. One day soon, however, the Revelator tells us, when Jesus appears again as King of kings and Lord of lords to inaugurate His kingdom of glory, He will manifest His sovereignty by riding out of the heavens on a 'white horse' to the sound of trumpets and with a vast retinue of holy angels.

When the Pharisees witnessed the excitement of the multitude and heard the ascriptions which they applied to Jesus, they were angry and alarmed. They were angry at the popularity of Jesus and they were alarmed that the Romans might think the commotion foreshadowed a revolt. They knew they were impotent to quieten the crowd themselves and so they appealed to Jesus. 'Master, rebuke thy disciples,' they remonstrated. But Jesus replied, 'I tell you that, if these should hold their peace, the stones would immediately cry out.' This acclamation was a fulfilment of prophecy and a final witness to the rulers and people of Jerusalem that they were about to reject their rightful King.

There were three routes from Bethany over the ridge of Olivet, as there are today. One lay between the central and northern summits of the mountain, the second on which Bethphage probably lay, ran over the highest point of the ridge; while the third, always the main road, followed the easiest ascent between the Mount of Olives and what is now called, though incorrectly, the Mount of Offence.

By the time the procession reached the summit ridge it was early afternoon, and as Jesus began the sharp descent into the Kidron Valley, the city of Jerusalem came into view in a blaze of April sunshine. Lying some three hundred feet below and half a mile away across the valley, the city must have been a wonderful sight with its mighty walls, the marble palace of Herod, the spreading suburbs and green gardens, all dominated by the glistening white towers, porticos, and courts of the temple, and the gilded façade and roof of the inner sanctuary.

But Jesus was not moved by the breath-

The seventh-century Byzantine Golden Gate, filled in by the Arabs in 810 AD. Jesus passed through the gate on this site on His triumphal entry into the city.

taking beauty of the scene. He was overcome with sorrow that the inhabitants of Zion failed to recognize that the great Antitype of the temple sacrifices had come among them. Jerusalem was about to reject its Redeemer and King and was drawing upon itself the inevitable retribution of utter destruction. Once the glory of the nations, Jesus realized that Jerusalem's doom was now sealed, and to the amazement of the crowds, whose acclamations were suddenly hushed into silence, Jesus wept for the glorious city and its unheeding inhabitants.

'If thou hadst known,' He cried, 'even thou, at least in this thy day, the things which belong unto thy peace! but now they are hid from thine eyes. For the days shall come upon thee that thine enemies shall cast a trench about thee, and compass thee round, and keep thee in on every side, and shall lay thee even with the ground, and thy children within thee; and they shall not leave in thee one stone upon another; because thou knewest not the time of thy visitation.'

Just under forty years later, in AD 70, this prophecy was fulfilled to the letter when the city was stormed and taken by the Roman general, Titus.

After sorrowfully beholding the city, Jesus continued His way down into the defile of the Kidron Valley, noting again the innumerable whitened sepulchres of the Jews to which He once compared the fair exterior but wicked heart of the Pharisees.

By this time the crowds in Jerusalem had seen the excited multitudes in the distance and had begun to stream across the valley to join them. Many of these were Jews newly come to Jerusalem from distant lands for the Passover feast, and when they inquired as to what the commotion was about they were told, 'This is Jesus the prophet of Nazareth of Galilee.'

As the rulers of the Jews saw the two streams of people mingled around Jesus their fury and alarm knew no bounds. 'Perceive ye,' they said to one another, 'how ye prevail nothing? behold, the world is gone after him.' And their fears were now heightened that Jesus might accept a crown at the hands of the people and precipitate a fatal revolt against the Romans. But they need not have feared. One day indeed Jesus would sit upon the throne of His father David, but that time was not yet. Now He was the King of grace, and His triumphant progress was to Calvary not to the throne.

Crossing the Kidron, Jesus began the ascent towards the city, soon reaching the Shushan or Golden Gate, which gave access directly to the outer court of the temple.

Here the guards restrained the crowds lest the tumult should spread into the temple itself, and Jesus was able to descend from His mount and slip quietly into the Court of the Gentiles.

We are not told what happened to the borrowed ass and colt, but we can be sure that when their purpose was fulfilled the disciples who had requisitioned the animals would take them safely back to their owner in Bethphage. As a matter of fact, the preferable rendering of the final words of the disciples to the owner is 'and he will return them again'.

Meanwhile, Jesus began to look around Him in the Court of the Gentiles. All was unusually quiet now as the excitement on the road from Bethany had drawn most of the crowds away. But Jesus looked with sorrow as He saw the tell-tale signs that the temple traders were there in full force again for this most profitable feast. He saw the tables of the money-changers stacked in the porticos, and the animal pens, now empty but which He knew on the morrow would be filled with bleating sheep and bellowing cattle. As He 'looked round about upon all things', nothing escaping His piercing eye, His decision was made as to His first task the next morning.

Then, as the sun went down red over the towers of Herod's palace and the priests returned to their quarters to eat their portion of the day's sacrifices, Jesus slipped out of the Golden Gate again and

The tear-drop shape of the Dominus Flevit nestles among the trees on the slopes of the Mount of Olives.

The simple, serene chapel of Dominus Flevit (the Lord wept) which recalls the anguish Jesus felt by the obstinate refusal of Jerusalem to accept God's offer of love. Here also Jesus foresaw the cruel end that would come under the Romans. The view from the chapel window is across the Kidron Valley to the site of the Temple, now an Islamic shrine. A hen and her chicks on the beautiful mosaic illustrates Jesus' words in Matthew 23:37.

returned with the disciples over the Mount of Olives.

He may have gone back to the home of Lazarus and his sisters, but as the night was warm and dry He may have chosen to spend it in some quiet spot on the mountain where He could prepare Himself for the ordeal that drew ever closer.

This chapter is based on Matthew 21:1-11; Mark 11:1-11; Luke 19:29-44; John 12:12-19.

The temple cleansed again

Descending into the Kidron Valley once again, Jesus mingled with the crowds going through the Golden Gate of the temple into the Court of the Gentiles.

Looking around He saw the temple traders already doing a brisk trade in sacrificial animals and birds, and this was also the last day for the purchase of the paschal lambs. Crowds were milling around the penned animals, the dove cages, and the stalls of meal, oil, and salt, and other ingredients for the sacrifices, while the clinking of coins at the tables of the money-changers told of the large amounts of money which were changing hands as the worshippers purchased their temple half-shekels for offerings.

In its proper place in the markets of the

Herod the Great's temple in a model of Jerusalem in AD 66. The building on the right is the Antonia Tower. The Pools of Bethesda are in the foreground.

city, and even in the streets leading to the temple, this trading was entirely right and proper, as the majority of the worshippers came from a distance and relied on the local merchants to purchase their offerings and change their money for temple coinage. But it was sacrilegious to carry the buying and selling into the temple courts, and the practice was made worse, if that were possible, by the cheating and extortion to which the worshippers were subjected.

Besides the profaning of the outer court by the greedy traders, Jesus noticed also that the city porters had turned it into a thoroughfare, making it a short cut in carrying their burdens from one part of the city to another.

The heart of Jesus had been distressed by such scenes every time He had come to the temple, but as He had not interfered with the traders since the occasion, three years before, when He had driven them

out, they thought that He had accepted the situation as He found it, and the market at this Passover was busier than ever.

But as His earthly ministry was drawing to a close Jesus was impelled for the last time to teach them the sanctity of God's house and of the symbols of His coming sacrifice. To their complete surprise, therefore, He walked straight across the court and began to drive out both 'them that sold therein, and them that bought' and to overthrow 'the tables of the moneychangers, and the seats of them that sold doves'. Likewise He turned back the porters who were crossing the court 'and would not suffer that any man should carry any vessel through the temple'.

On the earlier occasion Jesus had simply said to the greedy merchants, 'Make not my Father's house an house of merchandise', but this time, with the full Messianic authority of 'Messenger of the covenant', which He had assumed in His triumphal entry the previous day, He

The Islamic Dome of the Rock where once stood the Temple where Jesus attacked corruption and bigotry. (Below) The northern aspect of the Court of the Gentiles. Where the archways are seen stood Herod's Fortress of Antonia where Jesus was tried by Pilate.

cried, 'Is it not written, My house shall be called of all nations the house of prayer? but ye have made it a den of thieves.'

As the Gentiles were not permitted, on pain of death, to enter the temple proper, this 'Court of the Gentiles' had been specially provided so that 'the sons of the stranger' who desired 'to join themselves to the Lord, to serve him, and to love the name of the Lord, to be his servants', might come into His presence. Through this means the prophecy was to be fulfilled, 'Even them will I bring to my holy mountain, and make them joyful in my house of prayer: their burnt offerings and their sacrifices shall be accepted upon mine altar; for mine house shall be called a house of prayer for all people.'

How terrible it was, therefore, that the Sadducee temple authorities should permit traders to turn this 'house of prayer for all people' not only into a common market but into a 'den of thieves'. How could the Gentiles be attracted to the worship of the true God in the midst of such profanity and pandemonium? If this was how the rulers of the Jews addressed themselves to the sacred responsibilities to the 'nations', was it any wonder that God's patience was almost exhausted?

The news of Jesus' action travelled quickly through the temple and into the streets around, and it was not long before the blind and the lame and those afflicted with other maladies began to crowd in. Soon the court which had been filled with the din of buying and selling was resounding with the shouts of joy from sufferers restored at a touch or a word from Jesus.

By this time the rulers of the temple had been appraised of the happenings in the outer court and hurried to the scene. They were furious at Jesus' treatment of the traders who were there by their authorization and from whom they made much gain. They were also fearful that this signal demonstration of His authority might lead the people to proclaim Jesus Messiah and King there and then. Judge their surprise, therefore, when they found Jesus teaching quietly in the midst of an attentive crowd, while the children ran around crying, 'Hosanna to the Son of David'.

Finding no occasion in His gentle dignity to attack Him they could only bid Him, as they had done on the Kidron road, to rebuke the blasphemy of the children who saluted Him as 'the Son of David'. But Jesus replied that they were only acting in harmony with an age-old Messianic prophecy which, like all other prophecies 'must needs be fulfilled'. 'Have ye never read,' He asked them, 'Out of the mouths of babes and sucklings thou hast perfected praise?'

The priests were chagrined by the suggestion that, because they had failed to recognize and give praise to God for Messiah, He had put His praise into the mouths of little children. But in their rage they could find no words to reply; nor for fear of the people who 'hanging on his lips', could they find 'what they might do'. Gnashing their teeth in anger they slunk away to their council chamber to think out how they might 'utterly destroy' Him.

Left in peace, Jesus continued His work of healing and teaching until 'even was come'. Then once more He left the city and returned to Bethany.

The next day, the eleventh of Nisan, Jesus went into the temple to teach for the last time during His earthly ministry. To the end also the chief priests and elders dogged His footsteps, seeking to impede His work and amass evidence of which He could be condemned. The events of the past two or three days, His spectacular entry into the city, His second cleansing of the temple, His appropriation of the temple courts for His healing and teaching ministry, had completely undermined their authority as custodians of the temple. Their only hope now was to make a final attempt to humiliate Him before the people. So an imposing group of the temple rulers, including the chief priests, heads of the different courses of the priesthood, doctors of law, and other eminent members of the Sanhedrin, pushed their way through the crowds and confronted Him with the disdainful challenge, 'By what authority doest thou these things? and who gave thee this authority?'

Their carefully thought out plan was that if Jesus refused to declare His authority they would call the temple guards and expel Him as an unauthorized person. If, on the other hand, Jesus openly claimed the authority of God, they could accuse Him of blasphemy. Furthermore, if He claimed to be David's Son they would be able to accuse Him to Pilate of sedition and inciting rebellion against the Roman authorities.

It is perhaps strange that, in setting this trap for Jesus, they did not recall their humiliation on the last occasion that they had demanded His credentials. Apparently they thought that the time for decisive action against Him could not longer be delayed. Jesus, however, was not to be taken so easily in their snare. Adopting a tactic common in rabbinical debates, He replied, 'I also will ask you one thing, which if ye will tell me, I in likewise will tell you by what authority I do these things.'

Apprehensively they waited for His question. 'The baptism of John, whence

The Great Synagogue, an imposing modern building which serves as the centre of Jewish worship in Jerusalem.

117

was it? from heaven, or of men?' Jesus asked. This was a most disturbing subject for Jesus to introduce in public, and immediately there was a whispering among the rulers as to how they should reply.

'If we shall say, From heaven,' they argued, 'He will say unto us, Why did ye not then believe him?' for John had plainly testified that Jesus was the Messiah. 'But and if we say, Of men; all the people will stone us; for they be persuaded that John was a prophet.'

Eventually they decided not to involve themselves further in this question, and with their tongues in their cheeks, they replied, 'We cannot tell'.

It was bad enough for these recognized teachers of the people to have to confess themselves unable to appraise the work of so eminent a preacher as John, but they literally ground their teeth in frustration and anger when Jesus completed their discomfiture with the retort, 'Neither do I tell you by what authority I do these things.'

Thinking to get away before they were further humiliated, the chief priests and elders were about to slip through the crowd when Jesus stopped them. They had chosen to challenge His authority in public, so in public they should be further shamed.

'What think ye?' Jesus said. 'A certain man had two sons; and he came to the first, and said, Son, go work today in my vineyard.' The young man replied, 'I will not; but afterward he repented, and went.'

'And he came to the second, and said likewise. And he answered and said, I go, sir: and he went not. Whether of them twain did the will of his father?' Jesus asked.

The rulers could not see where this simple parable was leading, and gave the obvious reply, 'The first'. Their faces coloured when in front of the whole crowd Jesus approved their reply and went on, 'Verily, I say unto you, That the publicans and harlots go into the kingdom of God before you. For John came unto you in the way of righteousness, and ye believed him not: but the publicans and the harlots believed him: and ye, when ye had seen it, repented not afterward, that ye might believe him.'

The rulers thought that they had finished with the dilemma about John and his message, but now their attitude to him was publicly exposed and they were unfavourably contrasted with the publicans and sinners who had been converted and baptized by him. For all their fringes and phylacteries their profession was shown to be nothing more than a sham.

This shattering exposure of the hypocrisy of the Jewish rulers is not just an ancient story from the ministry of Jesus. It may well lead all who profess to follow the Lord to 'examine' themselves to see whether they 'be in the faith'. For just as God sent a message through John to prepare the way for the first coming of Christ, so in the last days He is sending His final appeal of mercy in preparation for Christ's second coming. And, as in the parable, when Christ comes in His kingdom He will gather to Himself a multitude of erstwhile sinners who have responded to His call, while many of those who have made a great profession of godliness will be found wanting.

How important then that we learn the lesson of this significant parable that when Jesus comes in glory we may be found among God's true sons.

This chapter is based on Matthew 21:12-17, 23-32; Mark 11:15-19, 27-33; Luke 19:45-48, 20:1-8.

Tribute to Caesar

Enraged by their public humiliation, the Pharisees retired for the second time to one of the council chambers within the temple precincts to consider what was to be done to rid themselves of Jesus.

As they could not find an excuse for ordering Him out of the temple on ecclesiastical grounds, someone suggested that they should try to entrap Him into a political offence which would involve Him with the Roman authorities. The idea seemed good and so it was decided to invite a number of Herodians to join with them in questioning Jesus on His attitude to the payment of tribute, that is, the poll or capitation tax which the Romans exacted from subject peoples to meet the costs of local government and maintain the occupation forces. It will be remembered that it was the imperial edict of Augustus Caesar for the registration of

every Jewish family for the assessment of this tax that brought Joseph and Mary to Bethlehem at the time of the birth of Jesus.

Ardent nationalists, like the Pharisees, deeply resented the humiliation, and the Zealots, the extreme wing of the Pharisee party, had raised several revolts against the tax, using as justification the scriptural injunction, 'Thou mayest not set a stranger over thee.' Such revolts, of course, stood no chance of success against the might of Rome and were savagely suppressed. Judas of Galilee is mentioned in the book of Acts as one Jewish leader who was put to death for subversive activities when his followers were scattered.

In contrast with the Pharisees, the Herodians took the line that as the nation was powerless to drive out the Romans, they might as well make the best terms possible with their conquerors. They were

the 'collaborators' of those days, who by currying favour with the Romans, derived considerable advantage for themselves. Some even enriched themselves at the expense of their fellow-countrymen by assisting in the collection of taxes for Herod and Caesar.

Being poles apart both politically and theologically, the Pharisees and Herodians had little association with one another,

and only on one occasion previously is there any record of a combined attack on Jesus. Now, however, in desperation, the Pharisees were ready to make any alliance to compass His destruction.

Even so, the leaders of the Pharisees could not bring themselves personally to approach their Herodian opponents, so they sent some of the younger Pharisees who were in training in Jerusalem to put

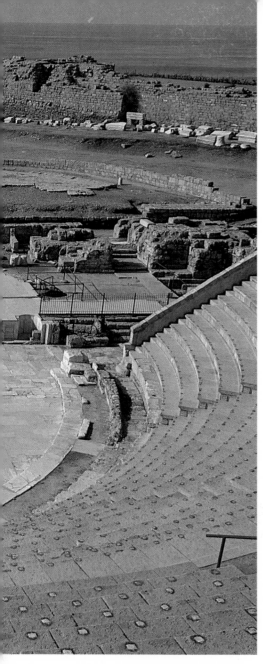

The magnificent setting of the Roman Theatre at Caesarea. King Herod's rebuilt city was the capital of the Roman province of Palestine, one of its administrators being Pontius Pilate. It was Peter who introduced the Gospel to the Gentile city but it was during Philip the deacon's ministry that this Christian church experienced its early, vigorous growth. Paul the apostle often made use of its harbour for his travels and finally spent two years in its prison.

'Master,' they said, with feigned reverence, 'we know that thou art true, and teachest the way of God in truth, neither carest thou for any man: for thou regardest not the person of men, Tell us therefore, what thinkest thou? Is it lawful to give tribute unto Caesar, or not?'

Jesus immediately saw through their cunning scheme. If He were to side with the Herodians and say that it was lawful to pay the tax, the Pharisees would be able to blacken His character in the eyes of the people as a traitor to the nation. On the other hand, if He agreed with the Pharisees that the tax was unjust, the Herodians would be able to 'deliver Him unto the power and authority of the governor,' Pontius Pilate, as an instigator of rebellion.

Looking straight into the eyes of His questioners Jesus replied, 'Why tempt ye me, ye hypocrites? Show me the tribute money.'

The Pharisees would certainly not have contaminated themselves by carrying pagan Roman coins in their satchels when they went into the temple, so it was probably one of the Herodians who produced 'a penny' or silver 'denarius', which had a value of about five and a half pence.

Jesus 'saith unto them, Whose is this image and superscription? They said unto Him, Caesar's.' Actually Julius Caesar was the first to put his head on Roman coinage. Augustus Caesar followed suit, and in

the proposition to them. The Herodians hated Jesus as much as the Pharisees, though for different reasons, and so it was not long before a joint deputation was arranged to interview Jesus.

Pretending that they had been discussing the question of tribute among themselves and had come to Jesus, as a highly respected and fearless Teacher, for counsel, they set their trap to catch Him.

121

The subjugating power of Rome left many elegant, architectural reminders of its building skills. Illustrated here are Roman remains from the ancient Phoenician port of Tyre, a region visited by Jesus during His Galilean ministry.

Christ's day the head was that of Tiberius Caesar.

Handing the coin back to the one who had presented it to Him, Jesus said quietly, 'Render therefore unto Caesar the things that are Caesar's; and unto God the things that are God's.'

The deputation was completely taken aback by this reply. They were sure that Jesus could not avoid committing Himself one way or the other, but it was impossible to 'take hold' of what He had said and use it against Him, for He had left the onus on them to decide what were Caesar's rights of possession.

The Jews indeed had a rule with reference to their contacts with other nations to the effect that, 'Wherever any king's coinage obtained, there his authority should be acknowledged.' The fact that they were using Roman coinage thus required them, by their own rule, to acknowledge Caesar's authority and his rightful demands.

Whether the subjection of the nation to the Romans was right or not was not the issue. The Romans ruled the country and protected it with their military forces; it was obvious therefore that they would be required to meet the costs of government. It was not a question of whether they should *give* tribute to Caesar. They were clearly required to *tender* it as a legal due and political necessity.

In actual fact they were entirely responsible for the situation in which they found themselves. If they had been true to God, His protection would have guaranteed their independence. Their subjection successively to Babylonians, Persians, Greeks, and now the Romans was the inevitable consequence of their disloyalty. God had declared through Moses that if they persisted in their sins He would finally bring against them 'from afar, from the end of

the earth', a 'nation of fierce countenance' whose 'tongue' they would 'not understand' and who would put 'a yoke of iron' upon their necks, a most remarkable prophetic description of the Romans. This had now come to pass and they could not expect to escape from the consequences of their bondage. One of the obvious consequences was the payment of tribute, and to refuse to pay the tax, was not only rebellion against the Romans but against the righteous judgement of God.

All this was implied in Jesus' injunction, 'Render therefore unto Caesar the things that are Caesar's.' But Jesus did not stop there. He added another declaration which confronted both the Pharisees and the Herodians with a much more serious issue. Render 'unto God', he said, 'the things that are God's'.

While they were hair-splitting as to whether they should pay the tax demanded by Caesar, they had sadly neglected the unquestionable duty of rendering to God 'the things that are God's'. Indeed it was the failure of all factions of the Jewish rulers to be faithful in their duty towards God which had brought them to their present position of subservience. If they had been true to Him they would never have had to decide whether or not it was right to pay tribute to Caesar.

Their wicked plotting was thus doubly exposed and there was nothing that they could say in their defence. Shamefacedly, therefore, they 'left him and went their way'.

There was, however, very much more in Jesus' reply than an adroit escape from the trap the Pharisees and Herodians had laid for Him. In His concise pronouncement Jesus strikingly summarized the Christian's relationship to earthly rulers and to

God as long as time shall last. These profound principles the apostle Paul elaborated in his discussions with the pagan Greeks in Athens and with the Gentile Christians in Rome.

God, explained Paul, not only created men upon the earth but He also determined 'the bounds of their habitation'. Hence 'the powers that be are ordained of God'. They may be righteous rulers or tyrannical powers, but at any given time the disposition of the nations is according to His permission. For this reason the Christian is to be 'subject to principalities and powers, to obey magistrates', and comply in all things to the requirements of earthly governments, provided that their demands do not conflict with the law of God.

'Whosoever, therefore, resisteth the power,' Paul says, 'resisteth the ordinance of God . . . for he is the minister of God, a revenger to execute wrath upon him that doeth evil. Wherefore ye must needs be subject, not only for wrath, but also for conscience sake.'

'For this cause,' he goes on, 'pay ye tribute also: for they are God's ministers, attending continually upon this very thing. Render therefore to all their dues: tribute to whom tribute is due; custom to whom custom; fear to whom fear; honour to whom honour.'

Peter likewise gives the same counsel to believers. 'Submit yourselves to every ordinance of man for the Lord's sake: whether it be to the king, as supreme; or unto governors, as unto them that are sent by him for the punishment of evildoers, and for the praise of them that do well.'

More than this, the Christian has a particular duty to pray for rulers that they may preserve peace and give freedom for the extension of the Gospel.

Though the old empires have gone and new nations have taken their places, it is still true today that the 'powers that be' rule by permission, if not by the approval, of God and so, whether they are righteous or tyrannical rulers, the Christian is in honour bound to render cheerfully all the dues which may properly be demanded of him.

However, above the Christian's duty to the State by which he is governed, he has a duty to God. Into this sphere the secular power has no right to intrude, and if it does, the true follower of God has a right and duty to resist even in the face of suffering and death.

When Daniel and his companions were confronted with the demand of heathen monarchs to desist from the worship of the true God or to worship false gods, they very rightly refused, even though their lives were threatened.

When the rulers of the Jews forbade Peter and John to preach Christ they plainly told the tribunal before whom they were called that they must 'obey God rather than men'.

In pagan Rome and during the Dark Ages, thousands of Christians perished rather than deny God. And today in many lands where religious liberty is denied either by over-reaching secular dictators or authoritarian Churches, Christians are continually facing prison and even death for conscience sake.

How grateful then should we be who dwell in lands where there is complete freedom, for liberty to render to God 'the things that are God's', and how much the more ready should we be to 'render unto Caesar' the things that rightly belong to him.

This chapter is based on Matthew 22:15-22; Mark 12:13-17; Luke 20:20-26.

The great commandment

Some of the scribes came again with new questions to try to confuse Jesus. Some way had to be found, and found quickly, to bring Him into disrepute in the eyes of the people for the prestige which Jesus was gaining from these encounters was driving them to desperation.

'One of them, which was a lawyer,' therefore, 'asked him a question, tempting him, and saying, Master, which is the great commandment in the law?'

It was one of the popular exercises of the rabbis to arrange the 248 affirmative and 365 negative commands of the rabbinical code in what they considered to be the order of their spiritual precedence. Those of absolute importance they classified as 'heavy', while the lesser ones which could be carried out by those who had time to fulfil them they regarded as 'light'.

If Jesus had been prepared to commit Himself to any particular order it would have started a debate in which the lawyer and his fellow scribes could, at least, have displayed their erudition in the presence of the people and thus restored some of their prestige.

But Jesus was too wise to be caught up in any rabbinical argument. Instead of 'weighing' commandment against commandment as the lawyer had hoped, He drew attention to a fundamental principle of Scripture which the Jews regularly recited in their morning and evening prayers, and which they even wore on their forehead and arm in their phylacteries.

'The first of all the commandments,' He replied, 'is, Hear, O Israel; The Lord our God is one Lord: and thou shalt *love* the Lord thy God with all thy heart, and with all thy soul, and with all thy mind, and with all thy strength: this is the first

An Arab mother, son and baggage are conveyed by conventional four-legged transport.

commandment.'

The Jews could claim to fear God and give Him divine honours, but they did not 'love' Him, and this vitiated all their worship. Because they did not realize that 'the first commandment . . . is *love*', all their worship was reduced to a joyless ritual rather than a happy fellowship; and

125

their obedience had become a burden rather than heartfelt response to the love of God.

To complete His exposure of the hollowness of the whole rabbinical system of calculated righteousness, Jesus gratuitously added a second command to the first for which the lawyer had asked.

'The second,' He said, 'is like, namely this, Thou shalt *love* thy neighbour as thyself,' and He added: 'There is no other commandment greater than these. . . . On these two commandments hang all the law and the prophets.'

This too was a quotation from the Old Testament, with which they should have been familiar, and it revealed that 'love' and not personal glory should have been the motive of all acts of benevolence to

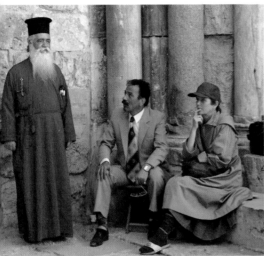

Some of the people and characters that give Jerusalem its unique multicultural flavour. A Jewish family gathers at the Western Wall for photographs; side ringlets and black clothes distinguish the Hassadim; the ever-present military reminds the visitor of the fragile nature of Israel's peace; every section of Christendom seems to have staked its claim to 'Holy' places; and of course the characters, an Arab coffee vendor, and the expert lady who can balance thirty eggs (with no hands) on her head.

their fellow men. Only on the basis of love could men reach this high standard of loving their fellow men 'as themselves.'

There was nothing selfless about the Pharisees' attitude to others. They did everything with the greatest publicity and ostentation in order that it might reflect credit to themselves, not because they cared for the poor and desired to satisfy their needs. Their failure in this respect was, Jesus intimated, a consequence of the fact that they did not love God. If they had loved God as they should, they would have loved their fellow men also. Because they did not truly love God, they did not truly love their fellow men.

127

The Pharisees indeed were quite wrong in classifying the second half of the Decalogue as 'lighter' than the first half. The second commandment was actually 'like' or equal to the first because each was dependent on the other. From these two commandments jointly every other commandment sprang.

It was to offset the prevailing Jewish idea that there were degrees of obedience that James in his epistle to the Church declared, concerning the commandments of the law, 'whosoever shall . . . offend in one point, he is guilty of all.' No commandment of God or of Christ can be neglected without undermining the basis of obedience to all the rest.

The scribe who had approached Jesus with the avowed purpose of catching Him was visibly impressed with the profundity of Jesus' reply and declared, 'Master, Thou hast said the truth: for there is one God; and there is none other but he: and to love him with all the heart, and with all the understanding, and with all the soul, and with all the strength, and to love his neighbour as himself, is more than all whole burnt offerings and sacrifices.'

Despite his pharisaic upbringing he could not but admit Jesus' point that mere ceremony has no value in itself, and that acts of worship and service are only pleasing to God if they spring from love in the heart.

Sensing the profound change in the man's attitude, Jesus said earnestly to him, 'Thou art not far from the kingdom of God.'

It is not recorded whether this lawyer went on to take the final step and associate himself fully with Jesus, or whether, like the rich young ruler, he drew back on the very verge of the kingdom, but we do know that since his day many who have set out to criticize the Bible and its

teachings have, as a result of a similar experience, been brought to realize its truth and to prostrate themselves in humble contrition before the Saviour they found in it.

The remarkable effect of Jesus' talk with the lawyer for a while silenced others who had hoped to follow up with further theological problems, and so it was Jesus' turn to put their professed knowledge to the test.

'What think ye of Christ?' He demanded of them, 'whose son is he?'

Not suspecting where the question would lead, they answered readily, 'The Son of David.' They did not need any profound knowledge to give this answer, for it was so declared time and again in the

writings of the prophets. 'Hath not the Scriptures said,' they declared on another occasion, 'That Christ cometh of the seed of David, and out of the town of Bethlehem, where David was?'

Receiving their answer without comment, Jesus next asked the rabbis, 'How then doth David in spirit call him Lord?'

They ought to have been able to answer this second question as easily as the first, for the prophets had equally clearly declared that this Child 'out of the stem of Jesse' would be no ordinary Son, but the incarnate Lord from heaven. Had not

Artists' Alley in Jaffa. An important port in Bible times, called Joppa, it is now part of Tel Aviv. It was the home of Dorcas, the helper of the poor, whom Peter raised from the dead.

Isaiah said, 'Behold, a virgin shall conceive, and bear a son, and shall call his name Immanuel'? And again, 'Unto us a child is born, unto us a son is given: . . . and his name shall be called Wonderful, Counsellor, The mighty God, The everlasting Father, The Prince of Peace.' (Isaiah 7:14; 9:6.)

But though the rulers knew the answer they now dared not give it, because if they admitted that Messiah would be both Son of man and Son of God they had no right to dismiss Jesus with such contemptuous remarks as, 'We know this man whence He is', 'Is not this the carpenter's son? is not his mother called Mary?' They should have been prepared to investigate the evidence of His miraculous birth, the source of His wonderful works and words, the testimony of John the Baptist, and the remarkable fact that in harmony with Messianic prophecy the common people and even the children had involuntarily hailed Him as both Son of David and Son of the Highest when He entered Jerusalem just a few days earlier. Either His claim could be proved a blasphemous lie or they must admit that it was true.

Recognizing now the dilemma into which Jesus' questions were leading them, the Pharisees and scribes extricated themselves hastily from the discussion and none dared 'from that day forth' to 'ask him any more questions'.

The rulers of the Jews had had their last chance to accept the irrefutable evidence that Jesus was the Messiah, and they had finally refused to recognize Him. There was nothing now for Jesus to do but to denounce them publicly and pronounce upon them the inevitable consequences of their sin.

This chapter is based on Matthew 22:34-46; Mark 12:28-37; Luke 20:39-44.

When shall these things be?

It was late on Tuesday afternoon when Jesus, still followed by the remnant of the temple crowd, descended from the Golden Gate into the Valley of the Kidron. The disciples had been profoundly affected by the dire judgement which Jesus had pronounced upon the city and temple. Yet, as they looked up at the colossal foundation stones of the Herodian walls, some of them sixty feet long and ten feet high, and beheld the great gates faced with gold, silver, and brass, they could not believe that this mighty edifice could ever be overthrown.

'Master', one of them remarked to Jesus, 'see what manner of stones and what buildings are here,' and what 'gifts' have gone into their enrichment. 'Surely,' he said in effect, 'You cannot suggest that all this magnificence is soon to be laid in ruins?'

Jesus turned, and, looking in the direction the disciple indicated, He said solemnly, 'See ye not all these things? verily I say unto you . . . the days will come, in the which there shall not be left one stone upon another, that shall not be thrown down.'

Fearful that Jesus' words might have been overheard by some of His priestly enemies, to whom they would be flagrant treason, the disciples hastily dropped the subject and hurried on, until, by the time they had crossed the Kidron, the crowd had dispersed on their various ways and they were alone.

They climbed the steep path through the olive groves and fig orchards of the Mount of Olives, and near the crest of the ridge, Jesus sat down to take a last look at the rejected city.

Across the valley, about half a mile away in a direct line and a little below where He sat, lay the complex of the temple buildings, the snow-white marble of the terraced courts, porticos, and stairways tinged pink in the setting sun, which glinted and sparkled on the gilded gates, roofs, and pinnacles. It was a scene of surpassing beauty and the pride of the nation. 'He who never saw the temple of Herod,' someone said, 'has never seen a fine building.'

But the thoughts of Jesus were not upon the splendour of the sanctuary. In His mind's eye was a vision of the tragedy which was soon to fall upon the blind and impenitent inhabitants of the once-holy city.

Peter and James, John and Andrew, sat for a while beside Jesus as the shadows lengthened. Then, breaking the silence, one of them, probably Peter, raised the question which was uppermost in their minds, but which they dared not ask Him in the hearing of His enemies.

'Tell us,' he said, 'when shall these things be? And what shall be the sign of thy coming, and of the end of the world?'

It was clear to them now that Jesus was leaving the city to its deserved doom. They hoped that this would save Him from the sufferings and death about which He had spoken so frequently in recent months, and that when judgement had fallen, He would be able to return and reveal Himself in all His glory as Israel's Messiah. So in their question they associated together as successive events, the 'things' connected with the destruction of the city, and His 'coming' to end this dark episode in the nation's history. When could they expect these 'things' to begin to happen, they asked, and what would be the 'sign' of the approaching climax?

Jesus did not immediately correct their thinking by telling them that the 'end' of Jerusalem and the 'end' of the world,

The Pater Noster (Our Father) Church stands on the Mount of Olives where Jesus gave His prophetic warnings of Jerusalem's destruction and the events preceding His second coming. It is built on the site of an early Christian church built by Helena in AD 333. The present building also presents the Lord's Prayer in forty-four languages on tiled panels recalling how Jesus taught the disciples to pray.

when His glory would appear, were to be separated by many centuries. If He had done so just before the ordeal of the cross, He knew it would have been more than they could bear. So He withheld the time sequence of events from them, and in the great prophecy which He now uttered, He mingled the two events; providing on the one hand the guidance they needed for the immediate future, and on the other an outline of the great interim which would be unfolded to the Church down the centuries as it was needed. Finally, He

131

delineated the 'signs' which would alert the last-day Church and prepare them for the final crisis.

Sketching in the course of events leading to the fall of Jerusalem, Jesus first warned His disciples against the deceptions by which Satan would seek to divert the attention of the Church from the opening providences of God.

'Take heed,' He said, 'that no man deceive you, for many shall come in my name, saying, I am Christ, and shall deceive many.'

The warning was needed, for, as Jesus declared, many fanatical prophets, professing to be messengers of God, did arise, contradicting the message of doom which Jesus had pronounced, and many were deceived into a false sense of security and into actions which cost thousands their lives.

In the procuratorship of Fadus of Judea, for example, a certain Theudas led a multitude to the Jordan, declaring that the waters would part before him. They did not, and he was quickly apprehended by the Romans and beheaded.

Another, who came from Egypt, gathered his followers on the Mount of Olives proclaiming that at his word the walls of the city would fall down. His career too was quickly terminated and his followers killed or scattered.

Warned by Jesus, however, the Christians were not deceived by these false prophets and so they were not involved in any of these abortive revolts or in the catastrophe of Jerusalem's end when it came.

'Ye shall hear,' Jesus went on, 'of wars and rumours of wars, be ye not troubled: for such things must needs be; but the end shall not be yet. For nation shall rise against nation, and kingdom against king-

dom: . . . and there shall be famines, and pestilences, and earthquakes, in divers places.' All these, He delcared, would be only 'the beginning of sorrows'.

This too was fulfilled in the days before the fall of Jerusalem. While the temple of Janus was shut at the time of Christ's birth, indicative of peace throughout the Roman world, the later years of the century were filled with insurrections within the empire and wars on the frontiers. The Roman historian, Tacitus, opens his history of this period with the remark that it was 'fertile in vicissitudes, stained with the blood of battles, embroiled with dissensions, and horrible even in the intervals of peace.'

Not only did strife increase as the first century wore on, but natural catastrophes like famines, pestilences, and earthquakes caused havoc in different parts of the empire. The Acts of the Apostles records a famine in Judea in the days of Claudius Caesar, while earthquakes followed by pestilence were recorded in the Aegean region, Macedonia, Asia Minor, and even in Rome itself in the middle decades of the century.

With the rising tide of catastrophe, declared Jesus, the wrath of the wicked would be turned against the faithful people of God. 'They shall deliver you up to be afflicted, and shall kill you: and ye shall be hated of all nations for my name's sake.'

True to His prediction the infant Church did become the object of attack by both Jew and Gentile. By the Jews they were persecuted as heretics. Said Jesus, 'They shall deliver you up to the councils; and in the synagogues ye shall be beaten.' Peter and John and Paul were more than once apprehended by the Jews, and Stephen suffered death at their hands.

The elegant façades of Rome meant little to the many faithful Christians whose lives were brutally sacrificed in the arena.

By the Romans the Christians were persecuted for undermining the worship of the national gods and the authority of the emperors. 'Ye shall be brought before rulers and kings for my sake, for a testimony against them,' Jesus had said. James was the first to suffer death at the hands of the political power of Herod. Paul was later haled before Gallio, Felix, Festus, and Agrippa, and was finally beheaded by the Emperor Nero in Rome. It was this emperor who instigated the first general persecution of the Christians.

Faced with increasing persecution the believers were encouraged by Jesus' promise of divine aid. 'When they shall lead you, and deliver you up,' He had said, 'take no thought beforehand what ye shall speak; neither do ye premeditate: but whatsoever shall be given you in that hour, that speak ye: for it is not ye that speak, but the Holy Ghost. For I will give you a mouth and wisdom, which all your adversaries shall not be able to gainsay nor resist.'

True to His promise the Bible records that the judges of Stephen 'were not able to resist' his words; while not a few of the Roman captors and executioners of the Christian martyrs found Christ themselves as a result of their fearless witness.

Because, however, of the severity of their trials, Jesus declared, the faith of many of the Christians would fail. 'Because iniquity shall abound, the love of many shall wax cold.' And 'many shall be offended, and shall betray one another, and shall hate one another. . . . Brother shall betray brother to death, and the father the son; and children shall rise up against their parents, and shall cause them to be put to death.'

In confirmation of this we have the independent authority of Tacitus again, who mentions that 'first they were seized who confessed that they were Christians, and then on their information a vast multitude was convicted.'

Yet while persecution would cause 'the love of many' to grow 'cold', the very opposition to the Gospel would result in its being disseminated as the persecuted Church was scattered abroad to the ends of the inhabited world. Paul himself carried the Gospel to Asia Minor, Greece, Italy, and even beyond into Spain, and there are traditions of the widespread evangelistic labours of all the other disciples. Simon and Jude, we understand, went north into Syria and Mesopotamia and Persia, Peter and John into Asia Minor, Matthew into Parthia, Andrew and Philip into Scythia, Bartholomew into North and West Asia, Thomas east into Media, Carmania, and India, and Matthias into Ethiopia. So to every part of the empire and beyond, the early believers carried the Gospel. Dodderidge declares that churches were planted in all those places 'in less than thirty years after the death of Christ' and 'before the destruction of Jerusalem'.

The fact that 'prodigious numbers' of Christians, according to Suetonius, and 'vast multitudes', according to Tacitus, could have been put to death in the first general persecution, shows how widely the faith had been spread by the days of Nero, and supports Paul's declaration that before his death the Gospel had been preached to 'every creature' under heaven.

Thus before the 'end' of the Jewish nation came, the words of Jesus, 'This Gospel of the kingdom shall be preached in all the world for a witness unto all nations, and then shall the end come', received their primary fulfilment.

To the Jews in Palestine and in the dispersion, the fall of Jerusalem was 'the end' of their national hopes, but for those whose faith was in Christ it was a confirmation of the outworking purpose of God.

Doubtless, when the 'end' came for Jerusalem many of the Christians expected the immediate establishment of the kingdom of glory, just as after the resurrection the disciples had inquired, 'Wilt thou at this time restore again the kingdom to

Israel?' But gradually, as time passed and Jesus did not return, they began to see that this cycle of persecution and witness, apostasy and triumph through endurance, which had characterized the first phase of the Church up to the 'end' of the Jewish nation, was to have a wider fulfilment both in time and in extent before the 'end of the world' and the coming of the Son of man in His kingdom.

This sequence of events leading up to the 'end' of Jerusalem, was indeed a miniature of a vastly wider fulfilment in the story of the Church in the world through the centuries leading up to the 'end' of all things.

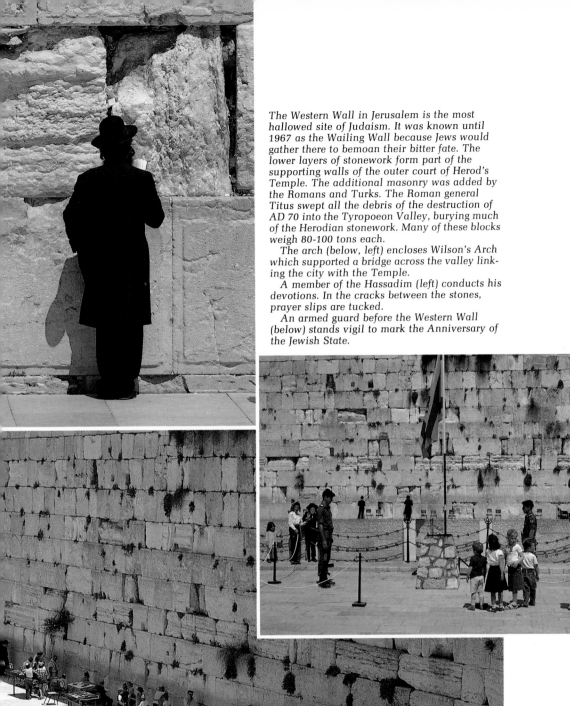

The Western Wall in Jerusalem is the most hallowed site of Judaism. It was known until 1967 as the Wailing Wall because Jews would gather there to bemoan their bitter fate. The lower layers of stonework form part of the supporting walls of the outer court of Herod's Temple. The additional masonry was added by the Romans and Turks. The Roman general Titus swept all the debris of the destruction of AD 70 into the Tyropoeon Valley, burying much of the Herodian stonework. Many of these blocks weigh 80-100 tons each.

The arch (below, left) encloses Wilson's Arch which supported a bridge across the valley linking the city with the Temple.

A member of the Hassadim (left) conducts his devotions. In the cracks between the stones, prayer slips are tucked.

An armed guard before the Western Wall (below) stands vigil to mark the Anniversary of the Jewish State.

135

Jesus foretold that the 'last days' of the world would be an era of unparalleled war and strife.

As the Gospel continued to go forth into the world, other false prophets would arise with false teachings concerning Christ's kingdom to deceive those who were not fortified by the 'blessed hope' and these, as later Bible writers were to reveal, would culminate in the great apostasy designated 'the mystery of iniquity' and 'Antichrist'.

As the apostate Church of Christ's day persecuted the true remnant, so the apostate Church of subsequent ages would harass the true people of God. Many, in consequence, would lose their hold of the truth, but a faithful remnant, braced by faith and sustained by grace, would maintain their witness 'even unto death'.

As the story of apostasy and persecution would be repeated in subsequent centuries, so also would the increasing strife among the nations. The 'wars and rumours of wars' of the first century would be but the 'beginning' of centuries of national revolutions and international strife which would not cease till the Prince of peace Himself should come.

So the situation which obtained before the 'end' of Jerusalem would be duplicated on a world scale in the days before the 'end' of all things. The 'last days' of the world would be an era of unparalleled war and strife, abounding iniquity, natural catastrophes, moral decline, and spiritual apostasy. Yet against the background of a perishing world the Gospel of the kingdom in the form of God's last message of mercy would be preached for a 'witness', not this time merely to the Roman world, but to 'every nation, and kindred, and tongue, and people', on the face of the earth, for the gathering out of the last faithful remnant. Then would come the 'end' not of a city or a nation, but of the world.

To the wicked of the last days the 'end' will be a day of darkness and judgement, as it was for the sinful and unheeding inhabitants of Jerusalem, but for those whose trust is in God it will be a day of glorious realization as Jesus, according to His promise, 'comes' at long last in all His glory to establish His eternal kingdom.

This chapter is based on Matthew 24:1-14; Mark 13:1-13; Luke 21:1-19.

136

Not one stone!

In His great panoramic prophecy on the Mount of Olives, Jesus purposely gave no indication of the time which would elapse between the 'end' of Jerusalem and the subsequent 'end' of the world. At the same time He wanted to provide His people with adequate 'signs' of His out-working purposes for their immediate guidance and for the guidance of the Church in subsequent ages. So, following His initial survey of the trials and triumphs of the Church, Jesus began to set forth in greater detail the sequence of events in the drama of history.

His next words, 'When ye therefore shall see' clearly introduces what was to be a recapitulation of what He had pre-viously described in general terms, with the object of providing specific 'signs', first of the end of the Jewish age and then of the end of all things. These would enable the 'last days' of the Jewish nation and the 'last days' of earth's his-tory to be clearly recognized by the 'watching' ones.

'When ye therefore shall see the abomination of desolation, spoken of by Daniel the prophet, stand in the holy place, (whoso readeth, let him under-sand),' Jesus began, 'then let them which be in Judea flee to the mountains . . . and let them which are in the midst of it depart out; and let not them that are in the countries enter thereinto.'

The immediate sign of the end for Jerusalem, declared Jesus, would be the appearance before the city of the 'abomi-nation of desolation', spoken of by the prophet Daniel. Those who had 'read' and 'understood' his prophecies, as Jesus admonished, would have no difficulty in connecting this power with the 'abomina-tion that maketh desolate' referred to sev-eral times by Daniel, and identifying it as

the power of Rome. The 'idols upon the battlements' at the time of Christ's crucifixion were, of course, the pagan ensigns carried at the head of the Roman legions and the images of the emperors on their shields, for all the idols of the heathen were an 'abomination' to the Jews.

True also to Daniel's prophecy it was a

As Jesus prophesied, nothing remains of the Temple complex but excavations at the south-east corner of the Temple area have revealed the fine masonry of the retaining walls of the outer court built by Herod. The walls were very high at this point and it is believed this was the 'Pinnacle of the Temple' where Jesus was invited by the devil to throw Himself down.

Roman 'prince' who had charge of the operations against Jerusalem, for when Vespasian left Palestine to become the tenth of the Roman Caesars, he left the Jewish campaign in the hands of his son Titus, who subsequently assumed the royal purple.

Now, said Jesus, if His people were on the watch for the first sign of the approach of the 'desolator', opportunity would be given them to 'flee' for safety to 'the mountains', as Lot was warned to flee from doomed Sodom. But there would not be much time and they would have to take immediate action.

If they were on the housetop, perhaps storing food, when the moment of escape came, they were not to 'come down to take any thing' out of their houses, but were to descend quickly by the outer stair and hasten from the city.

Likewise, if they were 'in the field' clad only in light, working garments, they were not to take time to go back home for their tunics or sheepskin coats, but at once to make their escape.

Because the emergency when it came would be a trying experience for all, and particularly for expectant mothers and those with young children, the Church were exhorted to pray that their escape would not have to be made during the 'winter', when the weather would be cold and travel difficult, and the Jordan would be in flood. They were also to pray that their flight would not need to be 'on the Sabbath day', in order that their worship might not be disturbed.

The latter reference is of special significance, showing as it does, that many years after the founding of the Christian Church, the believers would still be observing and worshipping on the Sabbath day. This makes it very clear that Jesus never intended, after His resurrection, that the seventh day of the fourth commandment was to be replaced by the first day of the week as the Christian's rest day. Indeed, contrary to the belief of many Christians today, both the Bible and Church history unite in confirming that the Sabbath was faithfully observed by many in the Christian Church not for decades but for centuries, until it was obscured by apostasy and neglect, in favour of the Christianized pagan feast day, Sun-day.

So the church watched and prayed through the years that followed Christ's ascension, as expectantly they waited for the final 'sign' Jesus had given them. And when, in AD 66, they saw the Roman forces under Cestius Gallus, prefect of Syria, approaching the city to quell the insurrection against the procurator Gessius Florus, they knew that the time was near.

Whether any Christians left Jerusalem on the approach of Cestius is not recorded. Possibly his descent upon the city was too swift for many to make their escape and the great majority remained in the city during the two years he unsuccessfully besieged it. Then for some strange reason, about the time of the Feast of Tabernacles in AD 69, Cestius withdrew his forces and beat a retreat. The Jews, thinking to emulate the heroic deeds of the Maccabees sallied out of the city in pursuit and only with difficulty did Cestius extricate his forces, leaving much spoil in Jewish hands.

The Christians, however, who had 'read and understood' both Christ's prophecy and the prophecies of Daniel, did not share the elation of the Jews, but saw in the raising of the siege a providential pause before the city's final destruction.

Mount Scopus, north-east of Jerusalem, has played a decisive role in battles for that city. It was on this strategic position in AD 70 that Titus gathered his Roman legions before he began his assault which destroyed the city and massacred or took into slavery its people.

And so, as they had prayed, just before the onset of winter, and we may well believe on some other day than the Sabbath, they made haste and left the doomed city, crossing over the Jordan to Pella, one of the cities of the Decapolis, about seventeen miles south of the Sea of Galilee. There, in the territory of Agrippa, who had remained loyal to Rome, they were safe from molestation. So, when the city fell, not a single Christian perished.

In one or two brief sentences Jesus went on to describe the catastrophe which descended upon Jerusalem after the escape of His followers:

'For these be the days of vengeance, that all things which are written (from Moses to Malachi) may be fulfilled. . . .

For there shall be great distress in the land, and wrath upon this people. And they shall fall by the edge of the sword, and shall be led away captive into all nations.'

If we had to depend solely on the Roman account of the taking of Jerusalem our information about it might have been comparatively meagre. It was surely, therefore, in the providence of God that there was in the service of the Romans, a Jewish general and historian, Josephus, who was able to record a vivid eyewitness account of the city's last tragic days.

The inspired resistance of the Jews who had pursued Cestius doubtless confirmed the Roman determination to break the spirit of the Jews once and for all, and towards Passover of AD 70, Vespasian, after restoring Roman power in the north, advanced against Jerusalem. On his way, however, he heard of the death of Nero. At once he set off for Rome to claim the imperial throne, leaving his son, Titus Flavius Vespasian, with orders to destroy

139

Jerusalem if the Jews refused to surrender.

Titus set up his camp on Mount Scopus on the fourteenth of Abib, just as Passover was beginning, and began to deploy his four legions of Syrian and Numidian auxiliaries, some 60,000 men in all, against the city.

The initial plan of Titus, whom the historian Suetonius has told us was 'most benevolent by nature', was to induce the Jews to surrender, and if they had been willing to capitulate they would doubtless have been treated with consideration. But their obstinacy, stimulated by their success against Cestius, forced Titus to do what was for him a 'strange work' and made certain the fulfilment of the prophecy of doom.

After some weeks of ineffective attacks, Titus ordered his troops to build a wall round the entire city, and in the incredibly short period of three days the task was accomplished by the tenth of the month Sivan.

Still the Jews, encouraged by false prophets to believe that the city could not be taken, refused to give in, and the Romans began their final assault.

As a result of some of the defence towers being deserted, Mount Zion fell first and the people who had not perished by famine were mercilessly slaughtered or burned in their own houses. The north wall was next breached and the Tower of Antonia was invested, leaving only the temple itself in the hands of the Jews.

Titus had been anxious to preserve 'this marvellous magnificence' as a monument to his victory, but it now became clear that he would have to take it also by storm. On the ninth day of Abib flaming braziers were thrust against the cedar doors of the temple area. The gold and silver coverings melted and the hard cedar wood was set alight. The Jews tried to arrest the progress of the Romans by setting fire to the outer courts themselves, but the soldiers advanced steadily into the sanctuary itself. A soldier threw a burning brand into a window of one of the rooms round the holy place and soon the building was in flames. Titus ordered the quenching of the fire, but the Roman soldiers, incensed by the stubbornness of the resistance, now paid no heed. Soon the whole sanctuary was a mass of flames. The walls fell in, the cedarwood roof collapsed into the inferno of fire which lit up the surrounding hills, and by morning the temple was a smouldering ruin.

As a reward for his victory in Palestine, Vespasian conferred upon his son the title Imperator, and at the Colosseum end of the Forum in Rome the great Arch of Titus was erected to commemorate his achievement further. On the inside of the arch are depicted the golden table of showbread, the golden candlestick, and two trumpets, being carried in procession in his triumph.

Josephus estimates that in the siege over a million Jews perished. In addition 90,000 were sent into slavery, the able-bodied to the Egyptian mines, while the rest were scattered through the provinces of the empire. No fewer than 11,000 perished while the separation and dispatch of the captives was in progress.

Moses had declared that if the Iraelites failed to follow the Lord they would be carried captive among the Gentiles. This was in part fulfilled in the Assyrian and Babylonian captivities, but after the war of AD 70 the Jews were literally scattered throughout the whole Roman world.

The total destruction of the city also

Amon at Karnak and Luxor are still massive ruins, not one stone of the magnificent temple of Jerusalem has been left in place.

Sixty years after its destruction the Emperor Hadrian built upon the site his city of Ælia, named after himself, and put a Roman colony in it, so that, as Jesus prophesied, Jerusalem was literally 'trodden down of the Gentiles'.

In AD 637 the city was surrendered to the Moslem Khalif Omar, and in AD 688 the Dome of the Rock was erected by Abd el Melek to cover the temple site. Thereafter, except for about a century from 1099-1187, when it was in Crusader hands, the Saracens and Turks held the city till 1917, while the scattered and persecuted Jews were hounded from country to country throughout Europe, Asia, and Africa.

fulfilled to the letter the words of Jesus that 'not one stone' would remain upon another when the Romans had done their worst. While the great pagan temples like the Parthenon at Athens, the temple of Jupiter at Baalbek, and the temples of

The great Arch of Titus in Rome (above) built to celebrate his victory over the Jews and the destruction of Jerusalem in AD 70. The relief inside the arch shows the laural-adorned Romans with their 'booty', the sacred objects from the Temple.

This chapter is based on Matthew 24:15-20; Mark 13:14-18; Luke 21:20-24.

The ten virgins

After His discourse on the Mount of Olives, Jesus walked with His disciples through the gathering darkness to Bethany, where they spent the night.

Of the next day, the thirteenth of Nisan, or Wednesday of the Passion Week, nothing whatever is recorded. Jesus did not go again to the Temple, and the approach of Passover kept the crowds away from Bethany, so that He was able to spend the day quietly with His hospitable friends.

Naturally the disciples would have further questions to ask about the coming of the kingdom, and it seems most likely that the parables of the ten virgins, the talents, and the sheep and goats, which are recorded only by Matthew, were told by Jesus in the quiet seclusion of the home at Bethany.

'Then shall the kingdom of heaven be likened unto ten virgins,' Jesus began, 'which took their lamps, and went forth to meet the bridegroom.'

On more than one occasion He had used the joyous picture of an Eastern wedding to symbolize the inauguration of the divine Son in His kingdom, and certainly the comparison was most meaningful.

Marriages in Bible times were invariably celebrated at night, and it will be following the darkest hour of earth's night that the dawn will break upon the kingdom of Christ.

There are clear spiritual parallels, too, in the procedures of a Palestinian wedding. When the time of the marriage came, the bridegroom would go forth from his father's house, accompanied by his friends, to the home of the bride. Then, having received her from the hand of her parents, he would return with the procession to his father's house for the wedding feast. In the same way when the great day of the marriage feast of the kingdom arrives, Jesus will come forth from His heavenly home, accompanied by a retinue of holy angels, to claim His bride, the Church, with whom He will return to the marriage feast in His Father's house in heaven.

For the purpose of this parable, however, the people of God are not represented as the bride of Christ, but as the friends of the bride who are waiting with lighted lamps to join in the procession to the marriage feast.

The symbol of virginity is used, as elsewhere, to typify the purity of their faith, their absolute loyalty to God, and the completeness of their separation from the world. And as ten was the usual number of lamp bearers in a bridal procession, the ten virgins fittingly represent the waiting remnant of God.

The lighted lamps which each guest carried well symbolize the bright flame of Christian experience which is the necessary preparation to meet Jesus when He comes. However beautiful the shape or highly decorated the exterior of the lamp, it is useless unless it is lighted. So also are we until our lives are lighted at the flame of the Spirit of God.

David realized this when he prayed that God would light his 'candle', or lamp. Paul, speaking to those who had found Christ, used the same picture when he said, 'Now are ye light in the Lord', and bade them walk as 'children of light'. Jesus similarly declared of His disciples, 'Ye are the light the world.'

Because of the smallness of the reservoir in the little oriental saucer-lamps they needed frequent refilling with oil. Likewise, the flame of spiritual experience needs not only to be kindled by God but must be daily replenished, as the Psalmist says, with 'fresh oil', through worship, meditation on God's

Oil lamps, excavated in Jerusalem, dating from the Roman period. The wick was placed in the 'spout' and the lamp was filled with olive or animal oil through the central hole. They were kept alight night and day, not only for light but as a means of providing fire.

Word, and prayer.

In His discourse on the Mount of Olives, Jesus had warned that not all would be waiting to receive Him at His coming, and in this parable He portrays five of the virgins as 'wise' and five as 'foolish'. The wise 'took oil in their vessels', that is, they maintained their readiness to meet the Bridegroom by the constant renewal of the flame of their spiritual experience. The 'foolish', on the other hand, represent those who, though they have taken the initial step of commital to God and accepted the invitation to the wedding feast, nevertheless fail to realize the importance of keeping their lamps 'trimmed and burning'. If such are not awakened to their need of 'oil in their vessels with their lamps', the coming of Jesus will find them unprepared like the foolish virgins when the bridegroom's approach was announced.

In His previous discourse Jesus had intimated that the difference between the ready and the unready would not be out-wardly apparent during the waiting period. On the housetops, in the fields, or at the household tasks they might be working together, and not until the moment of crisis came would it be manifest that one was ready and the other was not. So in this parable, while the bridegroom tarried they all 'slumbered and slept', snatching a little rest so as to be fresh and lively when the bridegroom came. Only in the excitement of preparation when at midnight the cry was heard, 'Behold, the bridegroom cometh', did the fatal lack on the part of the 'foolish' virgins become apparent. Not until 'all those virgins arose, and trimmed their lamps' did the foolish realize that their lamps were flickering out and they had no reserve of oil in their flasks. So in the coming day the profession of many will be tragically exposed as 'a form of godliness' devoid of any reserve of spiritual power.

In alarm the foolish virgins in the parable 'said unto the wise, Give us of your oil: for our lamps are gone out [lit., going out]'. But obviously the wise virgins could not take the risk of giving away some of their oil and not having enough to keep their lamps burning through the feast, and so they replied, very properly, 'Not so; lest there be not enough for us and you.' 'Go ye rather to them that sell,' they urged, 'and buy for yourselves.'

The spiritual application here is evident. If the loan of oil by the wise virgins to the foolish ones was possible though unfair to them, the transfer from one to another of the spiritual experience necessary to qualify for a place at Christ's table, is actually impossible. Our parents or friends may be instrumental in directing us to the Source of the 'oil' of grace, but character can be obtained only by one's self for one's self from the divine source of there will be 'a famine' of the Word. Men will run frenziedly to and fro seeking the Word they have so long neglected, but they will not find it. Doubtless, this was the experience of the foolish virgins, and when they hurried back to the bridegroom's house, their alarm was increased when they found that he had gone in and 'the door was shut'. In their distress they knocked repeatedly crying, 'Lord, Lord, open to us', but to their consternation the reply of the bridegroom came, 'Verily I say unto you, I know you not'.

Solemn indeed is the warning of this parable, that while today the door is open wide to sinners, and Jesus is still pleading, 'Him that cometh unto me I will in no wise cast out', a time is coming when the door of salvation will be shut and the decree will go forth, 'He that is unjust, let him be unjust still; and he which is filthy, let him be filthy still.' When that time comes the character of all will be fixed and the destiny of all will be sealed. Dreadful will be the words which will then fall upon the ears of the unprepared, 'I know you not'.

Once again, therefore, Jesus pleaded as He closed His parable, 'Watch therefore, for ye know neither the day nor the hour wherein the Son of man cometh.'

So, as the midnight hour of earth's history draws on, we will do well to examine the lamp of our spiritual life to see that it is 'trimmed and burning'. If perchance our lamp is burning dim or smoky through the accumulation of sin or the neglect of the means of spiritual grace, He will gladly rekindle the dying flame of our lives and refill our vessels with the oil of His Spirit; but we must ask Him to do it now, before it is too late.

This chapter is based on Matthew 25:1-13.

A sub-tropical shrub found in the Jordan Valley and locally known as the 'Sodom Apple' because its pleasant-looking 'fruit' are in reality poisonous seed pods.

supply. No proxy can make up for our neglect.

It is not stated in the parable whether the foolish virgins found any oil vendor still open, but the Bible makes it very clear that any who expect spiritual grace to be available to the unready in the day of Christ's appearing will be sadly disappointed. In that day, the Bible tells us,

The parable of the talents

In the parable of the ten virgins, the guests invited to the wedding slept while they waited for the bridegroom, in order that they might be rested when the marriage feast began.

This was, of course, true to the circumstances of an eastern wedding, but it was not intended to portray the occupation of the people of God as they await the return of the divine Bridegroom. To do this Jesus told another parable.

This time He likened 'the kingdom of heaven' to a 'man travelling into a far country, who called his own servants, and delivered unto them his goods'. Here Jesus is the Householder, the 'far country' was heaven to which He was to return after the conclusion of His earthly mission, while the servants represent those to whom He has committed the ministry of the Gospel during His absence.

In the work of God on earth each is given a responsibility proportionate to his God-given capacity to serve. This Jesus indicated when He went on, 'And unto one he gave five talents, to another two, and to another one, to every man according to his several ability; and straightway took his journey.'

In monetary value a silver talent would be equivalent to about £200, the two talents to £400, and the five to £1,000. The latter sum, though considerable, was not out of the ordinary for a trusted slave to handle for his master.

In the distribution of the master's resources an important difference will be noted between this story and the parable of the pounds which Jesus told as He came up the Jericho road. In the earlier parable the emphasis was on the acceptance or rejection of the gift of salvation which is common to all, and so each of the servants received the same amount, namely, 'one pound'. In this parable Jesus is dealing with the use His servants make of the differing gifts which He dispenses to each 'severally as He will', for the upbuilding of His Church and the hastening of His kingdom. As Paul mentioned in his epistles to the Corinthians and to the Ephesians, Christ appoints some to be apostles, some prophets, some evangelists, some teachers, and so on, according to the needs of His work and the capacity of the human instruments. For the use of these diverse gifts each is severally responsible, and will be called to render an account in the day of judgement.

Continuing His parable, Jesus told how the servants shouldered their various responsibilities. 'He that had received the five talents went and traded with the same, and made them other five talents. And likewise he that had received two, he also gained other two.'

These servants represent the faithful people of God who, while they watch and wait for the coming King, occupy themselves in diligent service for the advancement of the kingdom. Some are given great talents by means of which multitudes are gathered into Christ's Church. Others may have fewer gifts, but by using them faithfully, each is able to make a significant contribution to the cause of God.

The third servant, however, who had received only one talent, though he enjoyed all the amenities of his master's household, felt no responsibility to exert himself on his behalf. Aggrieved that he had only been entrusted with a single talent, and arguing that his small service would not count one way or the other, he decided that it was not worth while doing anything. So he 'went and digged in the earth, and hid his lord's money', so that

'Well done, thou good and faithful servant!'

he would be able to return it safely when the lord returned from his journey. Thereafter he doubtless occupied himself with his own selfish pursuits.

Sad to say, there are Christians who adopt this attitude. Because they have not been called to some great work for God they feel that there is nothing worth while which they can do, and so they do nothing.

To feel like this, however, is seriously to impugn God's purposes and providences. It was out of consideration for the lesser ability of the third servant that the householder gave him the responsibility of only one talent, but the fact that he did receive one was evidence that he could have used it to advantage. In the same way there is no soul upon whom Christ has conferred the gift of salvation who has not also received some talent for service in the place where His providence disposes, and for such he will be held as responsible as the most talented of God's servants on earth. To fail to use our one talent because that is all He has entrusted us with, is to despise the gift of God and to pass judgement on His wise providence. The lowliest task faithfully performed is as acceptable to God as the highest service, and is a necessary discipline for greater responsibility.

When at last the lord returned, the servants were called one by one to report their activities on his behalf. Then 'he that had received five talents came and brought other five talents, saying, Lord thou deliveredst unto me five talents: behold, I have gained beside them five talents more.'

The man who had received two talents next came to report that he also had gained 'two other talents beside them'.

To each of these faithful servants the

lord said, 'Well done, thou good and faithful servant: thou has been faithful over a few things, I will make thee ruler over many things: enter thou into the joy of thy lord.' It made no difference at all that one had brought five talents profit while the other had brought only two. Each had

The existence of traditional skills is very evident in Bible lands as demonstrated in a pottery shop in Hebron (above) and at an artist's studio in Caesarea.

served to the full extent of his ability and so each received the same commendation. And such will be the measure of Christ's welcome for each of His faithful servants in the day of final rewards. It is faithfulness in service, whether great or small, which will win the divine approval and bring the reward of entrance into 'the joy of the Lord' and higher and wider service in the kingdom of God.

When the man who had despised his one talent was called before his master he was full of excuses for his conduct. He 'knew', he said, that his lord was a hard taskmaster and that he always expected of his servants more than was right. Fearing, therefore, to incur his lord's wrath if he lost his money, he decided that he would keep his talent safe and return it intact.

'Thou wicked and slothful servant', was the lord's immediate and summary judgement. He was 'wicked' because he had sinfully maligned the character of his lord. Far from wanting to tax the man beyond his power, he had given him no more responsibility than he was capable of bearing, and all he expected of him was to do his best. Furthermore, the man was not only wicked in his assessment of his master but lazy as well; and it was for his sloth and not for his failure that he was condemned.

There is a solemn spiritual lesson in this, for all God-given talents, whether

147

many or few, are not given to us to be used or not used as we choose. They are a stewardship for which we must give an account, and to enjoy the privileges of the household of God while neglecting to bear our responsibilities as He directs, is ingratitude indeed. Spiritual indolence is, in fact, as sinful as active wickedness.

The final act of the householder in the parable was to deprive the condemned man of the talent of which he had proved himself unworthy. In nature it is a law that unused muscles and neglected func-

tions atrophy, and in the spiritual realm spiritual indolence must eventually result in the withdrawal of the grace man despises. Hence, the Psalmist's plea for God's patience, 'Take not Thy Holy Spirit from me.'

When we pray this prayer we will find that God is neither hard, demanding what we are not able to accomplish, nor lacking in patience with our weakness and frailty. But if we show ourselves unready to share the travail by which Christ's kingdom comes, we can have no grounds of complaint if at the last, like the unfaithful servant, we are 'cast out' from the enjoyment of its eternal privileges.

This chapter is based on Matthew 25:14-30.

The ancient art of the potter. The same techniques and equipment have changed little since Old Testament times, when pottery was the most common possession of both poor and rich alike.

Sheep or goats?

In the last of His three parables of the kingdom, Jesus drew a vivid picture of the final separation between the righteous and the wicked in the great judgement day when Christ returns.

When Jesus came the first time He specifically stated that He came 'not to condemn the world, but that the world through Him might be saved'.

When He returns, however, 'in His glory, and all the holy angels with Him', it will be to 'sit upon the throne of His glory' as King and Judge of all the earth.

In that day, Jesus said, there will be gathered before Him 'all nations', both Jew and Gentile, both the living and the dead, 'and He shall separate them one from another, as a shepherd divideth his sheep from the goats. And He shall set the sheep on His right hand, but the goats on the left'.

This allusion would be readily appreciated by the disciples. It was common for the shepherd of Palestine to tend both sheep and goats, the former for their wool and meat and the latter for their milk. During the day the flock would be pastured together; then at night they would be separated into different folds or into separate corners of one larger fold to sleep.

Between the two it was understandable that the shepherd should feel a deeper affection for the sheep, for while they were gentle, docile creatures, the goats were generally bad-tempered, quarrelsome, stubborn, difficult to control, and destructive animals. It was, therefore, easy to think of the sheep as the righteous and the goats as the wicked and to compare their separation when night came, to the separation of the righteous and the wicked at the end of the world's day of probation.

Setting the righteous on His right hand,

Sheep and goats are grazed in fields near Bethlehem, where angels announced the coming of the Messiah.

the side of favour and honour, Jesus will say to them, 'Come, ye blessed of my Father, inherit the kingdom prepared for you from the foundation of the world.'

Explaining the basis of their selection for their eternal reward, Jesus will say, 'For I was an hungered, and ye gave me meat: I was thirsty, and ye gave me drink: I was a stranger, and ye took me in: naked, and ye clothed me: I was sick, and ye visited me: I was in prison, and ye came unto me.'

When the righteous profess themselves unable to recall any such service rendered to their King, He will reply, 'Verily I say unto you, Inasmuch as ye have done it unto one of the least of these my brethren,

149

ye have done it unto me.'

On first thoughts it might seem that these grounds of reward sound rather like salvation by works, but, of course, there is no contradiction between the judgement scene here presented and the consistent teaching of Scripture that salvation is by faith alone.

As in the parable of the talents, Jesus was showing the inter-relation between faith and works. Faith is indeed the sole basis of salvation, but if by grace we are recreated by the divine Craftsman 'unto good works', these will provide the outward evidence of the inward transformation. The good works Jesus enumerates are not a source of merit but an evidence of faith.

By contrast, in phrasing His condemnation of those on His left hand Jesus will say, 'Depart from me, ye cursed, into everlasting fire, prepared for the devil and his angels. For I was an hungered, and ye gave me no meat: I was thirsty, and ye gave me no drink: I was a stranger and ye took me not in: naked, and ye clothed me not: sick, and in prison, and ye visited me not.'

When the rejected ones protest that they have no recollection of refusing to succour Him, He will reply, 'Verily I say unto you, Inasmuch as ye did it not to one of the least of these, ye did it not to me.'

In their case the absence of 'good works' clearly revealed that they had experienced no transformation of life through faith and that their profession was vain.

The separation completed, the righteous will enter 'the kingdom prepared . . . from the foundation of the world'. This kingdom was indeed first initiated in Eden, but through sin the plan was frustrated and its fulfilment had to be postponed. But when the age-long purpose of God is

consummated at the second coming of Christ and the earth is renewed again in all its Edenic beauty, the gates of the kingdom will be thrown open for the saints to enter and 'possess' it for ever.

But while the portion of the righteous will be glorious life in the kingdom 'prepared' for their eternal habitation, the fate of the wicked will be everlasting destruction in the fire 'prepared' for the Devil and his angels. Everything God's love can do to lead men to choose His salvation He has done. But if they reject it they thereby choose to share Satan's doom. Man's choice is free, but, according to his choice, his destiny is 'prepared'.

'These,' said Jesus of the rejectors of His salvation, 'shall go away into everlasting punishment: but the righteous into life eternal.'

What will be the nature of this eternal punishment? Jesus clearly indicated that it would be the opposite of 'life eternal', and the opposite of life eternal must be eternal

The Christian's faith provides the motivation for much of the care that is given in the form of food, water and agricultural know-how to the hungry; tents, clothing and sanctuary to the refugee; medical aid and preventive medicine for the sick; orphanages, schools and hope.

death. It will not be, as so many have erroneously taught, unending conscious suffering in the fires of divine wrath. This is not only a complete misrepresentation of Scripture, but a travesty upon the character of God.

If the wicked were to be miraculously preserved in order that they might go on suffering the pains of burning for ever, they would have 'eternal life' as surely as the righteous, the difference being only in the nature of that life! But nowhere does the Bible say that sinners will continue eternally. Instead, it declares categorically that they will become 'as though they had not been'. The Bible teaches not the 'eternal punishing' of the wicked, but their 'eternal punishment'. The 'wages of sin is death', eternal death.

Life without end will be the portion of the righteous. The fate of the wicked will be death without end.

This chapter is based on Matthew 25:31-46.

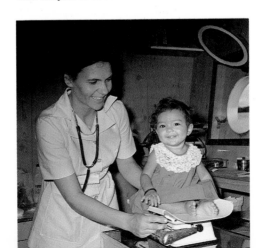

151

Preparing the Passover

After a quiet day of fellowship with His disciples and communion with God, Jesus rose on the Thursday morning to face the climactic ordeal of His earthly life.

The first three gospel writers, Matthew, Mark, and Luke all call this day, the thirteenth of Nisan, 'the first day of the feast of unleavened bread . . . when they killed the Passover'. So as soon as the disciples joined Jesus, they began to inquire about His plans for the celebration of the feast. 'Where wilt Thou that we prepare for Thee to eat the Passover?' they asked. As their number exceeded the minimum of ten for a Passover group, they assumed that they would partake of the paschal meal together, and quite evidently they expected to make all preparations that day to be ready for its celebration in the evening, that is, at the beginning of the fourteenth of Nisan.

These arrangements for the Passover, however, raise an important problem of chronology, for the record in John's gospel designates the next day, Friday, as the official preparation day, and indicates that the death of Christ synchronized with the slaying of the paschal lambs which were eaten on the evening of the fifteenth of Nisan. This is evident from the fact that the sentence upon Jesus, according to John, was delivered on the day of 'preparation of the passover', and that the priests would not defile themselves by entering the palace of the heathen Pilate just before the feast.

The question may well be asked, therefore, why the disciples inquired of Jesus about preparations for the Passover on Thursday morning and expected to be celebrating the feast on Thursday evening? The answer is that in the time of Christ there was some difference of opinion as to the time of celebration of the feast, when the fourteenth of Nisan fell on a Friday. In such circumstances the Sadducean temple authorities followed the normal practice of killing the lambs on that day, about the time of the evening

Innumerable pilgrims' feet which have followed the route covering the days prior to Jesus' death, have worn these steps which lead to the 'upper room'.

sacrifice, and eating the Passover meal on Friday evening. The more conservative Pharisees, on the other hand, put the feast back to the evening of the fourteenth of Nisan, that is Thursday evening, which involved having the meal ready as the sun began to decline on the thirteenth. It is thought that the Galileans followed the custom of the Pharisees, in this respect, and so Jesus was able to eat the last Passover meal with His disciples on the evening of the fourteenth of Nisan, while His death on the cross as the 'Lamb of God' coincided with the official slaying of the Passover lambs, and His resurrection, early on Sunday the sixteenth of Nisan, synchronized with the offering of the wave sheaf on the day after the first Sabbath of the feast.

As Jesus had not been into Jerusalem since Tuesday, the disciples may have thought that He intended to keep the feast in Bethany, which for the purpose of the Passover was regarded as within the city limits, but in order that antitype might meet type perfectly, Jesus had decided that He would eat it with His disciples in Jerusalem itself. When, therefore, the disciples approached Him, He selected two of them, probably Peter and John, and said, 'Go ye into the city, and there shall meet you a man bearing a pitcher of water: follow him. And wheresoever he shall go in, say ye to the goodman of the house, The

master saith, Where is the guestchamber, where I shall eat the Passover with my disciples? And he will show you a large upper room furnished and prepared: there make ready for us.'

It was the custom of the people of Jerusalem at Passover time to open their homes freely to visiting Jews for the celebration of the feast, and so there must have been many Galilean groups seeking similar hospitality that morning as Peter and John entered the city.

The disciples, however, did not have to make any inquiries, for no sooner were they inside the gate than they saw a man coming from one of the pools of Jerusalem, not with a water skin slung by a strap over his shoulder, but with a water pot such as was more commonly borne by women. The man was so conspicuous that Peter and John had no difficulty in picking him out and, as Jesus bade them, they followed him along the street. When he reached his destination, the disciples went in and spoke to the owner of the house as they were bidden. At once the man led them to the guest room of his house, where preliminary preparations for the Passover had already been made. In the centre of the carefully swept floor was a low table, and around it on three sides

153

were divans amply spread with cushions, for in the time of Christ the Passover was no longer eaten standing and in haste as when Israel left Egypt. Carpets surrounded the couches and clay lamps had been arranged in a central candelabra to illuminate the room.

The man may have prepared the room with the intention of extending hospitality to the first callers, but the fact that he invited the disciples in as soon as they mentioned 'the Master' suggests that he was himself a disciple. It could even be that a prior arrangement had been made by Jesus, including the plan by which the disciples would be led to his house. This secrecy may have been necessary in order to prevent Judas, the betrayer, telling the priests where they could find Him. This last supper was to have a deep significance for the disciples, and Jesus had much to say to them. It was essential, therefore, that they should be undisturbed.

The Bible does not give any indication where the House of the Last Supper was, but tradition has placed it on the hill of Zion in the south-west corner of the city. A church was built on the site in the fourth century which, after destruction by the Persians, was rebuilt by the Crusader, Geoffrey de Bouillon, much as it is today. The lower storey is now a mosque, claimed by the Moslems to be the tomb of David, but from the mosque twenty steps lead to an upper chamber of considerable size, with a vaulted roof supported by two central columns symbolically decorated with grapes and wheat ears. Some think that the original house was that of the parents of John Mark, which after the crucifixion provided a retreat for the disciples and the venue of the first church in Jerusalem. If so, the present building marks the site of 'the mother church of Christendom'.

Be that as it may, the disciples, after thanking their kind host for his hospitality, immediately set about assembling the food and utensils for the feast.

Residents in Jerusalem would probably have brought their lambs, unblemished animals of the first year, on the tenth day of the month, as the law of Moses commanded, but as it was impossible for those who came from a distance to bring their lambs with them, they were permitted to purchase them in Jerusalem any time up to the day before the feast. The obtaining of a lamb would thus be the disciples' first task.

Beside the lamb, a special bitter red sauce called charoseth, made of dried almonds, dates, figs, raisins, spices, and vinegar, had to be prepared; bitter herbs such as marjoram, bay, and thyme were obtained to represent the 'bread of affliction' which Israel experienced in captivity; and unleavened bread, to signify the putting away of the leaven of sin, had to be made or bought. The exact number of cups for the company who were to celebrate were placed in readiness, together with wine and water enough for the meal, and a large water jar and bowls were set by the wall for the ablutions on arrival and during the meal.

In the late afternoon, 'between the evenings', the lamb was taken to the temple to be slain and then brought back and roasted whole on a spit over an open fire, care being taken that no bones were broken in the cooking.

When all had been arranged, the owner of the house was left in charge, and the disciples returned to Bethany to report that everything was ready for the feast.

This chapter is based on Matthew 26:17-19; Mark 14:12-16; Luke 22:7-13.

154

A lesson in humility

Having received word from Peter and John that all was ready for the celebration of the Passover, Jesus waited until it was growing dusk to avoid observation, and then set off with His disciples for Jerusalem. It was dark when they entered the upper room which had been placed at their disposal.

Water and foot bowls had been set by the wall for the washing of the feet of the guests after their dusty walk from Bethany, but as no servant was at hand to perform this task, and none of the disciples offered to serve his brethren, they took their places round the table without washing. Jesus was grieved at this manifestation of pride in the hearts of the disciples. He saw that their thoughts were still upon the positions which thy would occupy in the kingdom of the Messiah – which they still mistakenly believed to be near – rather than upon the service and sacrifice to which He had called them. To have humbled themselves to perform the menial task of washing their fellow-disciples' feet, they felt would have prejudiced their chances of elevation in the kingdom. And so, as on many previous occasions, this last momentous gathering was marred by an undercurrent of tension

Rich splashes of colour from the beautiful trees and flowers of Israel are welcome relief during the 'parched earth' appearance of high summer.

and strife.

Jesus did not immediately comment on it. He allowed John to take his usual place on His right hand, with Peter next to him, while Judas ostentatiously placed himself on Jesus' left. When the disciples were all settled, each reclining on his left elbow, Jesus spoke to them. 'With desire I have desired to eat this Passover with you before I suffer.'

Up to this time Jesus had partaken of three Passover meals with His disciples, though not all had been present at the first two, as these were before the ordination of the twelve. This Passover, however, was to be the most fateful of all, for it was actually to climax the long succession of Passovers since Israel left Egypt.

This was the 'hour' to which all Jesus' earthly ministry had been directed, for on the morrow type and antitype would meet in His suffering and death, His work on earth would be finished, and He would 'depart out of this world unto the Father' to take up the next phase of His ministry as Mediator on behalf of sinners.

But though Jesus had looked forward to this final occasion of fellowship with His disciples, His heart was heavy with sorrow because He knew that they were far from ready to stand alone when His bodily presence should be taken from them. One of them was treacherously to betray Him, and the rest, in the last crisis, would flee for their lives, leaving Him to face alone the anguish of the cross. Yet 'having loved his own which were in the world, he loved them unto the end', and sought to prepare them for their own dread ordeal by His last loving counsels.

The Passover meal began in the usual manner, though the Bible record does not detail the first part of the service. Jesus, as head of the house, after giving thanks for the occasion, pronounced a blessing upon the wine, using the customary words, 'Blessed be thou, God, King of the universe, who createst the fruit of the vine.' He then passed a first cup around to each of the disciples.

This introduction to the meal was normally followed by the washing of the hands by all present. It may, therefore, have been at this point that Jesus decided to repair the omission before they came to the table, and teach the disciples a profound lesson. This is supported by the statement in John's account of the evening, 'And supper being begun (lit.) . . . he riseth from supper, and laid aside his garments; and took a towel, and girded himself.' Then, pouring water into one of the copper basins provided, He knelt down and began to wash the feet of the disciples, wiping them with the towel at His waist.

Amazed and shamed by the condescension of Jesus, the disciples accepted the service in silence until He reached Peter. When Jesus placed the bowl in front of him, Peter could contain his feelings no longer. 'Lord, dost thou wash my feet?' he cried incredulously.

'What I do thou knowest not now,' Jesus answered, taking Peter's feet in His gentle grasp; 'but thou shalt know hereafter.'

'Thou shalt never wash my feet,' Peter burst out impulsively, drawing his foot away. 'If I wash thee not, thou has no part with me,' Jesus answered quietly.

Peter was sobered by the warning. Although he still could not understand why Jesus should insist on washing his feet, the thought of being separated from Him affected him profoundly. 'Lord, not my feet only, but also my hands and my head,' he said. But this was not necessary nor appropriate to teach the lesson Jesus

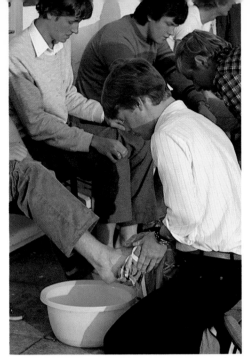

Young people taking part in a communion service at a Christian Youth Adventure Camp, follow the example set by Jesus in this simple but meaningful act.

intended. 'He that is washed [lit., had a bath],' He replied, 'needeth not save to wash his feet, but is clean every whit.'

By this Jesus meant that just as a person who had bathed his whole body in preparation for the feast was clean except for the dust of the journey upon his feet, so those who had committed their lives to Him needed only to be kept clean in heart by the purging away of every fleeting thought of sin before it had time to fix itself in the heart. And without a doubt, the symbolic service did accomplish this desirable end for the repentant disciples.

'Know ye what I have done to you?' Jesus asked as the chastened disciples resumed their seats at the table. 'Ye call me Master and Lord: and ye say well; for so I am. If I then, your Lord and Master, have washed your feet; ye also ought to wash one another's feet. For I have given you an example, that ye should do as I have done to you. . . . If ye know these things, happy are ye if ye do them.'

It is indeed a pity that most Christian Churches have forgotten this clear injunction, and no longer celebrate the beautiful ordinance Jesus instituted as a preliminary to the communion service; for it could be as efficacious today in breaking down pride, cultivating humility, and intensifying the spirit of fellowship in the Church as in that upper room in Jerusalem long ago. There are a few Protestant Churches in which the ordinance of feet-washing is still regularly celebrated as an essential preliminary to the communion service, with the consequent blessing to the participants as Jesus promised.

Having taught His beloved disciples this much-needed lesson in humility, Jesus had a wonderful word of encouragement for them. 'I appoint unto you a kingdom,' He said, 'as my Father hath appointed unto me.' If they would follow Him in service and sacrifice, a glorious reward would one day be theirs. If they drank now of His cup, they would 'eat and drink' at His 'table' in His kingdom. If they humbled themselves in service now, they would in due time be exalted to sit with Him 'on thrones judging the twelve tribes of Israel'.

Perhaps it was because Jesus saw the glint in the eyes of Judas at the mention of the kingdom that He added, 'I speak not of you all: I know whom I have chosen.' As Jesus looked at His disciples He knew who were His, and He knew who was not. Judas had ambitiously secured a place for himself in the disciple band, but from the beginning he was never really one of them. And soon he would be separated from them for ever.

The lesson of this solemn service must not be lost upon us, for only those who learn the lesson of humility will be exalted in the kingdom of God. 'Before honour,' said Solomon, 'is humility.' 'The meek,' said Jesus, 'shall inherit the earth.'

This chapter is based on Luke 22:14-16, 24-30; John 13:1-20; Matthew 26:20; Mark 14:17, 18.   157

At the Lord's table

When the disciples had resumed their places at table after the vivid lesson on humility which Jesus had given them, the main part of the Passover meal began. Before them were spread the roasted lamb, the savoury charoseth sauce, the unleavened bread, and bitter herbs. As head of the house, Jesus first dipped some bitter herbs into the sauce, ate them, and then distributed portions to all. A second cup of wine was next served, and when the youngest of the disciples, most likely John, asked the traditional question as to the significance of the Passover, Jesus explained its meaning. Wonderful must have been Jesus' discourse on this momentous occasion.

A Hallel, or hymn of praise, consisting of Psalms 113 and 114 was then sung, and a blessing pronounced upon the bread, Jesus doubtless using the customary words, 'Blessed be thou God, King of the whole world, who bringest forth bread out of the earth.' Then, dipping a piece into the sauce, He partook of it. The disciples followed suit, helping themselves also to pieces of meat from the common dish.

It was 'as they were eating' that Jesus interrupted once more the normal course of the meal to institute what was to be the counterpart of the Passover throughout the future history of the Christian Church. After His death on the morrow there would be no further need for blood sacrifices. At the cross, type would meet and be superseded by antitype. Never again would they need to kill an animal to symbolize the 'Lamb slain from the foundation of the world', for the memory of the cross would ever be with them. The bitter herbs, too, would cease to have their former significance, for the sacrifice of Calvary would for ever turn their mourning into joy. So, with the emblems of the bread

and wine which remained, Jesus inaugurated the Church's new service of commemoration.

Taking a piece of unleavened bread, He raised it in His hands towards heaven, and pronounced a blessing upon it. Then, breaking it in His hands, to represent the bruising and piercing of His body on the cross, He distributed the fragments to each of the disciples, saying, 'Take, eat; this is my body, which is given for you.' Appropriate indeed was the word 'given' for God had literally given His Son, and Jesus was about to give Himself for sinners by His vicarious sacrifice.

When the disciples had partaken of the emblem of His broken body which was to be 'given' for them, Jesus took a cup of wine and, after pronouncing a special benediction upon it, He passed it in turn to each of the disciples, saying, 'Drink ye all of it; for this is my blood of the new testament, which is shed for many for the remission of sins.' This corresponded with the third cup of the regular Passover meal, which was traditionally called the 'cup of blessing'. Paul recognized the even greater appropriateness of the title in connection with the new service of commemoration, and of it wrote, 'The cup of blessing which we bless, is it not the communion of the blood of Christ?'

Finally, to indicate His purpose in giving this new ordinance to His disciples at this time, Jesus added, 'This do in remembrance of me.' Until now the Passover service had kept in continual remembrance the deliverance of Israel from bondage in Egypt. The celebration of the Lord's supper would from now on keep in continual remembrance the ultimate deliverance of God's people from the bondage of sin through the cross.

As we partake of the sacred emblems we

Crushed grapes and grain supply the basic elements for symbols which represent a broken yet victorious Saviour.

are reminded that, through the broken body and the shed blood of our Lord, we have 'remission of sins'. In the papyri the word 'remission' was used for the release of a debtor from punishment, and Christ's sacrifice did indeed vicariously release man from the punishment due to him for his sin. The sacrifice of Christ could have secured remission for the sins of all the world, but actually it will avail only for those who are prepared by faith to accept its merits.

Besides symbolizing the justifying of the sinner through the merits of Christ's sacrifice, the ordinance Jesus instituted also vividly set forth the impartation of righteousness through the sharing of His life. As the disciples ate of the bread and drank of the wine, they symbolized the reception of the perfect holiness of His divine nature. As Jesus said on a previous occasion, 'He that eateth my flesh, and drinketh my blood, dwelleth in me, and I in him. . . . He that eateth me, even he shall live by me.' Just as the Israelites gained strength for their journey from the Passover meal, so we gain strength for the journey of life through partaking of the life of Christ typified by the bread and wine of the communion service.

Still further, the Lord's supper looked forward to Christ's final triumph, for after giving the wine to the disciples, Jesus added, 'I say unto you, I will not drink

henceforth of this fruit of the vine, until that day when I drink it new with you in my Father's kingdom.'

On more than one occasion after His resurrection, Jesus partook with the disciples in common meals, but He did not again partake of the 'fruit of the vine'. When the great day of the marriage feast of the Lamb comes, however, He will sit at the head of the table in the kingdom with all His redeemed around Him and drink with them of the 'new' wine of triumph and victory. Paul therefore reminded the believers that every time they partook of the sacred emblems, they showed 'the Lord's death till he come'. Thus the service was to keep bright both the memory of the past and the hope of the future.

Besides commemorating the blessings which are ours in Christ, the communion service was still further to manifest the fellowship of all believers with one another around the table of the Lord, and in the 'household of God'.

Of course, the disciples did not at the time fully comprehend all that this symbolic service was to mean to the Christian Church, but all were deeply affected by the words Jesus had spoken; that is, all save Judas. The fact that Judas was permitted to partake of the sacred emblems is, however, significant. There are those who assert that only professing and baptized believers can come to the table of the Lord. But Jesus set no such barriers to His table. If Judas the betrayer was allowed to partake of the sacred emblems when his heart was set to betray his Master, surely no Church has the right to exclude from the table any who wish to come. The invitation is extended to all, but the blessing of the service is received only by those who desire to receive the spiritual gifts of which the emblems are a symbol.

Garden and hedgerow flowers from Jerusalem and the surrounding countryside.

To partake 'worthily', however, does not mean that one must feel 'worthy'. We may come to the table of the Lord as conscious of our sins and weaknesses as the disciples themselves were, but if we sincerely desire the imputed righteousness of Christ to cleanse us from sin, and the imparted righteousness of Christ to enable us to do His will in all things, we will receive a blessing.

On the other hand, if we come, like Judas, unworthy in heart to the table of the Lord, we not merely lose the blessing, but incur God's curse, for instead of 'discerning the Lord's body' in the sacred emblems, we 'crucify him afresh'. No wonder, therefore, that the apostle Paul solemnly admonishes, 'Let a man examine himself, and so let him eat.'

When Jesus saw that His solemn words had made no impression upon Judas, and that the betrayer was still bent upon his evil purpose, He knew that the time had come for the final separation. So as the meal proceeded, Jesus said plainly to His disciples, 'I know whom I have chosen: but that the Scripture may be fulfilled, . . . I say unto you, that one of you shall betray me. . . . Behold, the hand of him

that betrayeth me is with me on the table.'

The words came as a shock to the disciples 'and they began to inquire among themselves, which of them it was that should do this thing'. It speaks well, however, for the new spirit which had come to them through the ordinance of humility that, instead of suspecting one another, they began to ask Jesus, 'Lord, is it I?' except Judas, whose silence the disciples did not notice amid their own personal apprehensions.

At last Peter leaned over to John as he reclined on Jesus' breast and whispered to him to ask Jesus who the betrayer would be. In an aside to John, Jesus replied, 'He it is, to whom I shall give a sop [or morsel], when I have dipped it.'

It was a common practice at a feast for the host to dip a piece of bread into the common dish and hand it to an honoured guest. By using this act as a means of identification, Jesus offered to Judas a last evidence of His love, and at the same time indicated, as prophecy had declared, that the betrayer would be a 'familiar friend' in whom He had 'trusted', who had eaten of His bread, yet who was now about to 'lift up his heel' against Him even as Ahithophel betrayed David.

As Jesus talked quietly to John, Judas sensed that he was the subject of conversation and, in an effort to cover up his intended treachery, he said sanctimoniously to Jesus, 'Rabbi, is it I?' He was taken aback when Jesus, dipping a piece of bread into the charoseth sauce gave it to him and said, 'Thou hast said.'

Up to this time there had always been the possibility that Judas might have repented of the ultimate crime he purposed to commit, but now the die was cast. The break between himself and Jesus was complete. Now 'Satan entered into him' and took complete control of his actions till his death.

None of the disciples except Peter had caught the words of Jesus to John, or understood the meaning of the giving of the sop, and so when Jesus said audibly to Judas, 'That thou doest, do quickly', they imagined He referred to some errand that the disciple needed to perform as 'keeper of the purse', such as buying food for the rest of the feast, or making some contribution to the poor during the Passover season. Only Peter and John realized, when Judas got up and went out, that he was going straight to the priests to arrange how they might take Jesus.

'It was night,' the Record says when Judas departed, and it was not merely the physical darkness which enveloped him. Judas went out from the presence of 'the light of the world' into the kingdom of darkness from which he was never to return.

When Judas first sought a place among the disciples, Jesus gave him his opportunity. All through the years they had been together He tried to win his love. If Judas had gained the victory over his pride and ambition he could have been a monument of grace. Instead, he allowed the sin in his heart to develop until no recovery was possible.

'The Son of man goeth [to his death] as it is written of him,' Jesus said to His disciples when Judas had gone out, 'but woe unto that man by whom the Son of man is betrayed! it had been good for that man if he had never been born.' It was necessary for the Scripture to be fulfilled because the death of Jesus was by 'the determinate counsel' of God for the redemption of lost mankind, but Judas was not himself predestined to be the betrayer. It was of his own free will that he had allowed Satan to use him as the tool of his evil design. And in so doing he turned his back upon God's purpose for his life. Rejecting eternal gain, he condemned himself to eternal loss.

This chapter is based on Matthew 26:21-29; John 13:21-30; Mark 14:18-25; Luke 22:17-23.   **163**

The Vine and the branches

It was late in the evening when Jesus ended His discourse to His disciples. At His request they all stood to sing the final Hallel of the Passover meal, comprising Psalms 115 to 118, and went out together into the night.

The most direct way from the suburb of Zion to the Mount of Olives was over the Tyropoeon bridge, and through the temple courts, but after dark none but the priests were allowed in the sacred precincts. So Jesus must either have turned north past Herod's palace, the house of the High Priest, and the fortress of Antonia, or else descended the Tyropoeon Valley and left by one of the southern gates, then following the upper slope of the Kidron gorge to the Sheep Gate. In either case He and His disciples would go down the street of steps leading from the Sheep Gate to the river. Traces of this road and the one which climbed the Mount of Olives on the other side are to be found less than a hundred yards from the modern bridge.

Most of the year the Kidron was a dry watercourse, but in the spring a torrent filled the river bed for a few weeks. As Jesus crossed by a shallow ford He doubtless recalled that David, His forefather according to the flesh, had gone over the Kidron probably at this very spot after he had been treacherously betrayed by his 'familiar friend', Ahithophel.

As the little group began to ascend the steep wooded hill, Jesus looked with compassion at His companions and sorrowfully said, 'All ye shall be offended because·of me this night: for it is written, I will smite the shepherd, and the sheep of the flock shall be scattered abroad.'

As usual it was Peter who hastened to assure Jesus of his loyalty. 'Though all men should be offended because of thee,' he said, 'yet will I never be offended.'

Peter was entirely sincere in his protestations of allegiance, but, as on so many previous occasions, he failed to realize his own frailty. And not until he had had the most severe test of his life did he learn the double lesson of humility and of utter dependence on Christ.

'Verily I say unto you,' replied Jesus to Peter's boast, 'That this day, even in this night, before the cock crow twice, thou shalt deny me thrice.'

At this Peter protested even more vehemently. 'If I should die with thee, I will not deny thee in any wise,' he asserted, forgetting the past occasions when the weakness of the flesh had belied his confident boasts.

'Simon, Simon,' said Jesus, the repetition of Peter's name indicating the solemnity of what He was about to say, 'Behold, Satan hath desired to have you, that he may sift you as wheat.' Already Satan had Judas in his clutches, and now he was seeking to wreck the experience of yet another of the disciples. 'But,' said Jesus, 'I have prayed for thee, that thy faith fail not.'

Though Peter would come near to the shipwreck of his faith through the machinations of Satan, yet in this crisis of his life he would be upheld by the prayers of Jesus. By God's grace he would learn his lesson and rise again.

Confident that Peter would not utterly fall, Jesus said to him, 'When thou art converted, strengthen thy brethren.' And out of that heart-breaking experience Peter did indeed gain a strength which enabled him to bring courage and hope to many during his long ministry to the Church.

But while Jesus had to warn Peter and

Spring flowers splash their colour across the wooded slopes of the Mount of Olives.

the other disciples of the trying hour
through which they would all pass, He
assured them that He would meet them
again before His return to His Father and
assign to them their future work for Him.
'After I am risen again,' He said, 'I will go
before you into Galilee.'

Very different, however, would they
find their work as messengers of the
Crucified One from their missionary
labours in the heyday of Jesus' popularity.
'When I sent you without purse, and scrip,
and shoes, lacked ye anything?' Jesus
asked. 'And they said, Nothing,' for
everywhere they had been welcomed as
the disciples of the Miracle-worker of
Galilee. Now, Jesus advised them, 'He that
hath a purse, let him take it, and likewise
his scrip: and he that hath no sword, let
him sell his garment, and buy one.' While
some would still receive them gladly, they
would also encounter hatred and opposition. And for this they must prepare
themselves.

There has been much speculation as to
what Jesus meant when He said, 'And he
that hath no sword, let him . . . buy one.'
Certainly He did not mean that His messengers would ever have to use physical
weapons to defend themselves, or to
advance the cause of the Gospel. If He
had, He would hardly have said, 'It is
enough,' when they told Him they had
two swords among the twelve of them!

The 'sword' to which Jesus referred was
the general purpose knife which Palesti-
nians of those days carried, as the Scots
used to carry a dirk in their hose. It was
commonly used for the cutting up of food,
and its name *ma'akeleth* was actually
derived from the word *ma'akel*, meaning
food. As homes would no longer be readily opened to them in their missionary
labours, they would need to carry food,

Looking across the Kidron Valley from the
Temple area to Gethsemane on the Mount of
Olives. The two buildings are (centre left) the
Church of All Nations and the Russian
Orthodox Church of Mary Magdalene.

money, and all necessary equipment as
they travelled from city to city. Hence His
timely counsel.

That Jesus would never tolerate His
messengers using material weapons either
for offence or defence, He showed shortly
after this when He rebuked Peter for drawing his knife against the high priest's ser-

vant. Paul said on a later occasion, 'The weapons of our warfare are not carnal'. The power of the Gospel is the power of love, not coercion. The 'quick and powerful' sword of the Spirit, the Word of God, is the only weapon which the messenger of Christ needs for the prosecution of his spiritual warfare.

Following the road up the slope of Olivet, Jesus and His disciples made their way towards a walled garden called Gethsemane where Jesus had often retired for communion with God, and on occasions had rested for the night when He did not wish to return to Bethany.

Its name, which means 'olive press', indicates it was an olive grove, though, as was customary, it would contain also some fig trees and vines. It seems likely that the grove belonged to one of Christ's disciples in Jerusalem, and if the upper room where Jesus had celebrated the Passover was in the home of John Mark, what would be more natural than that He should resort to the quiet seclusion of the family garden outside the city to meditate and pray.

Exactly where the Garden of Gethsemane was, it is impossible to say. Actually there are today three Gethsemanes on the slopes of the Mount of Olives, one cared for by the Roman Catholics, another by the Armenians, and still another, higher up the mountain, in the charge of the Russian Orthodox Church. All we can now say is that it was on the lower slopes of Olivet, not far from the Kidron crossing and probably less than half a mile from the city walls.

In the Franciscan garden, which Queen Helena and Constantine the Great in the fourth century believed to be the true Gethsemane, there are among the beautifully laid-out beds of Palestine flowers, eight gnarled old olive trees, twenty-four to thirty feet in circumference, which are certainly many hundreds of years old. One is known as the Tree of the Agony, but it is hardly likely that any of them go back as far as the time of Christ.

As the little band neared the gate into the garden the moon shone down upon a flourishing vine beside the road. Before it Jesus stopped to give His disciples yet another reminder that their strength for living and for service would ever be dependent upon their connection with His omnipotent power through the promised Spirit.

'I am the true Vine,' He said, pointing to the tree, 'and my Father is the Husbandman. . . . Ye are the branches: he that abideth in me, and I in him, the same bringeth forth much fruit: for without me ye can do nothing.'

The ancient prophets had often compared Israel to the familiar vine, but here Jesus suggested that really He was the Vine and His people were the branches, entirely dependent for their life on their constant connection with the divine stock. The reason ancient Israel failed to bear fruit, and bore only 'wild grapes', was because they had lost their vital connection with Him. At this time the nation was rapidly withering, and soon, like the dead branches of the vine, they would be gathered up for destruction.

To replace the dead wood, the branches of the new Israel were to be grafted in. If these new branches continued to 'abide' in Him through the efficacious presence of the Holy Spirit, they would, as Jesus declared in His earlier parable of the vineyard, 'bring forth' the good fruit of righteousness. But if, like Israel, they lost their connection with Him, they would become fruitless, and would eventually have to be rejected as ancient Israel had been.

This parable of the Vine and the branches is a parable also of the individual Christian life. In our own strength we can do nothing. Only by constant, daily partaking of the divine nature, can we mature and bear fruit 'unto righteousness'. As the branches of the vine have no life apart from a living connection with the stock, so we have no life apart from Christ. As the branches are nourished by drawing the vital sap from the trunk of the vine, so we are to draw daily strength by feeding upon God's Word and through a living prayer connection with Him. Thus do we literally become partakers of the divine nature, fortifying our weakness with His strength and our frailty with His enduring might.

Failing to abide, on the other hand, will inevitably result in a withering of our experience and eventual spiritual death. And if we become dead branches we can expect no other fate than to be gathered up in the day of judgement and destroyed. 'If a man abide not in me,' declared Jesus solemnly, 'he is cast forth as a branch, and

Grapes only reach succulent maturity when pruned and tended, and securely connected with the life-giving vine.

is withered; and men gather them, and cast them into the fire, and they are burned.' But, He added, 'If ye abide in me, and my words abide in you, ye shall ask what ye will, and it shall be done unto you.'

Moreover, Jesus explained further, just as the fruit-bearing vine is improved and caused to bear more fruit by careful pruning, so through testing and trial, God 'purges' our lives that we may bear 'more fruit'. The pruning process is drastic to the plant, as also the trials of the Christian life seem to us, but neither are haphazard or careless. Carefully the pruning knife is applied in our experience, and though the process may bring pain, the result will be for our good that we may bring forth 'much fruit'.

'Herein is my Father glorified,' Jesus concluded, 'that ye bear much fruit; so shall ye be my disciples.'

This chapter is based on Matthew 26:30-35; Mark 14:27-31; Luke 22:31-38; John 15:1-8.

Agony in Gethsemane

When Jesus had ended His prayer for His disciples and Himself, they continued up the road and, reaching the entrance to the garden, they went in. Just inside Jesus bade His disciples sit down to rest, while He took His three closest companions, Peter, James, and John, with Him into the recesses of the grove. 'Sit ye here,' He said, 'while I go and pray yonder.' Jesus had chosen these three disciples to witness the raising of Jairus's daughter. They had been with Him on the Mount of Transfiguration, and now He desired the comfort of their presence in His hour of greatest need.

Penetrating deep into the silence of the garden, Jesus halted beneath one of the trees and, turning to His disciples, He said, 'My soul is exceeding sorrowful, even unto death: tarry ye here, and watch with me.' As they looked into His face they saw an anguish of spirit such as they had never before beheld. But though they could not begin to enter into the agony of soul which was settling upon Him, Jesus felt the need of their nearness and sympathy in this hour of decision.

Leaving them, Jesus moved on into the gloom, and about a stone's throw away He fell upon the rocky ground in earnest prayer. As the disciples watched in silent awe they saw Him raise Himself from the ground, and the light of the full moon shone through a gap in the trees upon His upturned face. Resisting the exhaustion which was coming overwhelmingly upon them, they listened as Jesus talked with His Father.

'Father,' they heard Him say, 'if it be possible, let this cup pass from me.' Strange words these might seem upon the lips of One who had come down from heaven expressly to give His life a ransom for sin, and who so many times during His ministry had referred to His vicarious sacrifice. Why then, at this moment of supreme decision, should He ask His Father if there was any way whereby the bitter cup of suffering might be taken from His lips?

We may be certain that the words did not indicate any shrinking from the ignominy of the cross, or from the agony of pain and torture which He knew it involved. Nor do the words suggest any weakening of His resolve to fulfil the purpose of His advent. Rather do they reveal the complete humanity as well as the deity of the Son of man.

Fully man, the sinless Jesus experienced, in all its terrible intensity, the physical and mental anguish of the doomed sinner. As the prophet Isaiah foretold, God had 'numbered' Him with the transgressors. He had laid on Him 'the iniquity of us all'. The sword of justice was unsheathed against Him, and the Innocent One was about to be 'smitten' for the sins of a rebellious world.

No wonder then, as the dread weight of the world's sin and guilt pressed upon Him and the terrors of the shame and death of all the sinners whose place He was taking began to close around Him, that His anguished mind and heart shrank from utter and final abandonment to the doom He had chosen to accept. Jesus recoiled not from the agony of death, but from the black gulf of eternal separation from His Father.

It was in this terrible extremity that

Ancient olive trees in Gethsemane. The word Gethsemane has come to us from the Aramaic word Gath Shemanî, meaning 'oil press'. The trees under which Jesus spent His night of agony were felled, along with all the trees around Jerusalem, by the Roman general Titus during the siege of Jerusalem in AD 70.

170

Satan made his last desperate bid to defeat the divine plan of salvation. He sought to persuade Jesus that man was not worth the sacrifice. Not even His disciples deserved it. He had already got one of them to betray Him, and before long the rest would forsake Him and leave Him alone. So Satan urged Him to turn from His purpose and give up the contest.

But though the terrible sense of abandonment forced a last appeal to His Father from the lips of Jesus, there followed, without a moment's hesitation, the words which declared that the victory was already won. 'Nevertheless', He prayed, 'not my will, but thine, be done.' He had come down from heaven to do not His own but His Father's will, and it was God's will which should prevail to the end.

For a time the disciples watched Jesus. They saw him fall prostrate to the ground in an agony of grief. Then, overcome by physical weariness accentuated by their sorrow at His distress, they fell asleep. For all their confidence that they were 'able' to stand by Him, they had failed; and when Jesus rose and made His way with difficulty back to them, 'He found them sleeping'.

Going over to Peter, the disciple who had been loudest in his protestations of loyalty, Jesus roused him, and in tones of disappointment and gentle reproof said, 'Simon, sleepest thou? Couldst not thou watch one hour?' Then as the other two

The Basilica of the Agony or the Church of All Nations, so called because it was built with funds from many countries. The first church on this site to mark the struggle Jesus endured in Gethsemane was built in AD 380. the Crusaders built another structure on its ruins. Evidences of both buildings can be seen in the precincts of the present church which is noted for its beautiful mosaics.

disciples stirred, He went on 'Watch and pray, that ye enter not into temptation: the spirit indeed is willing, but the flesh is weak.'

Beyond His disappointment at their failure in His time of need, Jesus wanted them to realize that the crisis which was coming to Him was their crisis too. If He had come to the greatest test of His earthly life, they had also. If He needed the sustenance of communion with His Father, they needed it more.

When the disciples were fully roused, Jesus left them and went again to pray. 'O my Father,' He cried, 'if this cup may not pass away from me, except I drink it, thy will be done.' No more did He ask if there was another way to redeem a world of lost sinners. He knew there was not, and now He only sought strength to be obedient even to death.

As Jesus prayed, Satan continued desperately to press his last and greatest temptation upon the mind of the Saviour. Men would reject Him even if He made the sacrifice. His sacrifice would be in vain. The conflict was terrible, but Jesus remained unmoved.

Once again Jesus sought a respite from the struggle in communion with His disciples, but 'when he returned, he found them asleep again, (for their eyes were heavy),' and when He awakened them they knew not 'what to answer him'. They had not intended to fall asleep, but sorrow and the weakness of the flesh had overcome them.

For the third time Jesus left them and prayed, repeating the same words. And as the approaching agony of death came fearfully upon Him, 'His sweat was as it were great drops of blood falling to the ground'.

When Satan tempted Christ at the beginning of His ministry, he made three

'In prayer Jesus gained the victory.'

attempts to break His resolve before retiring defeated. Again in Gethsemane, God allowed Satan three times to seek to undermine His purpose. But as Isaiah had prophetically declared, Jesus did 'not fail'. Three times Satan pressed his attack and three times he was beaten back by Christ's reiterated declaration of submission to His Father's will. Jesus could not be turned from His mission. He took the cup and drank it to the dregs. Victory was now sure. The way of salvation could now never be closed. The gates of death had been forced open for all who wished to go forth free.

No sooner had Satan retired defeated than God dispatched an angel from heaven to the side of Jesus to strengthen Him after His fearful struggle. As the angel wiped the bloody sweat from the Saviour's brow, the agony passed from His countenance and the peace of absolute surrender to His father's will possessed Him. The evil angels fell back in defeat, while relief and joy filled the hearts of the watching angels. If the disciples could have shared that wonderful moment they would have been fortified to face the crisis coming to them with calm and confidence, but again they were asleep.

In prayer Jesus gained the victory. Now He was calm, assured, resolute, and indeed eager to go forward to meet His destiny. The disciples, by sleeping, had failed to prepare themselves, and before long would be fleeing in terror from those who came to take Jesus. If only they had heeded the Master's urgent exhortation, 'Watch and pray, that ye enter not into temptation'!

This chapter is based on Matthew 26:36-45; Mark 14:32-41; Luke 22:40-46; John 18:1.

Arrest in the garden

As Jesus looked down at the sleeping disciples, not so much disappointed that they had failed Him, as sad that they had failed to receive strength by watching with Him, He heard sounds in the distance. They told Him that the crisis hour of His earthly life had come.

Very early in His ministry His enemies had determined that He must be put out of the way, and on three occasions Jesus had foretold His arrest, trial, suffering, and death. Time and again attempts had been made to set the mob on Him, or to have Him arrested for disturbing the peace of the temple precincts, but always His assailants had been restrained, as by an unseen hand, because His time had not come. Until Jesus had finished the work which God had given Him, no man had power to do Him harm. Now the witness of His life was completed and He was ready to finish His work on earth by the witness of His death. This time He would make no attempt to escape from the net which was being drawn around Him.

The composition of the party which set out to arrest Jesus strikingly portrayed the forces which had combined against Him. First there were the Sadducean 'chief priests'. They desired Jesus' death because He was undermining their ecclesiastical administration, and had even dared to interfere with the lucrative temple trade.

Next there were the 'scribes', the leaders of the conservative Pharisees. They were anxious to be rid of Jesus because He had poured scorn on their 'traditions' and had condemned their formalism and hypocrisy.

Besides these two usually antagonistic parties, now united in opposition to Jesus, there were also some of the 'elders', heads of rich Jewish families, whose chief fear was that Jesus might start a revolt against the Romans and bring disaster upon the nation and upon themselves.

To carry out the actual arrest, the priests and elders had called out the temple guard, normally employed to keep order in the temple courts, and anticipating that the disciples of Jesus might put up some resistance to His arrest, they had also contacted the chief officer of the Roman garrison and secured the services of a 'band' of soldiers under their officer or tribune. How many there were in this band is not certain, as the term is a vague one, but there may have been fifty.

Lastly, following the temple police and the soldiers, was a motley rabble of ruffians armed with sticks and staves, who had been hastily mobilized by the priests in case of need.

Though the moon was at the full, the guards carried lanterns and torches in case Jesus fled into the dark recesses of the olive grove. Leading the party was the betrayer, Judas Iscariot. The particular mention that he was 'one of the twelve' again emphasizes that, as in the case of David's betrayer, he had been Jesus' 'familiar friend'. Judas would probably have preferred to have kept in the background after leading the priests and rulers to the garden, but as not all the guards and soldiers knew Jesus, he had to arrange a sign to make sure they seized the right person. So he told them, 'Whomsoever I shall kiss, that same is he.' And remembering previous occasions when Jesus had escaped from His enemies he added, 'Hold him fast'.

When Jesus heard the tramp of armed men, and saw the gleam of swords and spears in the red glare of the torches, He could still have foiled His would-be captors, but He did not. 'Behold,' He said calmly as He roused the disciples, 'he is at

175

hand that doth betray me,' and He began to walk slowly towards the multitude.

Moving stealthily forward, as they thought to surprise Jesus, the crowd suddenly came upon Him in a clearing among the trees, His form radiant in the light of the Passover moon. Following the pre-arranged plan, Judas, in pretended friendship, advanced to meet Jesus, and with his customary greeting, 'Hail, Master,' he kissed Him. In sacred art Judas is usually represented as kissing Jesus on the cheek, though the more usual salutation of a rabbi by a disciple was by a kiss on the hand. Whatever the form of greeting, the word suggests that he kissed Jesus repeatedly and fervently, keeping up his dispicable hypocrisy to the end.

'Friend,' said Jesus, gazing in sadness upon this erstwhile disciple, 'wherefore art thou come?' Then, without waiting for a reply, He added, 'Betrayest thou the Son of man with a kiss?'

As soon as the soldiers recognized the signal they moved forward to seize Jesus. Turning from Judas He faced them calmly. 'Whom seek ye?' He asked.

'Jesus of Nazareth,' they replied.

'I am he,' Jesus said. At once they rushed upon Him, but as they approached, the supernatural power which had thrown back His attackers at Nazareth flashed from His face and the crowd 'went backward', cowering in disorder 'and fell to the ground'.

By this momentary manifestation of divine power, Jesus showed that His enemies could do nothing against Him save by permission of God. His submission was to be as voluntary as His sacrifice was vicarious.

When nothing happened to them, those in the foremost ranks slowly rose to their feet and found Jesus still standing motion-less before them.

'Whom seek ye?' Jesus asked them again.

'Jesus of Nazareth,' they said, not menacingly now but apprehensively, fearing what He might do to them.

Quietly Jesus answered, 'I have told you that I am he: if therefore ye seek me, let these,' and He motioned towards His disciples, 'go their way'. Even in this critical moment Jesus' first thought was for the safety of His disciples. But Peter, brave and impulsive as ever, was not prepared to stand aside and see his Master taken from them.

'Lord, shall we smite with the sword?' he cried, and, quickly as a flash, he drew his knife from its sheath and struck at the man nearest to him. It happened to be Malchus, the personal servant of the high priest, who had doubtless come along to take immediate news of the arrest to his master. His name suggests that he was not himself a Jew, but most likely a Nabatean or Syrian slave.

Malchus tried to dodge the blow and the knife glanced the side of his head, almost severing his right ear. Quickly Jesus waved Peter aside and with the words, 'Suffer ye thus far,' He put the ear back into place, and the gash was immediately healed. How significant that Jesus' last miracle was an act of unmerited mercy towards an enemy!

Turning then to Peter He said, 'Put up thy sword into the sheath, . . . for all that take the sword shall perish with the sword.' By this foolish act Peter had laid himself and the other disciples open to instant reprisal, and if Jesus had not taken prompt action they might easily have been massacred to a man.

If Jesus had wished to repel His assail-ants, He had no need of Peter's puny

Before Annas

It was about one o'clock on Friday morning when the priests and soldiers, with their Prisoner, began the return journey to the city. Descending the Mount of Olives they crossed the Kidron and went up the street of steps from the river. The priests may have exercised their right to enter by the Golden Gate and cross the temple courts, forbidden to the people at night, or they may have gone in at one of the southern gates and up the Tyropoeon Valley to the palace shared by the high priest, Caiaphas, and his father-in-law, Annas. This stood on Mount Zion not very far from the house where Jesus had celebrated the Last Supper with His disciples.

Had Jesus been an ordinary prisoner He would have been detained till daybreak, as it was not lawful to convene the Sanhedrin court until after the morning sacrifice, but the chief priests feared that if His arrest became known too widely, His sympathizers might gather and demand His release before He could be tried. The high priest knew too that there were some members of the Sanhedrin, like Nicodemus, who were not in favour of taking action against Jesus, and if the trial were delayed they might influence others and make His condemnation difficult. Caiaphas, therefore, had decided that Jesus must be tried and sentenced that very night, and turned over to the Romans the next morning, so that His execution could be all over before the feast of Passover began.

So as soon as Jesus was securely in the palace of the high priest, an urgent summons was sent out to all the 'safe' members of the Sanhedrin to assemble for an emergency session. While Caiaphas was arranging this, he sent Jesus into the apartments of his father-in-law for a preliminary unofficial examination.

At this time Annas was without doubt the most influential of the chief priests after Caiaphas, for he was the patriarch of a family which had held the high priestly office for more than a quarter of a century. He himself had been appointed high priest by the Legate Quirinius, governor of Syria, back in AD 7, the accession year of Tiberius, and had office till AD 14. Though deposed by Valerius Gratus, the immediate predecessor of Pilate, he so completely dominated ecclesiastical circles in Jerusalem that he was able to get five of his sons and a son-in-law appointed to the office of high priest in the next twenty-five years. He was immediately followed by his son, Israel Ben Phabi, then another son, Eleazar, and in AD 18 he got his son-in-law, Joseph Caiaphas, appointed. Caiaphas held the office of high priest for the unprecedented period of eighteen years until AD 37. Probably it was because he was so well in with Pontius Pilate that he was deposed by Vitellus, prefect of Syria, within a few months of the procurator's removal and departure for Rome.

After Caiaphas, three more sons of Annas reigned, Jonathan, Theophilus, and Annas the Younger, before the family losts its influence. It was in the three months' tenure of office by the last-mentioned that James, the first martyr apostle, was beheaded. One of the last high priests before the disaster of AD 70 was Matthias, son of Theophilus and grandson of Annas. Annas himself lived through the hey-day of his family to a great age, and his traditional tomb is pointed out to the south of the city.

Besides holding the highest ecclesiastical offices in the nation, the family of Annas also controlled the temple trade from the 'booths of Annas' in the Kidron

179

Valley, and it was against the extension of their lucrative activities into the temple courts that Jesus had struck on the two occasions when He cleansed the temple. The house of Annas was noted for its profiteering; one instance, the raising of the price of doves, the humblest of offerings, evoking an indignant protest from one of the grandsons of Hillel. Even the

A bougainvillaea-covered bell tower near Mary's Tomb on the Mount of Olives.

servants of Annas went about with an air of superiority and did not hesitate, when walking in the streets, to drive the common people out of their way with rods. No wonder the Pharisee Talmud of later days pronounced a curse on 'the house of Hanan' and their 'viper brood'.

From all this we can guess how deep was the hatred of the powerful and avaricious Annas for Jesus, and how he welcomed the opportunity of examining Him.

When Jesus was ushered into his presence about two o'clock in the morning, His fetters were removed, as it was illegal to question a prisoner while still bound. Annas then set about formulating a charge against Him so as to expedite the trial when the Sanhedrin assembled.

He began by asking Jesus about His disciples. Such information would be very useful in convincing the Roman authorities that He was a dangerous revolutionary, and it would also enable them to be rounded up after Jesus had been dealt with. But Jesus detected the cunning old man's purpose and would give him no help.

Annas next turned the questioning to His doctrine, hoping to get Jesus to give them some lead towards His condemnation, but again He was quite uncommunicative. 'I spake openly to the world,' Jesus said; 'I ever taught in the synagogue, and in the temple, whither the Jews always resort; and in secret have I said nothing. Why askest thou me? Ask them which heard me, what I have said unto them: behold, they know what I said.' If His enemies had been massing evidence against Him for the past two years, surely they did not need any further explanation of what He had taught.

Without doubt, the officers of the guard

had had experience before of obstinate prisoners who would not talk, and one of them, feeling that it was his duty to coerce Jesus into confessing His crime, struck Him 'with the palm of his hand, saying, Answerest thou the high priest so?'

Annas should have been the first to reprove the officer for striking a defence-less and uncondemned prisoner, but he said nothing. Jesus could well have called Annas a 'whited wall' as Paul did under similar provocation; but instead He turned to the man and said, 'If I have spoken evil, bear witness of the evil: but if well, why smitest thou me?' The officer made no reply, but he did not molest Jesus again.

After some further questioning, Annas realized that Jesus was not to be inveigled into condemning Himself. He knew, too, that it was a gross violation of justice to try to extract a confession from Him, and that Jesus was entirely within His rights in requiring them to produce evidence against Him, especially on a capital charge. So when Caiaphas announced that the Sanhedrin was ready, Annas desisted and commanded the officers to take Jesus across the open court to the council chamber in the high priest's wing of the palace.

This chapter is based on John 18:13; 19-24.   181

Before Caiaphas

In response to the call of Caiaphas all the available members of the Sanhedrin were assembled in the court of the high priest when Jesus was brought in. Apparently, however, Nicodemus and perhaps one or two others who were known to favour Jesus, had been deliberately excluded to avoid prolonging the trial. In the Sanhedrin there were three categories of members and all are mentioned as being present at this night meeting, namely, 'the chief priests, and the elders, and the scribes'.

The chief priests included the high priest and all previous holders of the office who were still living, other high officials, like the commander of the temple guard, who deputized for the high priest, and the chiefs of the three temple treasuries, also the heads of the twenty-four courses of the temple priesthood.

The scribes represented the Pharisee party in the Sanhedrin. Rabbi Gamaliel may have belonged to this group, as he was one of the chief teachers of the law at this time, and one of the instructors of Saul, later Paul. Nicodemus, though not present on this occasion, was also one of the scribes.

The elders were the lay leaders of the synagogue of Jerusalem elected from influential families in the city.

Originally the Sanhedrin met in the temple itself, in the 'House of Hewn Stones' or 'the hall where the law is spoken', in one corner of the temple area near to the bridge over the Tyropoeon. In the time of Christ, however, they seem to have moved their place of assembly to the council chamber in the palace of Caiaphas.

The court was arranged in a large semi-circle of tiered seats. In the centre, on his priestly throne, the richly robed Caiaphas presided. On his immediate right sat the eldest member, the Abd-Beth-Din, or Father of the House of Judgement, and on his left the Nasi or Prince of the Wise Men. At either end of each half circle sat the superintending scribes, one to count the votes for acquittal and the other for conviction, and in the centre, in front of the high priest, the recording scribe had his desk. Before the court stood Jesus, with guards on either side.

Absolute integrity was, of course, required of the judges, and to secure experienced judgement, only members over forty years of age were allowed to vote on a capital charge.

Absolute honesty was also required in the witnesses, and where perjury was proved the false witness was subject to the same punishment as would have been meted out to the accused.

In the case of a trial for life, a day of fasting and prayer was required for the consideration of the verdict, to assure the scrupulous administration of justice. This provision immediately placed the court assembled to try Jesus in a quandary. A capital trial could not legally be completed in less than two days and the Passover began in under twenty-four hours. But if they delayed the trial till after the morning sacrifice, which would be about four o'clock, as the rules of the Sanhedrin required, it might not be over till afternoon, and then the execution could not possibly be carried out before sunset. They, therefore, decided to waive both rules and get the trial over during the night, legalizing it by a quick session immediately after daybreak.

The next problem was that although they had been trying to collect evidence against Jesus for two years, they did not really have anything on which to condemn Him to death. The examination

the palace to testify on His behalf, Caiaphas was only too ready to proceed at once to the prosecution.

Doubtless the witnesses testified to His high-handed treatment of the temple traders, His alleged breaking of the Sabbath, His working on the emotions of the crowd at His triumphal entry into Jerusalem, and His Messianic references to Himself, but though they tried to outdo one another in

St. Peter in Gallicantu (meaning cockcrow) is situated east of Mount Zion just south of the Old City of Jerusalem. It commemorates Peter's denial of Jesus in the courtyard of the Palace of Caiaphas the high priest, the probable remains of which, along with the ruins of a Byzantine monastery, form the sub-structure of the present church. The mosaic (right) on the front of the church depicts the abuse Jesus received at the hands of the Sanhedrin.

before Annas had been intended to supplement the meagre accusations they had, but he had been able to extract nothing from Jesus. So, before the hearing, the unscrupulous Caiaphas gathered the witnesses and assured them that they would be well rewarded if they could secure Jesus' conviction.

Strictly, Jesus should have had opportunity first to present His case and bring witnesses for His defence. But as all His disciples had fled, and none appeared at

LES OUTRAGES CHEZ CAIPHE

presenting the most damaging case against Jesus, their exaggerated stories all broke down under cross-examination and the witnesses 'agreed not together'.

The council was exasperated and almost in despair at the lack of any clear accusation against Jesus, when 'two false witnesses' were brought who seemed to have the evidence they were looking for.

'We heard Him say,' one reported, 'I will destroy this temple that is made with hands, and within three days I will build another made without hands.' This, if true, was a serious crime, for doing harm to the temple was an insult to God Himself. Jeremiah, in fact, was judged 'worthy of death' when he foretold the destruction of the temple.

However, to sustain this charge another witness was needed, so the second was brought in. Unfortunately for them, he said: 'This fellow said, I am able to destroy the temple of God, and to build it in three days.' Here was a serious disagreement on a material point. Did Jesus say He would destroy the temple, or did He merely say He was able to do so if He wished? So even this evidence which came nearest to a charge on which a sentence of death could be passed, was invalidated by the inconsistency of the two accounts of what He said. The council was furious to be so near yet so far from its goal.

Realizing that if this contradictory testimony was pronounced void, the case against Jesus would fall to the ground, Caiaphas quite illegally tried to get Jesus to condemn Himself by admitting to one or other of these divergent stories.

'Answerest thou nothing?' he demanded of Jesus. 'What is it which these witness against thee?'

Jesus could have defended Himself by

Part of the ancient structures found beneath the Church of St. Peter in Gallicantu (see illustration on page 183) is this area thought to be the prison and scourging room where Jesus was kept while in the custody of the High Priest. Water cisterns and grain bins (right) unearthed outside the church walls.

declaring that neither story was true, for His statement on the occasion referred to had nothing to do with the temple at all. What He actually said was that they would 'destroy' the temple of His body, but that in three days He would 'raise it up' from the dead. But to Caiaphas's great annoyance Jesus 'held his peace, and answered nothing'.

In a last desperate effort to get Jesus to condemn Himself, the high priest stepped down from his throne and advanced towards Him. 'I adjure thee by the living God,' he said, 'that thou tell us whether thou be the Christ, the Son of God.'

Caiaphas couched his question very subtly. He did not simply ask Jesus if He claimed to be the Christ, for this would not have been enough to condemn Him to death. The popular expectation concerning the Messiah was that He would be a 'man of men' as Trypho expressed it. Recent documents about Bar-Cochiba, the last of the Jewish rebels in the second century, indicate that he was set forth by one rabbi as a human messiah. So Caiaphas asked Jesus also to say if He claimed to be the divine Son of God. If He would confirm this claim they would not need to press the lesser charge of His alleged words against the temple.

The council waited with bated breath for His answer, for although it was entirely out of order to expect the prisoner to condemn Himself, they were prepared to act on His confession if they had to.

Thus far in His trial Jesus had refused to give them any help by commenting on the evidence that had been given, but now He had the opportunity before the highest court of the land to make a final statement concerning Himself. He knew that it would be used to condemn Him, but it would also condemn them for their rejection of Him. And so He spoke.

'I am,' He categorically declared to both charges, and though in the existing circumstances this claim might seem fantastic, He added, 'Nevertheless I say unto you, Hereafter shall ye see the Son of man sitting on the right hand of power, and coming in the clouds of heaven.'

Brushing aside the fearful warning which Jesus uttered, Caiaphas seized on this self-confession as the decisive evidence they sought, and taking hold of his outer robe at the neck he tore it down to the girdle at his waist.

To rend one's garment was a symbolic act signifying deep emotion. Jacob rent his garment when he thought that Joseph was dead. Job rent his as successive calamities fell on him. King Hezekiah rent his clothes when Rabshakeh of Assyria pro-

A flight of Roman steps connecting the lower city of Jerusalem with 'Mount Zion'. Jesus would have used these steps to go to Gethsemane after leaving the upper room and quite probably was bundled roughly up them by His guards to the Palace of Caiaphas.

during the trial of Jesus, but whether all these can be sustained it is difficult to assess, as the only codified Jewish law we possess is the Mishna, and this was not compiled until about AD 200. How far, therefore, it corresponds with the Sadducean criminal code of Jesus' day we cannot now be absolutely sure. We do know, however, that the trial contravened a number of requirements of the Mosaic law, and of course the greatest illegality of all was that before the trial began the Sanhedrin had already determined that it should end with Jesus' condemnation to death. Jesus was not put on trial to test His guilt or innocence. The sentence had already been decided on, and the court only met to formulate a charge!

As soon as the sentence was passed, the court was in an uproar. Forgetting their supposed dignity, the priests and elders surged around Jesus to vent their spite on Him. They spat in His face, pushed Him about, and exposed Him to every indignity. Then, to make further sport, they blindfolded Him and, striking Him with the palms of their hands across His face, they demanded, 'Prophecy unto us, thou Christ, who is he that smote thee?'

When the Sanhedrin had tired of their shameful mockery and abuse of Jesus, they ordered the officers to take Him to the guard room of the palace to await the dawn for a final session of the council to make the sentence quite proper! Could hypocrisy have gone further? It was as Jesus was led away across the courtyard from the hall of judgement that He witnessed the end of another drama that had been going on there while He was on trial, in which one of His closest disciples, Peter, had been tragically involved.

nounced doom upon Jerusalem, and in the New Testament, Paul and Barnabas restraining the people of Lystra from worshipping them by rending their clothes. Now, in mock zeal for God's honour, Caiaphas rent his robe crying, 'He hath spoken blasphemy; what further need have we of witnesses? behold, now ye have heard his blasphemy. What think ye?'

In this pronouncement, Caiaphas again was out of order for, though supposedly the judge, he was now directing the court to find Jesus guilty. But the Sanhedrin were not worried about the niceties of legal procedure. They had, at last, the evidence on which He could be condemned, and with one accord they cried, 'He is guilty of death'.

It has been claimed that no fewer than twenty-seven illegalities were perpetrated

This chapter is based on Matthew 26:57-68; Mark 14:53-65; Luke 22:54, 63-65; John 18:24.

Peter's denial

When the disciples had recovered from the shock of Jesus' arrest, they followed the crowd at a safe distance and saw Him taken into the palace of the high priest.

Now it happened that John was known to the servants of Caiaphas, most likely by reason of his supplying cured fish from Galilee to the Jerusalem market. John may have regularly visited Jerusalem in connection with the family business, and so had become known to the porters at the high priest's house.

In view of this, Peter suggested that John should go to the palace and try to get him in as well. Then they could see what happened to their beloved Master. It was a daring idea, but as on so many earlier occasions, Peter did not ask himself whether his courage would be sustained if he got into difficulties. When they got inside, John sought a quiet corner where he would not invite attention, but Peter boldly went over to the charcoal brazier which was burning in the lower courtyard.

The April night was quite cool and the servants and soldiers who were not on duty were sitting around talking about the prisoner who had just been brought in. Thinking he would not be recognized, Peter listened and watched as he warmed himself at the fire, but in a short time the girl who had admitted him joined the group. When she took a closer look at Peter in the glow of the fire she suddenly said to him, 'Art not thou also one of his disciples?'

Taken aback by the question, Peter averted his face and replied abruptly, 'I am not'. Then, fearful that he might be questioned further, he moved away into the covered porch which led to the outer gate. As he entered the shadow of the arch a cock crew in a nearby courtyard.

In his stress of mind Peter did not connect the first crowing of the cock with the warning Jesus had given him some hours before, but as he was standing there another maid approached and renewed her friend's accusation. 'This fellow was also with Jesus of Nazareth,' she declared.

Really alarmed now that he would be found out, Peter denied the charge with an angry oath, crying, 'I do not know this man . . . neither understand I what thou sayest.' And he moved again across the courtyard.

Peter managed to avoid further questioning for about an hour, and then just as he thought the suspicions against him were allayed, one of the servants of the high priest, a kingsman of Malchus whose ear Peter had cut off, came by. Seeing him he stopped and said, 'Did not I see thee in the garden with him?'

Quickly an excited crowd gathered round and another joined in, 'Surely thou art one of them: for thou art a Galilean, and thy speech agreeth thereto.' Just as north country folk here speak with a broader accent than those in the south, the Galilean speech was noticeably different from the more cultured and polished speech of the capital, and in his agitation Peter unconsciously gave himself away.

At this Peter 'began to curse and to swear, saying, I know not this man of whom ye speak,' and immediately the cock crew again.

Even then Peter might not have remembered the words of Jesus, but at that moment the door of the council chamber opened and Jesus was led across the courtyard. As He passed Peter He heard his oaths and turning He 'looked upon' him, or literally He 'looked into' him.

It was a terrible moment for Jesus. The sentence of death had just passed upon

Him and now, as He was led away, He heard one of His closest disciples disown and deny Him utterly.

Yet Jesus did not look on Peter in anger, but only in disappointment and sorrow. As their eyes met, Peter remembered what Jesus had said to him, and he was overwhelmed by what he had done. The dreadful realization came to him that he was no better than the traitor Judas. For all his boasting that he would never desert Jesus, he had basely forsaken Him in the hour of His greatest need.

Profiting by the momentary diversion of attention to Jesus, Peter slipped through the crowd and, opening the wicket gate in the great door, he went out into the street. The Bible does not tell us which direction Peter took. A grotto at the south end of Mount Zion, over which a church was later built, is called the Grotto of the Cockcrowing, but it seems more likely that he would go back to Gethsemane to the spot where Jesus had knelt only a few hours before. There he fell to the ground and, burying his head in his cloak, he 'wept bitterly' at his failure. Now he remembered the words of Jesus when He had found them sleeping, 'Pray that ye enter not into temptation.' If only he had resisted sleep and watched with Jesus, this might not have happened.

The full and honest account in the gospels of the failure of one of the disciples closest to Jesus is surely a most striking testimony to the truth of the Bible story. If the disciples had been trying to foist a false story about Jesus upon the people of their day, they certainly would not have allowed the slightest stain on the character of any of the apostles to be recorded. Yet here faithfully set down is a full confession of Peter's treacherous denial of his Master in the crisis hour of His life.

Not only does the story of Peter's denial corroborate the truth of the Gospel story, but it also provides a solemn warning against false confidence in our capacity to resist temptation. Under Satan's attacks, Christ repulsed the adversary three times but in Peter's three temptations he was defeated every time because he felt himself quite able to cope with any situation which might arise. We need constantly to lean upon God, and never more than when we think ourselves strong.

Contrasting Peter in the garden and Peter in the palace yard, we realize also that physical courage may be easier to

achieve than moral courage. Peter was brave as a lion in the conflict in the garden, but a coward in the face of ridicule.

Finally, Peter's tragic fall shows how one sin leads to another more serious sin. Sin accelerates. The moral, therefore, is not to begin.

But Peter's experience has in it also great encouragment, for it shows that if, in true repentance, we confess our sins and seek God's forgiveness, He will lift us up and receive us back into friendship and fellowship.

How ready Jesus was to forgive His erring disciple is evident from the fact that when He revealed Himself to the women at the tomb after His resurrection, He told them to tell the other disciples 'and Peter'. Moreover, Peter was the first of the disciples to see Him alive from the dead, and when they went forth to preach the message of the risen Christ, it was he who led out in the first great evangelistic sermon at Pentecost.

That Peter never forgot the lesson he had learned is evident from the emphasis he places in his epistles on vigilance and steadfastness that we may not fall.

This chapter is based on Matthew 26:69-75; Mark 14:66-72; Luke 22:54-62; John 18:25-27.

189

The remorse of Judas

On the morning of Friday, the fourteenth of Nisan, and the preparation day for the Passover, as soon as it was light – which would be about half past five or six o'clock – the Sanhedrin court met again to ratify the sentence passed on Jesus during the night.

From the cell where He had been confined He was brought into the court room, where now the 'whole council' were assembled. This suggests that some who could not be reached during the night had now been contacted, though it is doubtful if Nicodemus and others who favoured Jesus were summoned even to this final session.

As all the charges respecting His doctrine and His alleged words against the temple had broken down through the confusion of evidence, the accusation had now been narrowed to two points, His claim to be the Messiah and His further claim to be the Son of God. To give all who had not been present at the earlier trial evidence of these charges, the high priest put to Jesus his two leading questions again.

'Art thou the Christ? tell us,' he first asked. This was the more important charge to establish to ensure the confirmation of the sentence by Pilate, because it had a political connotation. If they could prove that Jesus was seeking to make Himself the Messianic leader of the Jews, they could be certain that Pilate would condemn Him as a revolutionary. They knew, of course, perfectly well that Jesus had never claimed temporal power and that He had, in fact, refused the kingship offered Him by the people; but if they could get Him to admit Messiahship, they could put the most serious construction on it in their plea to Pilate.

Jesus saw through the cunning of Caiaphas and declined to make his task easy. 'If I tell you,' He said, 'ye will not believe. And if I also ask you [questions which would establish my innocence], ye will not answer me, nor let me go.'

If He had admitted the charge, He knew the court would ratify the sentence of death on Him; and if He declared that He was not, they would sentence Him as a confessed imposter. There was, therefore, no purpose whatsoever in keeping up the pretence of a trial. But, He warned them, whether they accepted His claim or not now, 'Hereafter shall the Son of man sit on the right hand of the power of God.' And then it would be too late for them to make their peace with Him.

Taking no notice of Jesus' demand that the hypocritical proceedings be brought to an end, the high priest pressed his second question, 'Art thou then the Son of God?'

This was the decisive charge in Jewish eyes. The claim to be the 'Son of man' was not enough to constitute blasphemy. But if He would claim divinity by saying that He was the 'Son of God', then the case would be proved to the hilt.

When Jesus replied quietly, 'Ye say [correctly] that I am,' they were exultant. Throwing up their hands in mock horror they cried with one voice, 'What need we any further witness? for we ourselves have heard of his own mouth.' And for the third time the sentence that He was worthy of death was pronounced on Him, followed by more mocking and inhuman abuse.

Now that the sentence had been passed at a legal session of the Sanhedrin, the priests and rulers were ready to proceed with their prisoner to the Roman governor, Pontius Pilate, for the confirmation and execution of the sentence. This Jesus Himself had foreseen when He said that He

would be 'delivered unto the Gentiles' and 'crucified'.

There was no need now for the secrecy in which the trial had, up to this time, taken place. In fact, the co-operation of the mob was now desirable to convince the governor of the heinousness of Jesus' crime. So the priests and rulers proceeded to the temple to call the people to accompany them to the Praetorium.

It was probably at this time that Judas, who had followed the proceedings of the successive trials with increasing alarm, could contain himself no longer. What he had expected Jesus to do we shall never know, but certainly he never thought that He would allow Himself to be put to death.

Hurrying to the temple with the bag of money he had received for betraying his Master, he pushed his way among the chief priests and elders, who were congratulating themselves on the success of their plans, and grasped the high priest's robe in an effort to gain his attention. 'I have sinned in that I have betrayed the

Hinnom, a valley which runs just south of Jerusalem. In Old Testament times the valley, called Gehenna, was a place of depravity and sin where Israel sacrificed its children to the pagan fire-god Molech. Haceldama (below) in the Valley of Hinnom is the 'field of blood', so called because it was bought with the silver that betrayed Jesus. The various 'caves' are tombs where through the ages pilgrims and strangers have been buried.

innocent blood,' he cried.

Shaking Judas off, the high priest turned in anger and contempt from him, saying shortly, 'What is that to us? See thou to that.' If Judas had a conscience about what he had done, that was his affair. They certainly had none.

Filled with horror and remorse at the enormity of his crime, Judas 'cast down the pieces of silver in the temple, and departed'.

He could not, however, rid himself of his sense of guilt by parting from his ill-gotten gains. Appalled and desperate, he decided he could end his agony only by taking his life. Rushing from the temple he ran through the streets and out of the city, and in some lonely spot beyond the walls he 'hanged himself'.

What a terrible end it was to which Judas came. When he first joined Jesus he had felt no real call to a higher life. He thought he was doing Jesus a favour by throwing in his lot with Him, and he continued with Him for what he hoped to get when Jesus assumed kingly power. Soon he was criticizing the way Jesus was carrying out His ministry. He was angry that He allowed John to be beheaded, that He refused to accept kingship from the grateful crowds after the feeding of the five thousand, and he was impatient at Jesus' repeated assertions that He would have to suffer and to die.

When he could not gain support from the disciples, Judas determined to force the issue and compel Jesus to declare Himself. Right up to the trial, Judas was sure that He would escape from His enemies; and when He did not, he realized too late that his carefully-laid plot had recoiled on his own head, to encompass not merely his physical death, but his eternal ruin.

When Judas left the temple, the priests picked up the coins he had hurled to the ground and debated what they should do with them. As the money was the reward of treachery they could not bring themselves to put it back into the treasury. 'It is not lawful,' they said, 'for to put them into the treasury, because it is the price of blood.' Jesus had more than once accused the Pharisees of being over-scrupulous in the petty details of their traditions while neglecting weightier moral principles, and this was indeed the climax of their hypocrisy. They had descended to abysmal depths to destroy Jesus, and yet when the price of treachery was returned to them by the tool of their villainy, they were too scrupulous to put it back into the temple coffers.

After consultation, the chief priests decided to buy with it a plot of land called 'the potter's field' as a place for the burial of strangers who died without friends while visiting Jerusalem. The name of the field suggests that it was a worked-out clay pit in the Hinnom Valley, on the south side of the city, near the Potter's Gate.

By their act they fulfilled yet another prophecy of the passion, for Zechariah by inspiration had not only specified the exact price of betrayal, but also added, 'And the Lord said unto me, Cast it unto the potter: . . . and I took the thirty pieces of silver, and cast them to the potter in the house of the Lord.'

The priests would have kept the whole unsavoury affair a secret if they could, but it was not long before it became known to the inhabitants of Jerusalem, and ever after, this field was called Aceldama, or 'the field of blood'.

This chapter is based on Luke 22:66-71; Matthew 27:1, 3-10; Mark 15:1.

192

To Pilate and Herod

As soon as the Sanhedrin had pronounced Jesus 'guilty of death' He was again fettered and led away to Pontius Pilate, the Roman governor, for confirmation of the sentence and immediate execution. This was necessary because, since Judea

The existence of Pilate the Roman governor of Judea AD 26-36, is demonstrated by an inscription in Latin bearing his name discovered in the theatre at Caesarea in 1961.

became a Roman province, the power of life and death had been withdrawn from the Jewish courts. So Jesus' own prophecy that, after suffering 'many things' of the Jewish rulers, He would be 'delivered unto the Gentiles' to die, was fulfilled.

Normally the Roman governors of Palestine lived in the Palace of Herod at Caesarea, but at festival times they took up residence in the capital to ensure the maintenance of order. At first the Roman governors used as their Praetorium the former Palace of Herod on the west side of the city near the Jaffa Gate, where Herodian masonry is still to be seen among the ruins of the Turkish barracks. Later, however, the Praetorium was transferred to the fortress of Antonia dominating the north-west corner of the temple area. This fits in with the statement that the rulers and people came 'up' to it from the city.

According to Josephus there had been a citadel here as far back as the days of Solomon to protect the temple on the north side. At that time it was called Bireh, or the 'tower of the house'. It was restored by the Jews after the return from captivity as the 'tower of Hananeel' and was strengthened further by the Hasmoneans. Simon Maccabeus and John Hyrcanus both used it as a residence and added to its fortifications. The castle was finally rebuilt 'like a royal palace' and doubled in size by Herod the Great, who made it into two courts with an enclosing wall and corner towers nearly 200 feet high. To it he gave the name Antonia after Mark Anthony.

The inner court was used by Pilate as a residence and a 'hall of judgement'. A Moslem school now stands on this portion of the site. It was richly paved with agate and lazuli, the ceiling was of gilded cedar wood, and it was lavishly furnished. Philo mentions the gilded tables in Pilate's

193

apartment.

An outer colonnaded court, used by the garrison, lay to the north and has been found extending across the street called Via Dolorosa and under the convent buildings on the other side. It was flagged with great stone slabs a yard square and half as thick, which were found scored by the tracks of horses and chariots. Sockets are discernible, which may have held posts for tethering horses or the flags of the legion. Cut into the surface also are the geometrical figures of a dice game called margella, with which the soldiers amused themselves when off duty. This must be the Gabbatha or 'Pavement' of the palace.

Beyond the colonnade to the east were the buildings which housed the garrison. Usually this consisted of six hundred men, but when the governor took up residence it was reinforced by a cavalry detachment.

The entrance of the Praetorium was a monumental gateway of three arches with a total width of seventy feet. The central gate still arches over the Via Dolorosa near the Turkish barracks, while one of the smaller arches can be seen in the building on the north side of the road. From the gateway a road sixty feet wide descended to the town.

An esplanade on the south side of the palace fort looked down into the temple courts and two flights of stairs gave the soldiers quick access in case of rioting. Extensive foundations and a honeycomb of passages have been discovered beneath the present Moslem buildings which occupy the area, as well as an underground pool which supplied water to the fortress.

The governor or procurator of Judea at this time, Pontius Pilate, was the fifth holder of the office since the deposition of

The Antonia Fortress, rebuilt by Herod the Great, reconstructed as part of a model showing Jerusalem in AD 66. Christians re-enact the carrying of the cross (below) from the site of the Fortress along the Via Dolorosa.

Archelaus. He owed his appointment in AD 26 to Sejanus, the chief prefect of Tiberius, and he was removed from office in AD 36, not long after the fall and murder of his benefactor. The name Pontius suggests that he may have been connected with the Pontii, an old Roman family, while Pilate may indicate that he was a cavalry officer.

Josephus and Philo both agree that Pilate was proud, brutal, unjust, and corrupt, and Agrippa I, writing to the Emperor Caligula about him after his deposition from office, said that 'he was of an unbending and ruthlessly hard character', and that in his day 'corruption, violence, robbery, oppression, humiliations, constant executions without trial, and unlimited, intolerable cruelty' were rife. While we might expect a Jewish historian and a Jewish king to be prejudiced, these estimates are fully borne out by what we know outside the Bible of his actions.

His first act, in defiance of Jewish religious susceptibilities, was to order the Roman insignia bearing pagan symbols and the emperor's effigy to be carried into Jerusalem and planted in the citadel near to the temple. For five days he obstinately held out against a deputation who came to Caesarea to complain, and only when they declared themselves willing to be slaughtered rather than depart unsatisfied did he have the offending insignia removed.

Not long after, however, he repeated the offence by having gilded votive shields to the emperor set up in the former palace of Herod. This time the Jews appealed directly to Caesar, who compelled Pilate to desist from such provocative actions.

In spite of this rebuke, Pilate later robbed the temple treasury for the construction of a water conduit from the Pools of Solomon, near Hebron, to Jerusalem, and ordered a massacre of the crowds who gathered to demonstrate against the desecration.

The gospels record the slaughter of a party of Galileans in the temple forecourt for alleged revolutionary activity, and it was a similar act of violence against the Samaritans that finally caused Vitellus, prefect of Syria, to send him back to Rome.

These incidents reveal Pilate's contempt of the Jewish rulers, but they also show why he was afraid to go too far in provoking them, lest they should denounce him again to Caesar.

The record states that 'it was early', probably around 6.30 am, when the priests with their Prisoner reached the Praetorium. There was nothing unusual in this, as Roman governors generally held court before the day became hot, so that midday could be devoted to rest and the

afternoon to social life and amusement. In Rome business began about 6 am, and the law courts opened at eight. Even so it was rather too 'early' for Pilate and it was with no good grace that he dressed and prepared to see them.

Because they did not wish to incur defilement by going into a Gentile house just before Passover, the priests asked if he would come to the entrance of the Praetorium to give judgement. Pilate was still further annoyed at the request, but not wanting to give unnecessary offence, he had a portable tribunal set up at the gate, where it now crosses the Via Dolorosa, and ordered Jesus to be brought before him. 'What accusation bring ye against this man?' Pilate demanded when he was seated.

Instead of making a formal charge against Jesus, the rulers replied, 'If he were not a malefactor, we would not have

Beneath the Convent of the Sisters of Zion, which is situated within the area of the Antonia Fortress, is an original Roman pavement or Lithostratos. Off-duty legionaries have left for posterity their version of knuckle-bones and the Game of the King (above) engraved in the flagstones. Great slabs of limestone (below) with chiselled grooves to prevent horses slipping on surfaces made smooth by innumerable feet.

delivered him up unto thee.' It was an insult to Pilate to imagine that he would be prepared to endorse their decision without even knowing what it was, and Pilate showed his anger by curtly ordering them to depart. 'Take ye him and judge him according to your law,' he said.

Realizing that they would have to treat Pilate with greater respect if they wanted him to condemn Jesus, they replied obsequiously: 'It is not lawful for us to put any man to death.'

Now that they had to state their accusation against Jesus they realized that it was no use charging Him with blasphemy, as Pilate would have dismissed this as a purely religious matter in which he had no competence. But they had prepared for this contingency at the earlier trials by getting Jesus' confession that He was the Messiah, which had a political connotation, and they also had the evidence about the tribute money. So they now charged Jesus with treason against Rome on three counts. He was, they said, a revolutionary agitator who had been seditiously 'perverting the nation', He had sought to restrain the people from giving 'tribute' or taxes 'to Caesar', and He had proclaimed Him-

197

The courtyard of the El-Omariye school standing in the area of the Antonia Fortress where, in the 'hall of judgement', Jesus was tried by Pilate.

self 'Christ a King'.

These charges, if true, were very serious ones, of which Pilate would have to take notice. But, of course, they were absolutely false. Jesus had always discouraged violent action against the Romans, He had counselled the people to 'render . . . unto Caesar' the things that were Caesar's, and He had refused to allow the people to make Him King.

As Pilate looked at Jesus, even he could not believe that this calm, dignified Man was a hot-headed revolutionary. So he determined to examine Him himself. Bidding the soldiers bring Jesus inside, he went back into the judgement hall, while

the priests waited at the gate. Mounting the raised semi-circular dais or 'tribunal', which may have been the golden throne of Archelaus, Pilate ordered Jesus to stand before him.

'Art thou the King of the Jews?' he asked as he began his examination. Jesus meant no disrespect when He replied, 'Sayest thou this thing of thyself, or did others tell it thee of me?' What He wanted to know was whether Pilate understood what sort of king the Messiah of the Jews was according to the Scriptures.

Pilate at once pointed out that not being a Jew he could not be expected to understand such matters. He had to rely on what he was told. 'Thine own nation and the chief priests have delivered thee unto me: what hast thou done?' he demanded.

Then Jesus replied plainly, 'My kingdom is not of this world: if my kingdom were of this world, then would my servants fight, that I should not be delivered to the Jews: but now is my kingdom not from hence.'

Pilate found it difficult to imagine a kingdom which was 'not of this world' and not supported by force of arms, and in a puzzled tone he repeated his question, 'Art thou a king then?'

Jesus replied, 'Thou sayest [correctly] that I am a king,' and added, 'to this end was I born, and for this cause came I into the world, that I should bear witness unto the truth. Every one that is of the truth heareth my voice.'

The kingdom which Jesus was founding in the earth was not a temporal kingdom. It claimed no territory in this world order, though its sway was wide as the world. Its throne was the throne of grace, and its subjects were those who received His truth by faith into their hearts. Its laws were not fleshly ordinances, but the eternal law of God. It was extended not by force of arms but by the Gospel of love, yet when all earthly nations had passed, it would endure for ever.

Jesus' answer satisfied Pilate that he was neither a political revolutionary nor a rival of Caesar. He was evidently an idealist who thought He knew ultimate 'truth', but He was not a disturber of the peace. So, with a rather contemptuous reference to the 'truth' being a very debatable subject anyhow, Pilate took Jesus back to the gate of the Praetorium and told the Jews, 'I find no fault in this man.'

At once there was a fierce outcry from the disappointed priests, who began to assert with greater vehemence, 'He stirreth up the people, teaching throughout all Jewry, beginning from Galilee to this place.'

It was at this point that Pilate manifested the first evidence of the indecision which was to result in his defeat at the hands of the astute Jews. If he had been just he would have said, 'I have given my verdict', and dismissed the case. But he knew the rulers hated him, and for the sake of expediency he wanted to extricate himself without antagonizing them. So he turned to Jesus and said, 'Hearest thou not how many things they witness against thee?' But to Pilate's amazement Jesus 'answered nothing'.

The governor now found himself in a serious quandary. He was sure that Jesus was the victim of a plot and he wanted to release Him, but he dared not stir up any more animosity against himself. Suddenly he recalled that the Jews had said that Jesus had preached in Galilee. Here was a way of getting rid of the case by passing Him on to Herod Antipas, who still ruled Galilee and Perea as a vassal of Rome. He probably hoped that Herod would view

the case as he had done and acquit Jesus. Thus justice would be done without his personally incurring the anger of the Jews. At the same time it provided an opportunity for a diplomatic courtesy which might patch up his relations with Herod which had been strained since the slaughter of the Galileans in the temple.

Fortunately, Herod had come up to the feast of Passover, not so much from conviction, for he was half Samaritan and half Idumean, but for the sake of appearances and to participate in the social life of the capital at Passover time. So Jesus was bound again and sent under guard to the Hasmonean palace on the Xystus Square just across the Tyropoeon Bridge from the east gate of the temple.

The dissolute king Herod Antipas, youngest son of Herod the Great, the murderer of John the Baptist and the incestuous husband of Herodias, had long wanted to see Jesus. When he had first heard of Him he was afraid, thinking He might be John the Baptist come back to life. When this fear was dispelled he was curious to see Him, hoping that Jesus would work a miracle for his amusement. But though Herod asked Jesus many questions He 'answered him nothing'.

Herod was angry and humiliated that Jesus should treat him with such contempt, but he was as unconvinced as Pilate that He was guilty of the accusations the chief priests repeated to him. To Herod, Jesus was just another deluded religious fanatic, and mockingly he ordered Him to be decked in one of his discarded robes of royal purple and sent back, still uncondemned, to Pilate, with a cordial greeting, restoring friendly relations between the two rulers.

This chapter is based on John 18:28-38; Luke 23:1-12; Matthew 27:2, 11-14; Mark 15:2-5.

Pilate pronounces sentence

When Herod sent Jesus back to the Praetorium, Pilate was annoyed and disappointed. He had hoped to dispose of Jesus without incurring the displeasure of the Jewish rulers, but now he had Him on his hands again, and he would have to make some decision. So once more Pilate went out to the Jews who had congregated at the entrance gate and said to them, 'Ye have brought this man unto me, as one that perverteth the people: and, behold, I, having examined him before you, have found no fault in this man touching those things whereof ye accuse him: no, nor yet Herod: for I sent you to him; and, lo, nothing worthy of death is done unto him.'

Even if they could not understand the crime of Jesus, Pilate argued, they could not deny the weight of Herod's opinion, and if he found nothing worthy of death in Him, Jesus could not in justice be condemned. If it would meet their wishes, however, Pilate suggested, he would 'chastise' Jesus and then 'release him'.

This was the second evidence of Pilate's fatal weakness. If he agreed with Herod's judgement, he should have set Jesus free at once. To try to appease the Jews by scourging an innocent man was despicable and cowardly. But they would not even consider this. Nothing less than a sentence of death would satisfy them.

Pilate was caught on the horns of a fearful dilemma. Justice demanded that he should release Jesus, but he knew that if he did this the Jewish leaders would stir up a riot, the consequences of which, with Jerusalem packed with Passover pilgrims, he dared not contemplate. As he sat before the people, undecided what to do, an attendant brought a letter from his wife. It may be that Jesus had been talked about in the palace, and when Pilate was called early to deal with His case, his wife fell asleep again and dreamed of Him. In her dream she was given a divine premonition of what would befall her husband if he condemned Jesus, and she hastened to send a warning message to him. 'Have thou nothing to do with that just man,' she wrote: 'for I have suffered many things this day in a dream because of him.'

Pilate quailed at the contents of the letter, believing that it was a message from the gods, and at that moment a last loophole of escape occurred to him. It was customary among the Romans to declare an amnesty on the occasion of feasts in honour of the gods, and to release a certain number of convicted criminals, and a similar practice seems to have been instituted in Palestine in the days of the Maccabees to keep the peace among the warring factions of their day. It occurred to Pilate that this custom might help him in his perplexity.

In prison at the time there was a notorious bandit called Barabbas who, under the guise of patriotism, had ravaged Roman outposts and the roads leading to Jerusalem. Recently, when he carried his activities into the city itself, he had been captured and cast into prison together with many of his followers. His name Bar Abba suggests that he was the wayward son of a rabbi, and some manuscripts give his full name as Jesus Barabbas.

Pilate knew that the chief priests and rulers held no brief for Barabbas, who was a public terror, and he could not believe that the crowd would ask for his release rather than that of Jesus, so he said to them: 'Ye have a custom, that I should release unto you one at the Passover: . . . Whom will ye that I release unto you? [Jesus] Barabbas, or Jesus which is called the Christ?'

If they had not been prompted, the

crowd, from a sense of justice, would have asked for the release of Jesus, for many among the multitude had listened to Him in the temple and witnessed His miracles. But when the priests began to cry out that He had been condemned by the Sanhedrin, they felt that He must be evil, and joined in the cry, 'Away with this man, and release unto us Barabbas.'

'What will ye then that I shall do unto him whom ye call the King of the Jews?' Pilate demanded in exasperation. And the murderous cry went up, 'Crucify him.'

Pilate saw that his plan had failed and that he would have to release Barabbas as he had offered, but he still hoped that the crowd would relent, and be content with some lesser punishment for Jesus. So he asked them again, 'Why, what evil hath he done? I have found no cause of death in him: I will therefore chastise him, and let him go.' But instantly the people cried out loudly and more insistently, 'Let him be crucified.'

Seeing that argument was useless, Pilate ordered the guards to take Jesus back into the 'common hall', or outer court of the Praetorium, and to scourge Him preparatory to His execution. There Jesus was stripped and thrown to the ground or tied to a pillar in the sight of the multitude crowding the gate. Then the soldiers proceeded cruelly to scourge Jesus with the terrible Roman flagellum consisting of leather thongs to which were affixed metal spikes, jagged pieces of bone, and lumps of lead capable of flaying the bare skin of a victim to shreds.

When Jesus had been scourged almost to the point of exhaustion, the soldiers threw over His shoulders a discarded purple or scarlet cloak of one of the legionaries and 'plaited a crown of thorns' from the flexible branches of a sharp thorny plant, which has now come to be know as *rhamnus spina Christi*, and pressed it onto His head until it drew streams of blood. Into Jesus' hands they thrust an elm flogging rod in imitation of a sceptre, and in mock homage they knelt before Him crying, 'Hail, King of the Jews.'

Throughout this terrible ordeal Jesus uttered no word of condemnation against His torturers. As prophecy had declared, 'As a sheep before her shearers is dumb, so He openeth not his mouth.'

After the mocking and scourging, Jesus presented a pitiable appearance. Blood streamed down His face where the sharp thorns had pierced His brow and His body was gashed and lacerated by the barbs of the scourges. Thinking to arouse the pity of the crowds who were waiting to follow the soldiers to the place of execution, Pilate ordered Jesus to be set beside Barabbas in the entrance gate. Standing to one side he pointed to Jesus and said, 'Behold the man!' This declaration, in latin 'Ecce Homo', is perpetuated in the name given to the ancient arch over the Via Dolorosa. Pilate thought that the sight of Jesus would have softened the hardest hearts in the crowd, but at once the priests started to cry again, 'Crucify him, crucify him,' and the crowd echoed the fearful demand.

With a contemptuous wave of the hand Pilate cried, 'Take ye him, and crucify him: for I find no fault in him.'

Jubilant that they had at last gained their object, the chief priests replied, 'We have a law, and by our law he ought to die, because he made himself the Son of God.' Pilate was startled by the words. This was the first time he had heard this charge, and when the words 'Son of God' fell on his ears he recalled his wife's

dream. This must be what had troubled her, and the terrible fear came over him that the Man standing before him might be a god in human form.

Stopping the soldiers as they were about to lead Jesus away, Pilate took Jesus again into the judgement hall and asked Him anxiously, 'Whence art thou?' If Jesus had wished, He could have given Pilate such evidence of His divine nature that the governor would have been compelled to release Him. But He said nothing. Jesus

At the gate of the Praetorium, Pilate, the weak and vacillating but cruel governor, made a last attempt to arouse the pity of the mob in the courtyard below.

had never used His supernatural power for His own benefit before, and He would not now use it to save Himself from death.

At his wits' end to know how to extricate himself from his terrible predicament, Pilate demanded, 'Speakest thou not unto me? Knowest thou not that I have power to crucify thee, and have power to release thee?'

Calmly Jesus replied: 'Thou couldst have no power at all against me, except it were given thee from above: therefore he that delivered me unto thee hath the greater sin.'

Conscience-stricken that Jesus should pronounce his guilt less than that of the Jews, Pilate was the more anxious to save Him, but now the patience of the chief priests and rulers was exhausted. As he began once more to plead for Jesus they cried, 'If thou let this man go, thou art not Caesar's friend: whosoever maketh himself a king speaketh against Caesar.'

Pilate knew what they meant. If he did not put Jesus to death they would denounce him to Caesar for allowing sedition against the Emperor to go unpunished. And he knew that he could never survive this charge. If it was a choice between his life and that of Jesus, Jesus must die. He must save his own life and position at all costs. So he ordered Jesus to be brought again to the gate. The protracted trial had been going on for three hours. Pilate was weary and the crowd was on the point of rioting. Seating himself on the tribunal, Pilate waved his hand towards Jesus and said ironically, 'Behold your King!'

The Jews took the remark as an acknowledgement that Jesus was guilty of sedition and vociferously cried out, 'Away with him, away with him, crucify him.'

'Shall I crucify your King?' Pilate demanded in a final sarcasm. The chief priests answered, 'We have no king but Caesar.'

In a last gesture of self-justification, Pilate ordered an attendant to bring a basin of water and set it before the judgement seat. Putting his hands into it he 'washed [them] before the multitude, saying, I am innocent of the blood of this just Person: see ye to it.' But though he went through the motions, no external washing could cleanse his guilty heart. If he had taken 'much soap' and even 'nitre', as Jeremiah once taunted Israel, he could not have cleansed away the stain of his sin. He had sacrificed justice to expediency, principle for self-interest, and in doing so had perpetrated 'the greatest injustice in history'.

But while Pilate sought vainly to rid himself of responsibility for the fate of Jesus, the chief priests and rulers arrogantly accepted full responsibility for their actions. 'His blood,' they said, 'be on us, and on our children.' Little did they realize the curse they were pronouncing upon themselves and upon their race. At that Pilate 'willing to content the people' rose and gave the order for the release of Barabbas and shamefully 'delivered Jesus to their will'.

The Procurator returned to his chambers worn out by the struggle, but relieved that he had saved himself from denunciation by the Jews. His cruelly won security was, however, short lived. Four years later he ran into serious trouble when he sought to arrest a Samaritan patriot who had gathered his followers on Mount Gerizim and proclaimed himself Messiah. In dispersing the crowds many were brutally killed and great numbers of prisoners were later executed. The Samaritans protested to the Syrian legate, Vitellus, who deposed Pilate and sent him for trial to Rome. The Emperor Tiberius died before Pilate arrived, but he was banished to Vienne in Gaul by Caligula, and not long after is said to have died by his own hand.

This chapter is based on Matthew 27:15-31; John 18:39-19:16; Mark 15:6-19; Luke 23:13-25.

The way of sorrow

Immediately Pilate gave the order for the execution, Jesus was divested of the purple robe mockingly put on Him, and His own garments were given back to Him. Whether the crown of thorns was left on His head we cannot be sure, though in sacred art He is usually portrayed as wearing it to the end.

The officer of the guard then selected the execution party of four soldiers, probably Syrian mercenaries, under a Roman centurion, the bar of the cross was brought from the barracks stores, and Jesus was led away 'bearing his cross'.

Jesus had hinted to Nicodemus that the suffering Messiah would be 'lifted up' for the salvation of men. Now this prophecy was to be fulfilled in the ghastly Roman punishment of crucifixion. Crucifixion was the most terrible death of ancient times. It is said to have been invented by the Persians on the grounds that the earth consecrated to Ormuzd was not to be defiled by executions. From them it was adopted by Alexander the Great and passed on to the Carthaginians, and finally to the Romans during the Punic wars. Cicero called it 'the most cruel and frightful punishment' and Josephus said it was 'the most wretched of all ways of dying'.

The Romans used the terror of crucifixion to keep order in the subject provinces, as many as two thousand Jews at a time being crucified by Quintilius Varus, while Titus crucified five hundred a day during the last terrible siege of Jerusalem.

No Roman was degraded by crucifixion, its use as a punishment for civil offences being reserved for slaves; hence Tacitus' designation of it as the 'slavish death penalty'. This explains Paul's reference to the voluntary humiliation of Jesus, suffering 'even the death of the cross'. Significant it is, therefore, that this sign of ultimate humiliation should become the symbol of infinite love.

It was now the third hour of the Roman day, or nine o'clock in the morning. The two trials before Pilate, together with the brief visit to Herod, had taken nearly three hours.

With Jesus, as He set out along 'the way of sorrow' to the place of execution, were two malefactors bearing their crosses. They may have been companions of Barabbas, and the cross which Jesus bore might, but for the fickleness of the crowd, have been on the shoulders of Barabbas himself. As the Scriptures had foretold, Jesus was 'numbered with the transgres-

The Chapel of the Flagellation stands within the confines of the Antonia Fortress where Jesus was given a flogging. The chapel is beautifully decorated in the Crusader style and incorporates a memorial to the apostle Paul's imprisonment in the fortress.

sors' in His final suffering and death.

The law of Moses forbade punishment by death within the camp and prescribed a place of execution in some prominent place outside the camp 'so that all the people shall fear'. Naboth in the Old Testament was stoned at Ahab's order outside Samaria, and Stephen in the New Testament was hurried out of the city and stoned in the Kidron Valley. Jesus had similarly indicated in His parable of the wicked husbandmen, that the son of the owner would be taken outside the vineyard and put to death.

From the Arch of 'Ecce Homo', the monumental entrance to the fortress of Antonia, the procession proceeded along the road now called the Via Dolorosa, or 'Way of Sorrow', then much wider than now, and descended in a westerly direction towards the road coming up the Tyropoeon Valley along the west wall of the temple area.

When this road was reached we are not sure which way they turned, as the site of Calvary is not certainly known. The Church of the Holy Sepulchre, which encloses the site of Calvary and the tomb of Christ, as located by Queen Helena, mother of Constantine the Great, in the third century, is today *within* the wall of the Old City, and those who believe this to be the authentic site assert that in Christ's day the west wall of Jerusalem formed an angle at this point, turning east at Herod's Palace, near the present Jaffa Gate, and then north towards the Damascus Gate. This would leave the whole north-west corner of the present walled city outside the walls of Jesus' day, until enclosed by the third wall of Herod Agrippa, and would satisfy the scriptural requirement that Calvary was 'without the gate'.

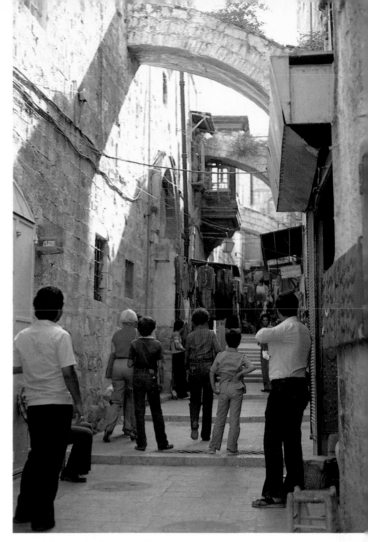

Part of the Via Dolorosa, the traditional route along which Jesus made His way from Pilate's judgement hall to Calvary.

However, there are many who do not accept the traditional location of Calvary, believing that the walls of the city in Jesus' day ran more or less along the line of the present wall. These locate Calvary some distance beyond the present north wall on an eminence to the east of the Damascus Road, not far from Jeremiah's Grotto, with the tomb of Christ in an ancient garden nearby. This spot is sometimes called Gordon's Calvary because he favoured this location when he visited the Holy Land. If this is the true site, then the Via Dolorosa must have turned north at the junction of the road up the Tyropoeon, 205 passed out of the city at the Damascus Gate, and continued along the Great North Road to the hill of Calvary or Golgotha. The geographical location of the cross, however, is really of little consequence. What matters is the event which was enacted there, and our own personal relation to it.

A great crowd followed Jesus and the soldiers, among them the chief priests, scribes, and elders, people from the city, and pilgrims who had come in for the Passover. The first mentioned were eager to see Him die, others went out of unhealthy curiosity, while still others followed sorrowing that an innocent Man should be sent to so terrible a death. Among the crowd also were the disciples and many of the women who had helped Jesus during His ministry. Mary of Bethany was there, together with Mary the mother of Jesus and Mary the mother of James the less.

As they 'led him away' it soon became evident that Jesus would not be able to carry even the bar of the cross up the steep road. Weak and exhausted from the scourging and ill treatment, He sank to the ground under the burden. Exasperated at the delay, the centurion looked around for someone whom he could press into service to get Jesus to the place of execution. The disciples could not have been far away, but none of them dared offer to help lest they should be denounced as accomplices, and perhaps even be put to death with Him.

It happened, however, that just at that moment there came by 'out of the country', where he was lodging during the Passover festival, 'a man of Cyrene, Simon by name.' Cyrene could have been Cyrenaica in North Africa, but was more probably Kyrenia or Cyprus, where there

was a considerable Jewish colony. In Peter's congregation at Pentecost there were men of Cyrene. Stephen also disputed with Cyrenians, and one of the teachers in the Christian Church which was later established in Antioch, was Lucius of Cyrene.

We are not told how Simon reacted to the service imposed on him. He may have been humiliated by the indignity, or he may have willingly helped out of pity for Jesus. But we do know that it changed his whole life, for Mark, in his gospel, mentions that Simon was the 'father of Alex-

ander and Rufus', evidently well known in the Christian community in after years. A

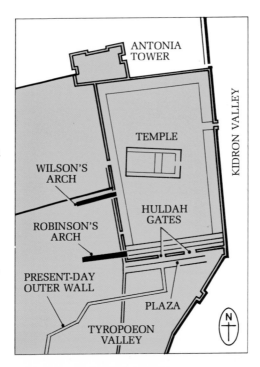

Excavations in the south-west corner of the temple precincts in Jerusalem. Many remains have been unearthed dating back to the time of Jesus. A street has been found which connected with the 'plaza' on which pilgrims assembled before entering the temple area through the Double (Huldah) Gate. The Tyropoeon Valley which ran between the west wall and the upper city (to the right) was bridged possibly by two arches. The remains of the lower, 'Robinson's arch', can be seen jutting out from the temple wall on the left. This conclusion is challenged by those who consider that this projection was a support for a great stairway to the temple from the valley below.

207

The 'Ecce Homo' arch was part of a triple triumphal gateway into Aelia Capitolina (Roman Jerusalem) built by Hadrian at the beginning of the second century. It was erected within the site of the Antonia Fortress where Pilate presented Jesus in a purple robe with the words, 'Behold the Man' (Ecce Homo!).

certain Rufus is mentioned by Polycarp in his letter to the Philippians, and tradition has it that Alexander was martyred for his faith.

In bearing the cross 'after Jesus', Simon not only found salvation for himself and his family, but he set an example to us, that we should take up our cross and 'follow him' in experience and service.

In the Talmud a vivid description is given of an execution procession. A herald went in front of the victim proclaiming his crime from a parchment charge sheet and demanding whether any desired to plead his innocence even at that late hour.

Two scribes accompanied the prisoner seeking to extract from him a confession of his crime in order to mitigate the wrath of God against him. A representative of the Sanhedrin followed to certify that the sentence had been duly carried out. Whether all this was mounted for Jesus we are not told.

As Jesus moved slowly along the road, followed by Simon bearing the cross, He passed a group of grief-stricken women, and even in this dark hour of His agony He found time to pause and speak with them. 'Daughters of Jerusalem, weep not for me,' He said, for in His suffering He was sustained by 'the joy that was set before him'. Instead they should weep for the terrible recompense which would overtake those who had rejected Him and were sending Him to the cross. 'If they do these things in a green tree,' He said, 'what shall be done in the dry?' If Jesus, a green and fruitful branch, was cut down in His innocency, what would become of the dead and withered tree of guilty Israel? If Jesus, who was guiltless, was so

A processional leaves the third station of the cross which recalls the first time that Jesus collapsed under the weight of His cross. There are fourteen stations, five within the Church of the Holy Sepulchre, although most of the sites are speculative in origin. These stations mark the progress of Jesus from His trial to the crucifixion.

treated, what would 'the end be of them that obey not the Gospel?'

At last the mournful procession reached 'a place called . . . in the Hebrew Golgotha', meaning 'the place of a skull'. In Luke the corresponding Latin name is given, Calvaria or Calvary. The name may have been derived from the shape of the round-topped mound or knoll, or it may have been so designated because it was a common place of execution, littered with the grim evidences of innumerable past victims. In the side of the hill called Gordon's Calvary there are two great holes which give the appearance of a skull, and have been used to explain its name, but it is unlikely that this configuration goes back to the time of Christ. They were more likely the result of weathering and quarrying of a much later date. Whatever its origin, however, the name has a deep significance in the Bible story, for it was in the place of death that death was for ever cancelled for those who accept the merits of Christ's vicarious sacrifice.

It was a merciful custom, going back to very early times, to offer to criminals about to die an opiate or narcotic of gall or myrrh to dull their final agonies. This kindly act is mentioned in the book of Proverbs, and in the time of Christ a charitable society of wealthy ladies, according to the Talmud, had taken it upon themselves to render this service. When, therefore, Jesus and the thieves reached the place of execution they were offered 'wine mingled with myrrh'. The thieves eagerly drained the cups, but Jesus 'would not drink'. He still had a ministry to perform on the cross, and if He had accepted relief of this kind He would have been too insensible to have helped any as He hung there. In His last hour, therefore, He would take nothing that would prema-turely terminate the saving work He had come to do, or separate Him from communion with God. With divine heroism, Jesus faced death conscious to the end.

On the hill of Calvary the soldiers proceeded to set up the crosses. There were four types of cross used in Roman times. The crux simplex was merely the pole of a waggon or chariot to which the victim was bound. The crux summissa had a cross bar placed on the top of an upright like a T. The crux decussata had the members placed diagonally like a St. Andrew's cross, while the crux immissa had the cross bar set in a mortise a little below the top of the upright. The last is generally regarded as the form of cross on which Jesus died.

The height of the cross varied, but normally the feet were not more than half the body height above the ground. It is unlikely that any block was used to support the feet, as is often portrayed in pictures of the cross, but a crutch may have been fixed between the thighs to support the weight of the body, which might otherwise have been torn away from the nails.

The upright beam, already on the site, was laid on the ground and the cross bar attached. Jesus was partially stripped, laid on the cross, and His hands were transfixed to the horizontal member by nails driven home with a wooden mallet. In representations of the crucifixion the wounds are usually shown in the palms of Christ's hands, but in all probability it would be necessary for the nails to be put through the wrists to bear the weight of His body. The feet were then nailed separately to the upright or impaled with a single spike through the crossed limbs.

Usually this cruel procedure forced shrieks of pain from the lips of the victim,

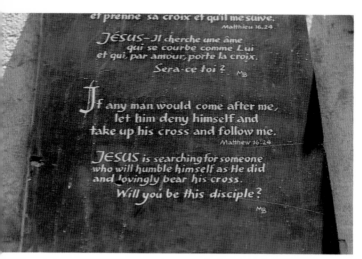

et prenne sa croix et qu'il me suive.
Matthieu 16,24

JÉSUS – Il cherche une âme
qui se courbe comme Lui
et qui, par amour, porte la croix.

Sera-ce toi ?
MB

If any man would come after me,
let him deny himself and
take up his cross and follow me.
Matthew 16:24

JESUS is searching for someone
who will humble himself as He did
and lovingly bear his cross.

Will you be this disciple?
MB

A pointed reminder on a wall in the Via Dolorosa that discipleship comes not from pilgrimages but humble commitment.

but through it all Jesus uttered no word of complaint. He only breathed a prayer to His Father for His tormentors. 'Father, forgive them; for they know not what they do.' Jesus' first word from the cross offered mercy and grace to the soldiers who in ignorance obeyed the command of the centurion, but not to them only. It speaks forgiveness to all who have since realized their soul's need at the foot of the cross.

At the top of the upright beam the charge against Christ was affixed. Pilate had commanded to be written on it, 'Jesus of Nazareth the King of the Jews', in the three languages of Palestine of that day — Aramaic, the language of the common people; Greek, the language of the Hellenistic world; and Latin, the official language of the Roman overlords, just as General Allenby, when he took Jerusalem from the Turks in 1917, issued his proclamation of occupation in Arabic, Hebrew, and English.

210   When the chief priests saw the inscription they remonstrated with Pilate, urging that it be changed to, 'He said, I am King of the Jews', but Pilate refused to alter it, saying abruptly, 'What I have written I have written'. And so it remained, by a higher ordination than that of Pilate, a witness to His enemies that He reigned even from His cross, and one day would reign in glory as King of kings and Lord of lord; a witness, too, to all who thereafter would learn of the Saviour-King to the ends of the world and to the end of time.

When all was done, the cross, with its divine-human burden, was raised up by the soldiers and dropped with a sickening thud into the hole prepared for it, dreadfully tearing the hands and feet of Jesus as the cruel nails took the full weight of His body.

On either side of Jesus the crosses of the two other condemned men were set up and then, collecting the clothes stripped from the victims as the customary perquisites of their distasteful task, the soldiers proceeded to divide them before settling down for their final watch.

The poor garments of the two thieves were first shared out and then they came to the clothes of Jesus. His sandles, girdle, headgear, and outer tunic or cloak were divided, but when they came to the inner garment He had worn they saw that it was 'woven from the top throughout' in one beautiful seamless piece, most likely by the loving hands of His mother. Feeling that it would be a shame to tear up so perfect a garment they decided to cast lots for it, and so yet another prophecy of His passion was fulfilled to the letter: 'They parted my raiment among them, and for my vesture they did cast lots.'

This chapter is based on Matthew 27:31-35; Mark 15:20-26; Luke 23:26-33; John 19:16-24.

Obedient unto death

When the soldiers sat down to watch at the cross they expected their vigil would be a long one; for though excruciatingly agonizing, crucifixion was a slow death. Sometimes the victims would linger on for two or three days before death ended their sufferings.

As Jesus hung upon the cross, His enemies vented their spite upon Him in insulting words. Forgetting their dignity as the leaders of the people, the chief priests and scribes and elders mocked Him, saying, 'He saved others; himself he cannot save. If he be the King of Israel, let

Calvary is believed by many to be within the walls of the Church of the Holy Sepulchre. The Romans built a temple to Venus here which was demolished and replaced with an immense basilica by Constantine in AD 336. It was destroyed by the Persians in AD 614. The present structure, the most important shrine in Christendom, was largely built by the Crusaders. Their defeat resulted in Moslems having overall control of the church to this day. The Franciscans, Greeks, Armenians, Copts, Syrians and Ethiopians have squabbled and jostled for rights within the building's dark and mysterious cloisters. Beneath its massive domes the sounds of strange liturgies, the pungent odour of incense, the icons and elaborate trappings of worship seem much removed from the humble Jesus whom it seeks to elevate.

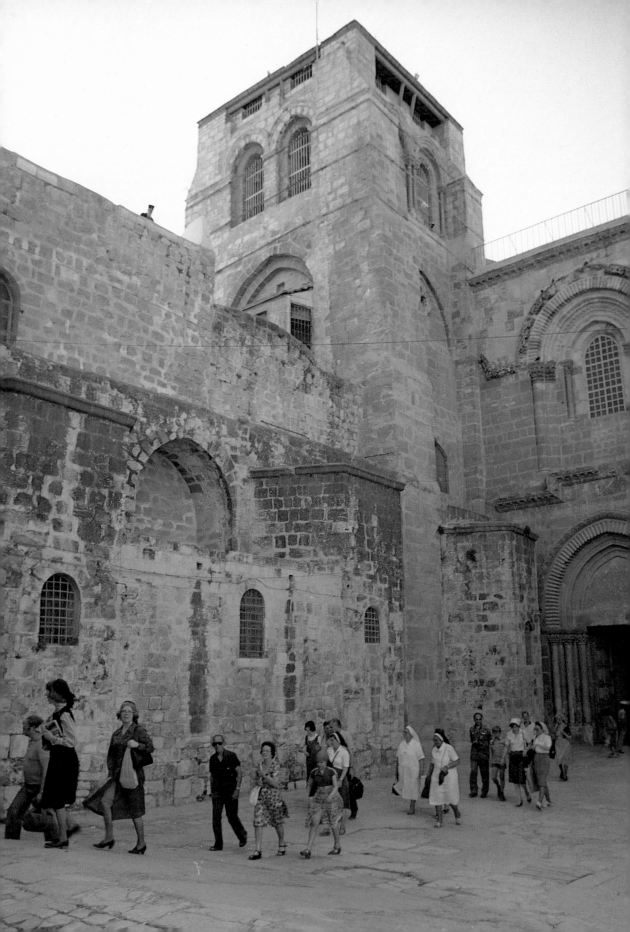

him now come down from the cross, and we will believe him. He trusted in God; let him deliver him now, if he will save him: for he said, I am the Son of God.'

Had Jesus wished He could have freed Himself instantly and brought swift judgement on His tormentors. But then the whole sinful race would have been eternally lost. It was because He would not leave man to his fate that He did not come down. By a miraculous descent from the cross He could have manifested the greatness of His power, but by the miracle of His vicarious sacrifice He revealed the depths of His infinite love.

Led by the rulers, the crowds of idlers who thronged the busy road joined in the mocking and derision. The soldiers, too, who had taunted Jesus in Pilate's palace, joined in the abuse, saying, 'If thou be the King of the Jews, save thyself.'

At first both the thieves also 'which were crucified with him, cast the same in his teeth', demanding in rage and despair, 'If thou be Christ, save thyself and us.' One, however, to whom tradition has given the name of Dismas, as he watched the patient Sufferer from whose lips no word of vengeance or self-pity fell in all His agony, realized that he was in the presence of a power beyond human; of One who, if He would not save him from physical death, could save him from eternal ruin. His heart was touched, and in true repentance he acknowledged Jesus as his Saviour.

Looking across at the other thief, who was still railing, he said, 'Dost not thou fear God, seeing thou art in the same condemnation? And we indeed justly, for we receive the due reward of our deeds: but this man hath done nothing amiss.'

Then turning his head towards Jesus on the central cross, he pleaded, 'Lord, re-member me when thou comest into thy kingdom.' Probably the thief's conception of Messiah's kingdom was no different from the popular idea of the Jews, but he did believe that though Jesus now hung on the cross, in some way he could not understand, Jesus would manifest His power and fulfil His destiny. Jesus hon-oured his imperfect faith. Oblivious of His own suffering He turned to him and said, 'Verily I say unto thee, To day thou shalt be with me in paradise.'

As the verse is punctuated in our Authorized Version it might be imagined – indeed it is commonly so interpreted – that Jesus assured the thief that He would return to His Father's home in heaven that very day, and that He would take the pen-itent thief with Him. But Jesus said noth-ing of the kind.

In harmony with the consistent teaching of the Bible, and as Paul later explained in one of his epistles, Jesus did not at His death 'ascend' to heaven; He 'descended first into the . . . earth,' there to sleep the 'sleep' of death until His resurrection. On the third day Jesus did not come back from heaven to meet His disciples; He came forth from the grave where He had been since His burial. Consequently, Jesus did not go to Paradise on the day of His death, and the thief obviously did not either.

What then did Jesus promise the peni-tent thief? All becomes clear when it is realized that there is nothing inspired about the punctuation of the Bible. This has been supplied by the translators ac-cording to their understanding of the meaning of Scripture, or in this case as a consequence of their misunderstanding of it. If they had placed the comma correctly after and not before the word 'today', they would have correctly rendered Jesus'

214

words. What He said, using a common Old Testament form of emphasis, was not 'I say unto thee, Today shalt thou be with me paradise,' but, 'I say unto thee today, Thou shalt be with me in paradise.' Jesus promised the penitent thief on that very day, the day of His crucifixion, that when He came into His kingdom – which He had explained many times before would be at his His second coming – the repentant thief with all the saints would be

The Chapel of Golgotha in the Church of the Holy Sepulchre (right). It is heavily ornamented with censors, lamps and icons which give a sense of unreality to the stark horror of the cross on Skull Hill. It is said to be on the actual hill of Calvary, although there is no clear evidence for this view. Tourists (below) gaze into the empty sepulchre. Its architecture is somewhat bizarre, bearing little resemblance to a rolling stone tomb.

raised immortal by 'the voice of the archangel and . . . the trump of God.'

So while the impenitent thief died as he had lived, without hope, the cross of the penitent thief became a stepping stone to the Paradise of God. At the very point of death Jesus triumphed over Satan and snatched another soul from his clutches and from eternal destruction.

The story of the penitent thief provides us with a wonderful assurance that it is never too late this side of death to seek the mercy of God, who never turned a

215

repentant sinner away. At the same time, the other thief provides a warning that to wait till the eleventh hour may be too late, for his heart was not softened by the sight of the dying Saviour, and for him repentance never came.

It was not long after Jesus had spoken His redeeming word to the penitent thief that He caught sight of His mother with the other Marys and His closest disciple John, standing at the foot of the cross. Concerned for her future care more than for the pain and anguish He was enduring, Jesus addressed His third utterance from the cross to her as He said gently, 'Woman, behold thy son,' and to John, 'Behold thy mother.' 'And from that hour,' the Record says, 'that disciple took her unto his own home.'

Tradition has it that when John left Palestine to care for the churches in Asia Minor, he took Mary with him and that she died at Ephesus at a great age. Another tradition, however, asserts that she was buried in a tomb in the Kidron Valley, near Jerusalem. Whatever the truth about her death, however, we do know that she was not translated body and soul to heaven to become co-mediatrix with Christ in the presence of God, as Rome promulgates in her dogma of the Assumption of the Virgin. Wherever she was laid to rest, Mary still sleeps awaiting, with all the saints, resurrection to immortal life. She identified herself with the rest of humanity in confessing her own need of a Saviour, and believed with Paul that there is only 'one mediator between God and men, the Man Christ Jesus.'

When John had led the mother of Jesus away, the other Marys remained to watch and wait. As the end drew on, the physical agony of Jesus was intensified. The weight of His body dragged upon His lacerated hands, the stiffened muscles were tortured by cramp, the lungs and heart were engorged by the impaired circulation, the veins swelled, and a mounting fever added to His exhaustion. But through all His sufferings, Jesus uttered no word of complaint. The penitent thief, too, was quiet now and only the other thief still railed at his tormentors.

The sun rose higher in the sky and then, as it reached its zenith at the sixth hour, suddenly the noon-day light began to fade and in a few moments the darkness of night overshadowed all the land. It was not an eclipse, for at Passover the moon was always at the full. It can only be explained as a supernatural phenomenon by which God mercifully veiled from mortal sight the dying agonies of His Son. It symbolized, too, the darkness which covered the earth when the Light of the world was withdrawn.

With the darkness a death-like silence fell upon all. The taunts and mockings died on the lips of the fear-stricken beholders. Many beat their breasts in terror and groped their way back to the city.

About the ninth hour, from the midst of the darkness the voice of Jesus was heard by those who still watched, 'Eli, Eli, lama, sabachthani,' He cried, which is to say, 'My God, my God, why hast thou forsaken me?'

Hearing the cry some said, 'Behold, He calleth Elias' for, according to the common belief, Elijah came to the help of those in dire distress. Others said, 'Let us see whether Elias will come to save him.' But it was not Elias for whom Jesus called. The cry which pierced the darkness came from His lips as He looked into the abyss of eternal separation from God for the sake of sinful man. In the garden an angel was sent by God to comfort Him after His fateful decision, but on the cross the face of God was hidden. Jesus' words were not so much a question, for He desired no release from the final sacrifice. Rather were they intended to provide a glimpse of the fearful fate from which man was to be saved by His taking upon Himself the curse of the world's sin. And the wonder of divine love is that, though it was in His power to turn back, He did not do so. Human wisdom can never hope to fathom the mystery of divine love, but in that cry we can perhaps dimly glimpse the miracle of the atonement.

For three hours the awesome darkness had persisted and then, at the ninth hour, it was dissipated as mysteriously as it had come, revealing Jesus on the point of

217

death. From His lips, parched by mounting fever, the cry came, 'I thirst'.

By the side of the cross there was an earthenware vessel 'full of vinegar', actually a kind of sour wine, with which the soldiers refreshed themselves during their vigil. One of them, taking pity on Him, picked up a stalk of hyssop, stuck a sponge on the end, and having soaked it in the wine, moistened Jesus' closed lips. This was not the stupefying drink like the wine mingled with myrrh which He had been offered earlier, and this time Jesus did not refuse it. Thus still another Scripture was fulfilled, 'They gave me vinegar to drink'.

When Jesus had received the drink, His lips parted and in a 'loud voice', heard by all who were standing near, He cried, 'It is finished'. To the Jews, blinded by prejudice, the death of Jesus was the end of an impostor. They believed that His claims had been proved hollow, that His teaching was overthrown, and His influence for ever destroyed. But for Jesus the cross was the culmination of His work on earth and the foundation and basis of the work which He was to take up in heaven at His resurrection.

The cross was the ultimate indictment of Satan and the exposure of the 'lie' which, in his rebellion, he had opposed to the 'truth' of God.

It was the final revelation of the malignity of sin and the manifestation of its inevitable consequences. It was the vindication of the holiness of the eternal law. It provided full satisfaction of the claims of divine justice. It was the last payment of the debt of sin.

It was the crowning evidence of the redeeming love of God in Christ; it testified that the basis of the atonement was fully provided, and that the way was opened by which man could be restored to fellowship with God.

It proclaimed that the battle with Satan was won, that his defeat was complete and his fate sealed.

The work of the cross was a 'finished' work; and as we look in faith upon the crucified Saviour, we cannot but echo the personal testimony of the apostle Paul, 'God forbid that I should glory, save in the cross of our Lord Jesus Christ.'

Immediately after His momentous declaration, 'It is finished,' Jesus spoke His last words on the cross. To His Father He said, 'Into Thy hands I commend my spirit.' Whereupon His head fell limply upon His breast and 'He gave up the ghost'. Literally 'He dismissed the spirit'. The expression is significant. Jesus could have held on to the life which was inherently His. None could take it from Him. 'I have power to lay it down,' He said, and this He voluntarily and vicariously did as the price of human redemption. To His Father He committed the life that was His that He might give it freely to those who by faith claimed the merits of His sacrifice.

As Jesus died 'the earth did quake, and the rocks rent,' as if in protest at the divine tragedy. In the traditional rock of Calvary in the Church of the Holy Sepulchre a crack is shown some two yards long and a foot wide, but this does not in any way identify the spot, for it is actually of much earlier seismic origin, this region having been from ancient times an earthquake zone.

The shock ran through the nearby city graveyard and many of the gravestones were moved out of their places, revealing yawning caverns from which, after Christ's resurrection, 'many bodies of the saints which slept arose, and came out of the graves . . . and went into the holy city, and appeared unto many'.

In the temple the officiating priest was standing before the altar with hand uplifted to slay the lamb of the evening sacrifice. Another priest had thrown back the first veil and stood with censer raised before the altar of incense, when suddenly the inner 'veil' of gold and purple embroidered linen at the entrance to the 'most holy place' was 'rent in twain from the top to the bottom'.

The priest in the holy place dropped his censer, the knife fell from the hand of the priest at the altar, and the lamb ran from him and made its escape. The last type had met the divine Antitype on the cross, the mediation of the Levitical priesthood was ended, and a living way was opened direct to the mercy seat inviting all sinners, Jew and Gentile, by faith to 'come boldly unto the Throne of grace'. Sacrifice and oblation were now superseded by the shed blood of the true Lamb of God. The age of types and shadows was ended; the new age of Gospel reality had begun.

'And all the people that came together to that sight, beholding the things which were done, smote their breasts, and returned' trembling from the cross and from the temple to their homes.

The leaders of the Jews were not softened by the divine dignity of Jesus' death, or by its catastrophic accompaniments. Their closed minds and hearts still persuaded them that Jesus was an impostor who had earned His due recompense. But there were others among the priests and the people whose consciences were smitten by what they had seen, who in the darkness and tragedy of Calvary were drawn to the Saviour, and at Pentecost they made confession of their faith.

A work of grace was accomplished too,

Within the darkness of this awful scene was the dawn of a great victory.

in the heart of at least one of the soldiers who had carried out the sentence of death. For when they 'saw the earthquake, and those things that were done, they feared greatly', and the centurion, to whom tradition has given the name Petronius, cried out, 'Certainly this was a righteous man: . . . this was the Son of God.' And he joined with Simon of Cyrene, the penitent thief, and the nameless multitude of priests and people who that day found 'life in a look at the crucified One'.

This chapter is based on Matthew 27:36-56; Mark 15:27-41; Luke 23:34-49; John 19:25-37.

219

In Joseph's new tomb

When the Jewish leaders recovered their composure after the earthquake and the other calamities attending the death of Jesus, they realized that the 'day of preparation' was nearing its end and that the Sabbath was drawing on. It was a rule that the bodies of executed criminals should never be left exposed to desecrate the Sabbath, and this was a particular Sabbath, being not only the weekly rest day, but also a 'high' Sabbath of the Passover festival. So they went to Pilate and asked that the legs of the victims be broken to hasten death 'that they might be taken away'.

Permission was granted by Pilate, and the soldiers, who were just as anxious to get away, proceeded to break 'the legs of the first and of the other which was crucified with him.'

When, however, they came to Jesus, they were amazed to find that 'He was dead already'. So another prophecy which specified that 'a bone of him shall not be broken', was fulfilled. Instead, one of the soldiers pierced His side with a spear 'and forthwith came there out blood and water'.

Many traditions have been built around the piercing of Christ's side. One claims that the blood was collected in a chalice and became known as the Holy Grail. Another asserts that the soldier who pierced Christ was called Longinus and that he too was converted at the foot of the cross and later died a martyr in Cappadocia. These traditions may be discounted, but the record itself is of deep significance. In the first place, the piercing of the heart of Jesus proved beyond all doubt that He really died. Sceptics have tried to explain away the resurrection of Jesus by asserting that He had only swooned and was in a coma when He was placed in the tomb. The spear thrust, however, proved conclusively that Jesus was dead when He was taken down from the cross.

There is also a profound significance in the fact that from the wound there poured 'blood and water', for this mingled stream could only have flowed if the pleural cavity had been ruptured. This is known in medical practice to result from distension following intense mental suffering, and reveals the terrible agony which Christ endured on our behalf. Literally, as the Psalmist foretold, He died of a 'broken heart'.

When the disciples and the devout women who were waiting on the edge of the crowd saw that Jesus was dead, the terrible thought seized them that His body might be cast into the burning pits of Gehenna like that of any common criminal, but they did not know how to prevent this. Suddenly they were surprised to see two of the rulers approach the centurion and engage in earnest conversation with him. They did not know at this time that one of these was Nicodemus, the doctor of law who had visited Jesus by night, and that the other was Joseph of Arimathea.

Nicodemus had followed the ministry of Jesus with the deepest interest ever since his searching conversation with Him early in His Jerusalem ministry, and he had endeavoured to secure justice for Jesus whenever His name was discussed by the Sanhedrin, but he had never dared to come out openly as a disciple. When Nicodemus looked upon Jesus dying on the cross he was ashamed of his fearfulness and gave his heart fully to Him.

Joseph, his friend, was a rich and devout leader among the Jews and 'an honourable counsellor' in the Sanhedrin. His home town is designated Arimathea, or Ramah, but as there were some seventy

An authentic rolling stone tomb thought by many Christians to be the more likely site of the burial of Jesus. This tomb says much more to the visitor than the official Holy Sepulchre, being simple, unadorned and set in a beautiful garden where many meditate, pray and take part in communion. The entrance to the tomb carries the great message of Christianity, 'He is not here, he is risen.' The Garden Tomb is located beyond the Damascus Gate on the north side of Jerusalem.

Ramahs in Israel we cannot precisely determine which one it was. Evidently he also had property in Jerusalem and most likely was a permanent resident there at this time.

Like Simeon and Anna, Joseph of Arimathea 'waited for the kingdom of God' and, through the influence of Nicodemus, had also become a 'secret disciple' of Jesus. With Nicodemus he followed the crowds to Calvary and there gave his heart to God.

In the zeal of their new-found faith, the two rulers realized that there was now something which only they could do.

They could save the body of Jesus from ignominy and give Him an honourable burial. So they spoke to the centurion, who himself was under conviction, and he readily agreed to take no action till they put their request to Pilate. Pilate could not understand why so eminent a Jew wished to espouse the cause of the crucified Jesus, but he at once granted the request. So Joseph returned to the cross with a roll of fine linen cloth, the best which could be bought, which he may have intended for the swathing of his own body at his death.

While Joseph was away interviewing Pilate, Nicodemus went into the city where he purchased about a hundred pound's weight (30 kg) of a mixture of 'myrrh and aloes'. These were not intended primarily as embalming materials, though they would have a temporary preservative quality, but were rather a sweet-scented tribute to the dead, much as we buy flowers to place on the grave of departed loved ones.

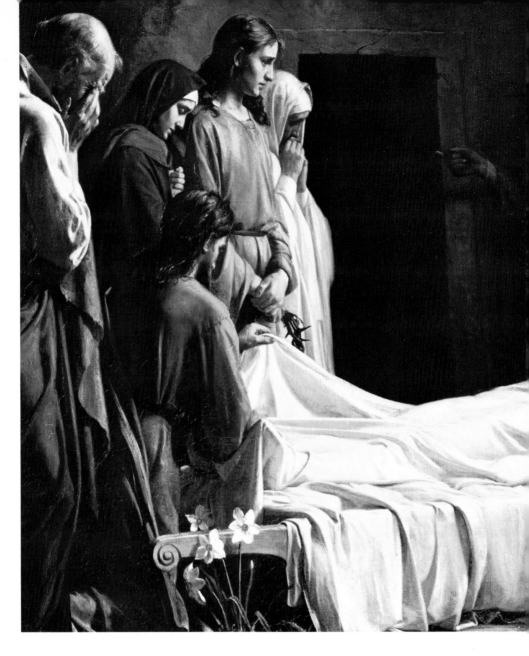

With profound relief and gratitude, Mary Magdalene and the other Mary, who had remained by the cross, watched the two rulers as they tenderly took the body of Jesus down and began to enfold it in the broad linen bandages, wrapping the spices in the folds. Realizing by their actions that these men must have loved Jesus dearly, the women came forward and made themselves known to Joseph and Nicodemus. Then they helped in the final preparations of the body for burial.

Meanwhile the soldiers had completed their task of dismantling the crosses, the bloodstained cross beams being unceremoniously thrown into a ditch or onto some nearby rubbish heap. More than two centuries later Queen Helena, mother of Constantine the Great, searching near the traditional site of Calvary, believed she had found the beam of Christ's cross, and erected over the spot a little chapel, later

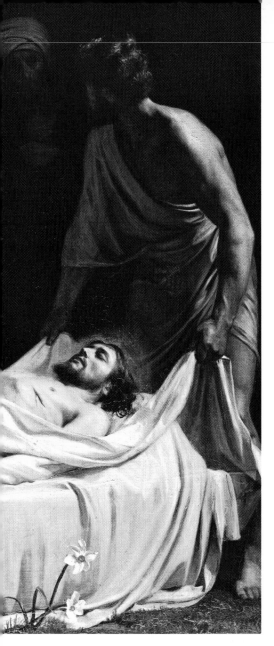

work was done. The important thing is what happened on the cross and how we relate ourselves to that redemptive act.

When the temporary embalming of the body of Jesus was completed, Joseph and Nicodemus lifted it onto a bier and, with the women following, carried it to a garden or orchard belonging to Joseph, in which was a 'new sepulchre' which he had had cut out of the rocky hillside as a family burial place, but in which no bodies had yet been laid.

The traditional sepulchre in the Church of the Holy Sepulchre, in its encasement of sculptured marble, certainly now bears no resemblance to an ancient rock tomb, but the so-called 'Garden Tomb' near Gordon's Calvary shows very clearly what it must have been like. This comprises two chambers, an outer ante-room and an inner tomb chamber, the latter being about six feet by three feet. Its 'newness' is attested by the fact that only one bench had been properly cut for the reception of a body. In front of the entrance doorway, just as in the Bible account, there is a rock groove along which the great millstone was rolled to close the tomb.

Reverently the body of Jesus was wrapped in an enveloping shroud. His arms were folded across His breast, His head was slightly raised on a stone pillow, and a napkin, a small square of linen, was laid over His face. Then returning through the outer chamber, the men removed the wedge holding the millstone back and rolled it across the entrance doorway. There Jesus, who had died in company with 'the transgressors', was left to rest, as prophecy had foretold, 'with the rich in his death'.

The holy women remained awhile after the men had gone. They were last at the tomb as they had been last at the cross.

to be replaced by the great Church of the Holy Sepulchre.

We can honour Queen Helena for her Christian faith, and for influencing her son to accept Christianity and become the first Christian Emperor, but we cannot but regret the part she played in starting the wave of relic worship which swept Europe for centuries as a result of her alleged discovery of the 'true cross'. It does not really matter what happened to the cross after its

223

Adjacent to the Garden Tomb is a rocky cliff that resembles a skull, known as Gordon's Calvary. General Gordon visited Jerusalem in 1883 and was convinced that here was the genuine Golgotha, the place of the skull where Jesus was crucified.

Then they too returned to the city to prepare 'spices and ointments' to complete the embalming of Jesus' body when the Sabbath was past.

According to Jewish law the washing and embalming of the bodies of the dead was regarded as a permissible duty even after the six trumpet blasts had announced the opening of the Sabbath. But as the rulers had made adequate provision for the temporary preservation of the body, the women were content to 'rest' upon the Sabbath day, 'according to the commandment', as they believed Jesus would have them do.

Yet while that Sabbath day was a day of physical rest for the disciples, as it had always been, it was a day also of mental and spiritual anguish. They had never believed that Jesus could really die, and now that He had been laid lifeless in the tomb they were so overwhelmed that they entirely forgot His promise that He would rise again. For them that Sabbath was a day of unrelieved darkness and despair. On the morrow they would see to the final embalming of His body and then would seal the tomb. After that they would be left with precious memories, but no hope.

But though the disciples forgot Jesus' promise that He would rise, the chief priests and rulers did not. Of course, they did not believe that He would really rise from the dead, but they were apprehensive lest His disciples should remove the body and hide it, and then declare that Jesus had risen, in an attempt to justify their faith and perpetuate the sect He had founded. So towards sunset on the Sabbath they went again to Pilate.

'Sir,' they said, when they were granted audience, 'we remember that that deceiver said, while he was yet alive, After three days I will rise again. Command therefore that the sepulchre be made sure until the third day, lest his disciples come by night, and steal him away, and say unto the people, He is risen from the dead: so the last error shall be worse than the first.'

But Pilate was not disposed to assume any further responsibility in the case. It had already given him enough worry and he did not want to get involved further, so he said to the priests and rulers, 'Ye have a watch,' meaning the soldiers who had been used in connection with Jesus' arrest and execution: 'go your way, make it as sure as ye can.'

So the rulers went 'and made the sepulchre sure', fastening cords across the stone and sealing them so that the stone could not be tampered with. Then 'in the end of the Sabbath' they set 'a watch' to make sure that no one came near during the night.

Little did they realize that all their elaborate precautions to make the sepulchre 'sure' against human interference would, in a few hours, provide 'sure' proof of the supernatural character of Christ's glorious resurrection.

This chapter is based on Matthew 27:57-66; Mark 15:42-47; Luke 23:50-56; John 19:38-42.

224

The broken seal

When the chief priests and rulers left the tomb of Jesus as the sun declined over the western hills, they felt confident that they had disposed once and for all of the movement He had started. The sepulchre had been made 'sure' by the affixing of the governor's seal, and the strong guard which had been set excluded any possibility of the disciples attempting to remove the body and then proclaiming that their Master was risen.

From dusk until nine o'clock the soldiers in the first watch did their spell of duty and were relieved. The second watch followed on until midnight and then the third watch took up their posts. Perhaps they were changed at three o'clock in the morning before anything happened. Luke says it was 'very early in the morning' and Matthew designates the fateful moment as 'as it began to dawn'. It would therefore seem that it was about four o'clock, just before the first glow of morning light, that there was a crash of thunder, the earth shook as it had done at the crucifixion, and a mighty angel in glimmering white raiment descended from heaven, scattering the unseen hosts of evil angels who sought to bar his passage, and stood before the tomb. As his hand touched the great stone in front of the entrance it rolled away as if it had been a pebble, and in a loud voice he bade Jesus, in His Father's name, to come forth.

Jesus had said before His death that He had power to lay down His life and power to take it again, and at His Father's call He broke the bands of death and stepped forth from the tomb.

We are not told the name of the angel to whom this momentous commission was given, but one cannot but believe that it was again the angel Gabriel. To him was given the honour of announcing the birth of John the Baptist to his parents and the birth of Jesus to Mary. If it was he also who ministered to Jesus after His temptation in the wilderness and who comforted Him in Gethsemane, it would indeed have been appropriate if he were sent to roll away the stone and call Jesus from the tomb.

It may seem strange that the Scriptures draw a veil over the actual moment when Jesus came forth Conqueror of death. Perhaps the scene was too sacred for mortal eyes to behold, or too wonderful for human language to describe. So it is left to the eye of faith to glimpse the stupendous sight as the grave-clothes fell away from the body of Jesus and He rose in all the majesty of His heavenly glory. Before Him the angel bent low in worship and the Roman guard, trembling with terror, fell at their posts in a death-like faint.

When the soldiers had recovered from the shock, Jesus and the angel had gone and all there was to recall what had taken place was the open tomb, which yawned dark in the flickering light of the torches planted in rock niches around.

The centurion in charge picked up a torch and staggered to the entrance of the tomb, followed by the rest of the guard, and to their consternation and horror they saw that it was empty. Fearfully he began to wonder what report he could take back to his superior officers to excuse his failure to keep the tomb. As there was no purpose in maintaining the guard around an open and empty tomb, the centurion led his men back to the barracks with the intention of reporting the alarming incident to Pilate. Word, however, soon reached the chief priests and rulers, who had the soldiers brought first into their presence. The officer of the guard felt that their safety lay in telling the whole truth, for even Pilate could not accuse them of dereliction of duty in the face of supernatural forces. But the high priest realized that if such a story got around it would confirm the validity of Christ's claim and the people would turn on them for crucifying a holy prophet, if not Messiah Himself.

So, asking the soldiers to wait until he had consulted the Sanhedrin, the high priest quickly summoned as many as he could gather and put the disturbing report before them. After a short session the soldiers were called in and offered 'large money' to say that the disciples of Jesus 'came by night, and stole him away' while they slept. A few days before, these priests had used money from the temple funds to pay the betrayer of Jesus, and doubtless it was from the same source that they now bribed the Roman soldiers to suppress the story they had brought. With their offer they assured the centurion that if the matter came to the notice of Pilate, and they were faced with the possibility of trial and perhaps execution for sleeping on watch, they would 'persuade him, and secure' their safety.

The captain of the guard discussed the matter with the soldiers. The 'large money' was certainly not to be set aside lightly, and if the priests could 'square' Pilate they would be in no danger of punishment. 'So they took the money, and did as they were taught.' And so authoritatively was the story put over to the people that Matthew reports that, when he was writing his gospel, around AD 60 or 70, it was still 'commonly reported among the Jews' in order to bring discredit on the Christian Church.

Examining the facts as they are recorded for us in the gospel narratives, however, we can see that the efforts of the Jews to cover up the evidence of the resurrection have only served to make more sure the central truth of the Christian Gospel.

The piercing of Jesus' side as He hung on the cross made it absolutely certain that Jesus was dead when He was laid in the tomb. The suggestion of some modern critics that Jesus was only in a coma when He was taken to the sepulchre, never occurred to the priests, because they made absolutely certain that He was dead.

The sealing of the tomb and the setting of a strong guard likewise, for all the story they put out, really excluded the possibility that the disciples, with nothing more than a few knives, could have forced their way to the tomb and absconded with the body.

The idea that the disciples could have got the body away while the guard were all asleep is also foolish in the extreme. For though at any hour of the night the guards off duty would have been asleep, it is inconceivable that all the watch on duty could have decided simultaneously to take a nap because everything was quiet. And if by some strange chance this could have happened, how could the soldiers possibly have known that the disciples came while they slept? When they woke up they would see that the tomb was open and empty, but they could not really tell whether the body had been stolen or whether Jesus had risen as He said He would. Moreover, the disciples could hardly have opened the tomb and got away with the body without waking someone.

Then again, if the story of the soldiers sleeping on watch had been true, as the priests asserted, surely their best policy would have been to denounce them to Pilate and have them put to death. Then they could have put out the story that, in

A member of the Garden Tomb's friendly staff explains to a group of visitors the unique message of the empty sepulchre. The gardens (below) are a popular haven from the noise and bustle of the nearby city of Jerusalem.

spite of all the precautions they had taken against fraud, their efforts had been frustrated by a neglectful Roman guard. The fact that they did not avail themselves of this wonderful opportunity of clearing themselves was because if they had tried it the soldiers would have exposed it as a dastardly lie.

Finally, if the theft story was true, why did not the priests bend every energy to find out where the body was and produce it as conclusive evidence of the fraud? That they never even instituted a search shows that the whole story was a concocted lie. The only reason they were able to get it over was because it was corroborated by the soldiers and had been accepted by Pilate.

To all, however, who examine the facts with an unbiased mind it is clear that the priests were caught in their own craftiness and succeeded only in providing conclusive evidence that Jesus did actually rise from the dead. Once again, therefore, the 'wrath of man' redounded to the 'praise' of God.

This chapter is based on Matthew 28:4, 11-15.

He is risen!

While the priests and soldiers were concocting the fraudulent story by which they hoped to explain away the resurrection, Jesus was giving decisive evidence to His followers of His triumph over death.

When Mary Magdalene and the other women left the tomb late on Friday they had agreed to meet on the morning of the first day to complete the work of embalming Jesus' body. Mary doubtless went home to Bethany, while the other women were probably lodging in Jerusalem during the Passover.

On Sunday morning, while it was still dark, Mary made her way over the Mount of Olives to the tomb in the garden, and though she had the greatest distance to travel, she was the first to arrive. The time was about five o'clock.

As soon as she got near enough, she was startled to see that the stone had been moved away and the cave-like entrance to the tomb yawned wide. Not knowing anything about the setting of the guard, the dreadful thought crossed her mind that the enemies of Jesus, determined to undo the honour that Joseph had given to His body, had taken it away and cast it, like that of any criminal, onto the refuse heaps of the Hinnom Valley. Without even looking into the tomb, therefore, Mary turned and ran to tell Simon Peter and John. When she found them she explained breathlessly, 'They have taken away the Lord out of the sepulchre, and we know not where they have laid him.'

It was not long after Mary had rushed from the tomb that the other women, including Mary the mother of James, Salome, and Joanna, arrived with the embalming spices which they had prepared before sundown on Friday. Like Mary they knew nothing about the setting of the watch so that the possibility of their not being allowed access to the tomb did not occur to them. What worried them, as they drew near, was the great stone which had been rolled in front of the entrance. 'Who shall roll us away the stone from the door of the sepulchre?' they said one to another.

Hoping that they would find someone around to help them they went on, and when they got there, they saw to their surprise that the stone had already been rolled away.

Mary had been so startled at the sight that she had run off without investigating further, but when they went up to the opening and looked in they saw an angel having the appearance of 'a young man . . . clothed in a long white garment' sitting on the right side of the antechamber, and they were afraid.

At once the angel reassured them. 'Be not affrighted,' he said. 'Ye seek Jesus of Nazareth, which was crucified: He is risen; He is not here.' And in his tone there was a gentle reproach that they, like the other disciples, had forgotten His oft-repeated promise.

'Remember,' he went on, 'how he spake unto you when He was yet in Galilee, saying, The Son of man must be delivered into the hands of sinful men, and be crucified, and the third day rise again.' As the angel spoke, it all came back to them and 'they remembered his words'.

'Come,' said the angel as he saw a look of amazement overspread their faces, 'see the place where the Lord lay.' At the angel's bidding they looked into the inner chamber and saw another angel sitting on the bench where Jesus had lain, but His body was nowhere to be seen.

When the women came out of the tomb they 'bowed down their faces to the earth' before the two angels. Then the first angel spoke again. 'Go your way,' he said, 'tell his disciples and Peter that he goeth before you into Galilee: there shall ye see him as he said to you.' How gracious it was that Jesus should have commissioned the angels to mention Peter particularly by name. He knew that Peter's repentance was sincere and He still had a great work for him to do. So in His first message to His followers, Jesus had a special word for Peter. Later in the day He was to give Peter personal assurance of forgiveness and reinstatement by revealing Himself to him first of all His disciples. Trembling and amazed at what they had seen and heard, the women hurried off to tell the wonderful tidings to the disciples.

Meanwhile, Mary had found Peter and John, who, fearing that she must be suffering from some hallucination due to her overwrought state, felt they should go along to see for themselves. They set off together, probably about half-past six, but John, being younger and more fleet of foot, outstripped Peter and reached the tomb first. There he found the stone rolled away and the tomb open just as Mary had said.

By this time Peter had come up. Impulsive as ever, he did not stay on the threshold but went straight into the antechamber and looked through into the inner tomb, where he saw that the niche where the body of Jesus had been placed was empty. He noticed something more. The linen bands in which the body had been swathed were folded up neatly and placed at one end of the bench, while the napkin which had covered His face had been folded and placed a little distance away by itself.

At once he called John to come and look. Instinctively both realized that this could not be the work of either friends or

The power and glory of God was the means by which Jesus was raised from the dead, 'the first-fruits of those who have fallen asleep'.

enemies of Jesus. If anyone had taken the body away to put it in another sepulchre they would certainly not have unwrapped it and taken it away naked. And no enemy who had intended to cast Jesus' body into the death pits of Hinnom would have folded the grave cloths tidily before making off with it. To Peter it was a mystery and he departed 'wondering in himself at that which was come to pass'. But John 'saw and believed'. To him the only explanation was that Jesus must have risen as He said He would.

No sooner had Peter and John hurried off to tell the other disciples, than Mary, who had followed after them, came again to the garden tomb. It was now about seven o'clock. This time she went up to the sepulchre, still silently weeping at the disappearance of her Lord, and as she stooped to look in she saw the two angels who had spoken to the other women a little while before. They had purposely not shown themselves to Peter and John, but now they were sitting 'the one at the head, and the other at the feet, where the body of Jesus had lain.'

As Mary knew nothing of their conversation with the other women, and still

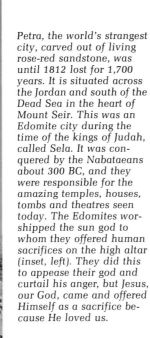

Petra, the world's strangest city, carved out of living rose-red sandstone, was until 1812 lost for 1,700 years. It is situated across the Jordan and south of the Dead Sea in the heart of Mount Seir. This was an Edomite city during the time of the kings of Judah, called Sela. It was conquered by the Nabataeans about 300 BC, and they were responsible for the amazing temples, houses, tombs and theatres seen today. The Edomites worshipped the sun god to whom they offered human sacrifices on the high altar (inset, left). They did this to appease their god and curtail his anger, but Jesus, our God, came and offered Himself as a sacrifice because He loved us.

believed that the body of Jesus had been taken away, when the angels asked her, 'Why weepest thou?' she replied, 'Because they have taken away my Lord, and I know not where they have laid him.'

Before the angels could reply Mary heard a step behind her, and turning, she saw a Figure, who repeated the angel's question, 'Woman, why weepest thou? Whom seekest thou?'

Whether it was the darkness of the morning or the fact that her eyes were blinded by tears, or whether it was that her eyes had been made 'holden', she took the questioner to be Joseph's night-watchman, employed to look after the orchard. Thinking that, as he had been there all night, he might know what had become of Jesus, Mary asked, 'Sir, if thou have borne him hence, tell me where thou hast laid him, and I will take him away.'

Then from the lips of the supposed gardener came the word 'Mary' in a voice which she instantly recognized as that of Jesus.

'Rabboni (my honoured Master),' was all that she could say as she fell to the ground, reaching out her hands to embrace His feet.

But Jesus restrained her. 'Touch me not,' He said; 'for I am not yet ascended to my Father: but go to my brethren, and say unto them, I ascend unto my Father, and your Father; and to my God, and your God.' In passing on Jesus' first message to the other women the angel had referred to them as His 'disciples', but now in Jesus' further word through Mary He called them by a name more endearing than any He had yet used. In spite of their disloyalty and cowardice He regarded them now not merely as His 'servants' or His 'friends', but as His 'brethren'.

Shortly after Jesus had spoken to Mary

He rewarded the faith and devotion of the other women by appearing to them also as they were on their way back to the city. 'All hail', He said to them, and with joy they fell before Him, clasping His feet in worship.

That Jesus should just a little while before have restrained Mary from touching Him and yet now He allowed these women to embrace His feet, indicates that in the interval Jesus had ascended to His Father for the acceptance of His sacrifice, and returned. No sooner had Jesus received the worship of the women than He again disappeared.

Hurrying on their way the women soon reached the house where the disciples were lodging and found Mary there, as well as Peter and John. Excitedly they compared notes as to what each had seen and heard. Mary and the other women told how they had seen the angels at the tomb and learned that Jesus was risen, and then had actually seen Him. For confirmation the disciples turned to Peter and John. Had they seen the angels? Had they seen Jesus? But they had to admit that neither had actually seen the angels or Christ.

The disciples were torn between hope that the report of the women was true and the fear that, in their agitated state, they had suffered some hallucination. They wanted to believe, but they could not rid themselves of their doubts. Until they had further evidence, therefore, they could not accept the women's story. 'Their words seemed to them as idle tales (lit., like non-sense), and they believed them not.' So the matter rested and the perplexed disciples waited for further news as to what had become of Jesus.

This chapter is based on Matthew 28:1, 5-10; Mark 16:1-11; Luke 24:1-12; John 20:1-18.

On the Emmaus road

Since the women had reported their meeting with the angels at the tomb, and subsequently with Jesus Himself, there had been no further news of the risen Lord. By the early afternoon, some of the believers, who had been waiting with the disciples in the upper room in Jerusalem for confirmation of the women's story, decided to return to their homes. Among these were two who lived in Emmaus. One was called Cleopas, which was probably short for Cleopatras. The name of the other is not given, but as they evidently lived together, they may have been brothers or near relatives.

All we know of the location of Emmaus from the Bible is that it was about sixty furlongs, or rather less than eight miles, from Jerusalem, but it is generally believed that it lay on the road descending through the foothills of Judea towards the coastal plain. Qubeibeh is exactly the right distance and is the most likely site.

As the two men went down the Lydda road between vine-clad hills they talked of the events of the day. Like the other disciples they wanted to believe, but could not bring themselves to accept the unsupported story of the women, and it was as they were trying to reach some conclusion about the matter that a Stranger caught up with them.

The fact that they did not recognize Him as Jesus, even after walking with Him all the way to Emmaus, was because their eyes were deliberately 'holden', as Mary's had been earlier. They assumed that He was a Passover pilgrim going home, and though they did not feel particularly sociable, they walked along with Him.

Jesus was grieved at their discouragement and sorrow, and would have liked to reveal Himself at once to them, but He desired that they should come to a realization of His resurrection through faith in the promises of Scripture rather than by a miraculous revelation of Himself. So He opened the conversation by kindly asking them why they were so cast down. 'What manner of communications are these that ye have one to another, as ye walk, and are sad?' He said.

An ancient route that passes through the village of Qubeibeh which many consider to be the biblical Emmaus.

The two disciples were surprised at the question, for if He came from the Passover, as they imagined, He should have known of the tragic happenings of the past few days, and have guessed why they were so solemn.

'Art thou only a stranger in Jerusalem,' Cleopas asked, 'and hast not known the things which are come to pass there in these days?'

'What things?' Jesus asked, feigning not to know what they were referring to.

The disciples answered, 'Concerning Jesus of Nazareth, which was a prophet mighty in deed and word before God and all the people. And how the chief priests and our rulers delivered him to be condemned to death, and have crucified him.'

Their description of Jesus is significant, for it shows that they still believed He was a 'prophet', though they had 'trusted' that He might have been the King-Messiah who was to have redeemed Israel from the Roman yoke.

The only ray of hope concerning His Messiahship, they said, was that He had said that He would rise 'the third day' and that 'certain women also of our company made us astonished, which were early at the sepulchre; and when they found not his body, they came, saying, that they had also seen a vision of angels, which said that he was alive.' Furthermore, 'certain of them which were with us went to the sepulchre, and found it even so as the women had said.' But, they added sceptically, 'Him they saw not.' They had not entirely abandoned hope, but they still could not accept the unsupported testimony of the women.

Jesus let the disciples finish their story, and then He began to direct their attention to the Scriptures which should have been their stay in this crisis hour.

'O fools,' He said, 'and slow of heart to believe all that the prophets have spoken: ought not (was it not necessary for) Christ to have suffered these things,' in order that He might 'enter into his glory', first as our Mediator and High Priest, and finally as the eternal King? Did not all type and prophecy declare that 'without shedding of blood' there could be 'no remission'? 'And beginning at Moses and all the prophets, he expounded unto them in all the Scriptures the things concerning himself.'

The two disciples were amazed as Jesus clearly distinguished the prophecies of the suffering Messiah from the prophecies of His 'glory', and showed how the former had been perfectly fulfilled in all that had happened in recent days. Doubtless He referred to the prophecy to our first parents in Eden of the bruising of the 'heel' of the Seed, the command to Abraham to offer up his only son Isaac, the smitten rock and the upraised serpent in the wilderness, the sacrifices of the sanctuary service, and Christ's predictions of His sufferings in the Psalms and in Isaiah. Never had they seen these scriptures so clearly before, and gradually the conclusion began to force itself upon their minds, that if Jesus had fulfilled the prophecies of the suffering Messiah, the prophecies of His resurrection 'must needs' have been fulfilled also. But still the perplexing problem held them back from complete faith. Why had Jesus shown Himself only to the women? If He had really risen, surely He would have shown Himself to His closest disciples, but as yet none of them had seen Him. Where was He?

By this time the travellers had reached the village of Emmaus and had stopped at the door of the house where Cleopas and

The two disciples felt strangely warmed as they listened to the words of this apparent Stranger.

his companion lived. Jesus, still unrecognized by them, made as if to take His leave and go on farther, but the desire to learn more from this wonderful Bible Teacher impelled them to invite Him to stay the night with them. 'Abide with us,' they insisted: 'for it is toward evening, and the day is far spent.' So Jesus, who will never force Himself upon anyone, but is always prepared to enter the hearts and lives of those who invite Him, 'went in to tarry with them'.

They were hungry after their long walk, and as soon as a meal had been spread they sat down, or rather reclined, at the table. It was customary in those days, as it still is in the East, to invite the guest of honour to preside over the table, and so

235

the disciples requested Jesus to ask a blessing and distribute the simple fare.

At their invitation Jesus 'took bread, and blessed it, and brake, and gave to them.' As He carried out the functions of host, the disciples noticed that their guest broke the bread just like Jesus used to do; He lifted His hands in blessing just like Jesus, and then, suddenly, as they looked at the upraised palms, they saw the nail prints. At once the truth came to them. It was Jesus. But as they rose to worship Him 'He vanished out of their sight'.

For a moment they were speechless at the realization that it was their dear Master Himself who had walked and talked with them all the way home. Then they began to think back and wonder why they had not recognized Him before.

'Did not our heart burn within us,' they said, 'while he talked with us by the way, and while he opened to us the Scriptures?' They might have known that no one could have explained the Scriptures like that but Jesus Himself. No one could have aroused such joy, such hope in their hearts as Jesus.

Thrilled that they had at last seen and talked with the risen Christ, their one desire was to get back to Jerusalem as quickly as possible and tell their brethren that the women were right and that Jesus was indeed alive from the dead.

Leaving their meal untasted, 'they rose up the same hour' and set off immediately up the hilly road to Jerusalem. They may have walked or they may have taken donkeys for speed, in which case they could have made the journey in two hours, say by half-past eight.

Through the Jaffa Gate they hurried in the darkness. Passing the palace of Herod they made their way along the narrow street to the house on Mount Zion where the disciples were lodging. The door had been barred 'for fear' of molestation by the rulers of the Jews, but at their specially arranged knock they were at once admitted. In the room were ten of the disciples and others of the company of believers who had remained with them.

Before they were able to speak, the disciples excitedly told them that the testimony of the women had been confirmed that afternoon after they left. 'The Lord is risen indeed,' they said, 'and hath appeared to Simon.' At this Cleopas and his companion told their experience of how Jesus had met them 'in the way', and how they had not recognized Him until He broke bread in their home at Emmaus.

Suddenly, as they talked excitedly together, 'Jesus himself stood in the midst of them, and saith unto them, Peace be unto you.'

The appearance of Jesus so startled the believers that, although a moment before they had been assuring one another that Jesus was alive, when He actually appeared in their midst they could not believe their eyes. Supposing that it was a 'spirit' they were 'terrified and affrighted'.

Gently Jesus assured them that it was really He. 'Why are ye troubled? and why do thoughts (of doubt) arise in your hearts? Behold my hands and my feet, that it is I myself: handle me, and see; for a spirit hath not flesh and bones, as ye see me have.'

As they looked they saw the undeniable evidence of His pierced hands and feet. Advancing towards Him they touched His garments and embraced His feet. The evidence of seeing, hearing, and touching convinced them at last that it was really Jesus.

To assure His disciples finally that He was no phantom, Jesus said to them, 'Have ye here any meat?' Quickly they set simple food on the table, 'a piece of a broiled fish, and of an honeycomb. And he took it and did eat before them.'

'Then,' says the Record, 'were the disciples glad.' Rapturous joy swept away their last doubts. John must have recalled this wonderful moment when he began his first epistle, 'That which we have seen with our eyes, which we have looked upon, and our hands have handled of the Word of Life; . . . declare we unto you.'

Convinced now that it was Jesus Himself who had come back to them, they gathered round Him as He sat at the table and He began to remind them of all He told them before His death.

'These are the words which I spake unto you, while I was yet with you, that all things must be fulfilled, which were written in the law of Moses, and in the prophets, and in the psalms, concerning me.' And He 'opened . . . their understanding, that they might understand the Scriptures.'

'Thus it is written, and thus it behoved Christ to suffer,' Jesus explained, 'and to rise from the dead the third day.'

Gently He 'upbraided' His disciples for their 'unbelief and hardness of heart, because they believed not them which had seen him after he was risen.'

When Jesus had shown His disciples the significance of His atoning death, He went on to set before them the task which He was about to place in their hands.

'Ye are witnesses of these things,' He said, and 'as my Father sent me, even so send I you.' From then on, He told them, it would be their responsibility to proclaim to the world the good news of 're-pentance and remission of sins . . . in his name among all nations, beginning at Jerusalem'.

The church at Qubeibeh (Emmaus) is set in a peaceful area of the rolling hills of Judea. Crusader and Byzantine churches and an earlier building have been found, confirming the tradition that this was Emmaus. A Crusader village has been discovered near the church, which straddled a Roman road to Jerusalem.

Not yet, however, were the disciples ready to embark on their great missionary task. First they needed to be empowered by the promised gift of the Spirit.

237

'Behold,' He said, 'I send the promise of my Father upon you: but tarry ye in the city of Jerusalem, until ye be endued with power from on high.'

As an earnest of this full outpouring of the Spirit, 'He breathed on them, and saith unto them, Receive ye the Holy Ghost', and then He vanished from their sight.

Far into the night after Jesus had left, the disciples talked of the events of the day, and their hearts welled up with the new joy which had come to them through the revelation of their risen Lord.

This miraculous change in the disciples, which was to astonish the people of Jerusalem in the days which followed, provides the final evidence of the truth of the resurrection. If the whole story had been an invention or fraud, it could hardly have bound the poor, scattered, and discouraged disciples into a united fellowship, and kindled in their hearts a burden to carry the message of a crucified and risen Saviour to the world. Certainly they would not have been prepared to endure the hardships of the long and dangerous journeys it entailed, to face persecution and suffering, and at last, almost without exception, to die a martyr's death for a lie. Clearly the only explanation of the conversion of the disciples from gloom and despondency to joy and confidence, from paralysed inaction to burning zeal, was that the crucified Jesus had returned as

Jesus explained His mission as Messiah to two amazed disciples while walking through the hills near Emmaus.

their empowering Lord.

The resurrection of Jesus placed the final seal upon His divine mission of redemption. Jesus was 'declared to be the Son of God with power, . . . by the resurrection from the dead'. By it the ignominy of the cross was wiped away, the efficacy of His sacrifice was demonstrated, and His advocacy on behalf of repentant sinners at His Father's throne was assured.

Not only was He enabled by 'the power of his resurrection' to quicken those who were 'dead in trespasses and sins', but, through Him, death itself was finally conquered. By His resurrection He possessed Himself of the keys of death and the grave, and Himself became the 'firstfruits of them that slept'. In His resurrection we have the pledge that at the 'last day' all who 'die in the Lord' will come forth from the dust of the earth to live for evermore. Finally His resurrection assures us that He will come at last to 'judge the world in righteousness', to 'destroy them which destroy the earth', and to restore all things according to His eternal purpose. No wonder the resurrection has been called the 'central fact' of time and of eternity.

This chapter is based on Luke 24:13-49; John 20:19-23; Mark 16:12, 13.

238

Doubting Thomas believes

Although Luke states that 'the eleven' were present when Jesus appeared to the disciples in the upper room late in the evening of the resurrection day, the expression was used in a general way to mean all the disciples who were in Jerusalem at the time, except for the betrayer, Judas. Actually John tells us that Thomas, called Didymus, was not there. Whether some occasion necessitated his absence or whether, hugging his discouragement, he had gone off by himself, not wanting even the company of his fellow disciples, we do not know; but he did not at that time see Jesus.

When the other disciples sought him out and told him, 'We have seen the Lord,' he refused to believe them until he should have visible evidence for himself. 'Except I shall see in his hands the prints of the nails, and put my finger into the print of the nails, and thrust my hand into his side, I will not believe,' he declared. And nothing they could say could convince him.

For a whole week the disciples saw nothing of Jesus, but, 'after eight days', which would be the following Sunday, when Thomas had at last been persuaded to come out of his seclusion and join their company, Jesus appeared to them again, despite 'the doors being shut, and stood in the midst, and said, Peace be unto you.'

The object of His coming was obvious when He spoke immediately to Thomas. 'Thomas,' He said, 'reach hither thy finger, and behold my hands; and reach hither thy hand, and thrust it into my side: and be not faithless, but believing.'

But Thomas did not now need such evidence. The sight of the Master was sufficient to dispel all his doubts and, casting himself at Jesus' feet, he cried, 'My Lord and my God.'

It must be said to the credit of Thomas that though he was slow to believe, when he was convinced, his confession was profound and full; for the words he used were the two chief divine titles in the Old Testament Scriptures. Now Thomas declared his belief that Jesus was none other than Jehovah Elohim, the 'Lord God'. And Jesus accepted the titles, as well as the worship of Thomas and the other disciples as they joined with him.

Because Thomas really wanted to believe, Jesus came specially to dissipate his doubts, but He took the opportunity of this occasion to point out for the benefit of all to whom the good news of the risen Lord would thereafter come, that the promise of Scripture, confirmed by the testimony of those to whom He had shown Himself not once but five times on His resurrection day, should be sufficient to evoke saving faith.

'Because thou hast seen me, thou hast believed,' Jesus said to Thomas, but more blessed would be the faith of the generations to come who might not have the privilege of seeing Him in person, yet who would believe on the strength of Scripture, attested by those who had been 'eye witnesses of his majesty'.

Having used His meeting with Thomas and the other disciples to teach this important lesson, Jesus vanished, not to appear again until He met His disciples in Galilee.

This chapter is based on John 20:24-29; Mark 16:14.

239

Lovest thou Me?

As soon as Passover week was over, the disciples left for Galilee as they had been instructed by Jesus, and while they waited to keep the appointment He had made them, they went to their homes in Capernaum.

One evening, soon after their arrival, several of the disciples were walking by the lakeside. There was Peter and Thomas, now freed from all his doubts, the sons of Zebedee, two other disciples, perhaps Andrew and Philip, and Nathanael, who had decided to stay in Capernaum rather than go back to Cana in the hills.

Like so many vigorous people, Peter found waiting around very frustrating, and as he saw the fishermen, many of whom he knew well, getting the boats ready to go out onto the lake at nightfall, he suddenly announced to the others, 'I go a fishing'. He felt that it would give him something to do, and the proceeds would help to replenish their meagre resources. At once his companions said, 'We also go with thee.' So, putting some nets into one of the spare boats belonging to the Zebedee family, they set off. But though they toiled all night 'they caught nothing'.

Disappointed at having apparently lost their skill, they were returning to the shore as dawn broke over the hills of Gilead, when they heard Someone calling from the shore, 'Children, have ye any meat?' or in other words, Had they caught anything? Not recognizing Jesus, either by reason of the morning mist over the beach or, as on other occasions, because their eyes were 'holden', they tersely replied, 'No'.

Then the Man on the shore called again,

St. Peter's Church at Tabgha by the shores of Galilee. It was in this tranquil yet beautiful place that Jesus again met His disciples with a ready-cooked breakfast; where He miraculously supplied them with an overwhelming catch of fish, and where He questioned Peter's loyalty. Churches have stood on this site since the fourth century. The inside of the present church has a simple dignity which gives it a timeless appeal. It invokes a sense of calm and thoughtfulness to those who understand the meaning of its historical setting.

'Cast the net on the right side of the ship, and ye shall find.'

Thinking that He had seen signs of a shoal close inshore, they threw the piled-up net into the sea as He indicated and soon 'they were not able to draw it for the mulitude of fishes.'

Staggered at such a haul when they had not caught anything during the best hours of the night, they looked again at the Fig-ure on the shore, and suddenly John whispered to Peter, 'It is the Lord.' It was John who first 'believed' at the tomb, and now again he was the first to recognize Jesus.

Peter was standing on the gunwale of the boat, clad only in a sleeveless tunic reaching to his knees. When he realized it was Jesus 'he girt his fisher's coat unto him' and jumped into the water. It was quite shallow just there and he waded easily to the beach, while the other disciples steered the little ship the remaining hundred yards to the shore, trailing the net full of fishes.

When they landed, they followed Peter along the beach, and soon saw 'a fire of coals', or rather of broken branches which Jesus had gathered along the shore, and 'fish laid thereon'. On a stone beside the fire were cakes of bread.

241

As there was not enough food for all the disciples, Jesus said to Peter, 'Bring of the fish which ye have now caught.' Obediently he went back to the boat, and with the assistance of the other disciples dragged the net 'full of great fishes' up the beach. He took some to Jesus and while they were cooking, he sat down with the others to sort and count the catch. They were surprised to find that they had netted no fewer than a hundred and fifty-three, 'yet was not the net broken'.

When enough food had been cooked, Jesus said to the disciples, 'Come and dine', and they all sat down round the fire with Him. Jesus took of the bread and of the fish from the common dish, blessed it as He always did, and distributed to the disciples who were hungry after their hard night's work.

When the meal was over, Jesus took Peter aside and walked with him a little way along the beach. Feeling instinctively that Jesus was going to talk about his disloyalty, Peter waited apprehensively. When they were out of earshot Jesus said to him, 'Simon Peter, Simon, son of Jonas, lovest thou me more than these?' Though Jesus made no actual reference to his denial, Peter realized what He meant. At one time such a question would have aroused him to a vehement protestation that his love was deeper than any of the others, but now he had no high opinion of himself. Far from loving Jesus 'more' than the other disciples, his recent conduct made it doubtful whether he loved Him as much as they. So he humbly replied, 'Yea, Lord; thou knowest that I love thee', but the word he used signified a lesser level of love than that which Jesus had put into His question. Jesus had used the word *agapao* which signifies the highest love, to which man can rise only by divine grace. Peter did not feel justified in claiming this and said in effect, 'You know that I regard you with a deep affection (*phileo*).'

Without commenting on Peter's reply, Jesus said, 'Feed my lambs.' By this He indicated to Peter that as he had been graciously restored to favour by Jesus, he should have a special sympathy for the mistakes and the hesitant faith of those who were new in the truth.

When they had walked a little farther Jesus said again, 'Simon, son of Jonas, lovest thou me?' Once more He asked Peter if his love was of the highest, but He did not this time ask him if he loved 'more' than his brethren. A little perplexed, Peter replied as he had done before, 'Yea, Lord, thou knowest that I love (have a deep affection for) thee.'

This time Jesus said to him, 'Feed my sheep.' Having experienced how Satan had followed him like a wolf to destroy him, he would be able to give pastoral care to the other sheep of God's flock.

After a few moments Jesus said to Peter for the third time, 'Simon, son of Jonas, lovest thou me?' But this time He followed Peter's lead and said in effect, 'Can you really say you have a deep affection for me?'

At this Peter was grieved. He had admitted that he could not claim to have manifested the highest level of love for Jesus, but when Jesus queried even his own estimate of his love he felt hurt. But he realized that his actions justified Jesus' doubts, and throwing himself upon the forgiving love of Him who could see 'into men', he replied, 'Lord, thou knowest all things; Thou knowest that (at least) I love (have an affection for) thee.' In reply Jesus said a third time, 'Feed my sheep.'

Peter had denied Jesus three times, and

242

After the anguish and pain of the events during Passover week, the disciples were reassured as Jesus ate and talked with them again.

so Christ's question was put to him three times that he might be able to give a threefold testimony to his repentance.

Having given Peter opportunity to show the genuineness of his repentance, Jesus went on to tell him of the ultimate sac-rifice which he would make in his Master's service. 'When thou wast young,' Jesus said, 'thou girdest thyself, and walk-est whither thou wouldest.' Then he was his own master and could do what he liked. 'But when thou shalt be old,' Jesus went on, 'thou shalt stretch forth thy hands, and another shall gird thee, and carry thee whither thou wouldest not.

Soon the disciples would permanently leave the familiar surroundings of the lovely shores of Galilee, and disperse far and wide with the good news of the risen Christ.

This spake he signifying by what death he should glorify God.' And by way of final encouragement to His beloved disciple, Jesus ended the conversation with the exhortation, 'Follow me.'

There was no question now as to Peter's readiness to follow Jesus in life and in death, and the book of Acts and his own epistles show how faithfully he did 'follow' the Lord. His death is not recorded in Scripture, but tradition has it that in Rome in AD 67, on the same day that Paul was beheaded, Peter was scourged and crucified. But so different was he then from the boastful Peter of earlier years, that he asked to be put to death head downward, because he did not feel worthy of the honour of dying as Jesus had done. Devotedly Peter glorified God in his life of service, and nobly he glorified Him in his dying.

As Jesus turned to go back along the shore of the lake, Peter saw John coming to join them, and asked, 'Lord, and what shall this man do?' Peter and John had always been companions in service and Peter wondered whether they would continue to work together and perhaps even suffer and die together for Christ. It was a natural enough question in a way, but Jesus did not satisfy his curiosity. Instead He replied, 'If I will that he tarry till I come, what is that to thee? Follow thou me.'

Jesus' words are a warning to all workers for God that associations in service must never become so close, that if they need be broken, invidious comparisons are made. Sometimes Christian workers feel that others have had privileges or advantages they have not had, and may even jealously aspire to the vocation of another, while despising their own calling. Jesus wanted to emphasize that it is His prerogative to decide how the talents of His servants shall be used, and that no comparisons with others should ever disturb their joy and satisfaction in service for Him.

In the case of these two disciples, John, in the providence of God, was permitted to continue in service long after Peter was martyred for the faith, and more than once he was himself delivered from a martyr's death. But, contrary to the belief of some that he would 'not die', he did eventually join the 'dead in Christ', and with Peter awaits the day when Jesus will return to awaken and reward His sleeping people.

So also with us, if we keep our eyes on Jesus, and are faithful in the work He gives us to do, we may be assured that His providence will sustain us in every experience we are called upon to meet, and at the last there will be a 'crown' and a share in the 'inheritance of the saints' reserved especially for us.

This chapter is based on John 21:1-23.

The great commission

When Jesus left His disciples by the lakeside, He bade them gather as many of His Galilean followers as possible to meet Him on a certain mountain and at a time which He indicated.

In harmony with these instructions the disciples passed the word around as widely as they could, and when the day came the believers made their way to the rendezvous by various routes in order not to arouse suspicion. At the appointed time there were more than five hundred gathered together, by far the largest number Jesus ever assembled between His resurrection and His ascension.

As the believers waited in groups on the mountain side Jesus suddenly appeared among them and 'when they saw him they worshipped him'. Even in this privileged company, however, there were some who 'doubted' at first that it was really He. But they were not in His presence long before, like Thomas, they knew that it was the risen Lord.

Why did Jesus bring all these believers together on this occasion? One important reason was to provide positive evidence of His resurrection to the disciples in Galilee as He had done in Jerusalem. As Paul later commented, it was the climax of the 'many infallible proofs' by which He 'showed himself alive' from the dead.

But Jesus had not brought all these believers together only to provide a final and conclusive witness to His resurrection. His further purpose was to commission His church for its great task. To the apostles and the believers in the upper room in Jerusalem, Jesus had first outlined their future work for Him. On that occasion there were perhaps a hundred or so Judean believers present. Now to the believers in Galilee He repeated the great commission.

First, Jesus proclaimed the authority which had been vested in Him by His Father. 'All power,' He declared, 'is given unto me in heaven and in earth.' Henceforth, seated at the right hand of the throne of God in heaven, He would have at His command all heavenly intelligences for the exercise of His mediatorial ministry. And on earth all power would be available to His appointed heralds for the proclamation of the Gospel of His saving grace.

'Go ye therefore,' He bade His followers, 'and teach all nations.' In the days when He Himself went about teaching and preaching, His call had been 'Come.' Now He bade His people 'Go.' The 'disciples' were now designated 'apostles'.

By 'ye' Jesus meant all who were then listening to His words, and all who would in due course hear the Gospel from their lips. All, in fact, who have learned the joy of salvation are to go forth and tell it to those who know it not.

When Jesus was on earth He went only to the 'lost sheep of the house of Israel', but now the opportunity of hearing the Gospel was to go to Gentile as well as Jew, to Greek and barbarian, to all peoples everywhere. They were to begin their new proclamation in Jerusalem, and spectacular indeed were the results of the first proclamation there on the day of Pentecost. Then from Jerusalem they were to go into 'Judea' and 'Samaria', and finally 'unto the uttermost part of the earth.'

Not only was the Gospel to go geographically to all the world, but it was to reach every stratum of society, from the highest to the lowest. Rich and poor, bond and free, learned and unlearned, all were to hear the saving truths of the Gospel of redemption. It was to go not only to 'all nations' but to 'every creature'.

245

Evidence of the spreading influence of Christianity over paganism is illustrated here where a very early Christian church (foreground) was constructed within the shadow of the giant columns of the Temple of Cybele. It stands among the ruins of Sardis in Asia Minor, what is now western Turkey. This great temple dedicated to the fertility god Cybele (or Diana) was built in the fourth century BC. The church in Sardis received a letter from the apostle John, warning of its spiritual condition (Revelation 3:1-6).

The Gospel which God's heralds were to carry was the 'Gospel of the kingdom', the kingdom of grace which He would first establish in the hearts of men, and the kingdom of glory into which He would gather His people at His coming.

The outward sign of the inward acceptance of the Gospel, and the rite of initiation into His Church, was to be baptism by immersion. As John baptized in Jordan with the 'baptism of repentance' in anticipation of the coming of Christ, and as Jesus instructed His disciples to baptize those who accepted His word during the days of His earthly ministry, so those who now received the Gospel of the kingdom were to be baptized 'in the name of the Father, and of the Son, and of the Holy Ghost', signifying their death and burial with Christ, their spiritual resurrection to newness of life in Christ, and their adoption into the family of God. In itself, of course, the act of immersion in water has no inherent regenerating power, as some teach. The thief on the cross was saved, though he was never baptized. It is belief in Christ that saves. But because we believe, we desire to manifest our belief through baptism.

The initial step of belief, followed by baptism into the Church of Christ, was to be followed by diligent instruction in 'all things whatsoever' Jesus had 'commanded'. There was a reason for this emphasis, for even in Paul's day there were those who perverted or diminished the true faith into 'another gospel', which was not the Gospel at all. And in our day likewise there are many who claim to be bearers of the Good Tidings, but who bear only half the Gospel, or even less!

There are those who declare 'all things' pertaining to grace and faith, but who fail to teach the 'all things' of obedience; forgetting that Jesus came to save His people 'from' not 'in' their sins. In all ages the true people of God are those who 'keep the commandments of God' as a result of their acceptance of the 'faith of Jesus'.

Then there are the proponents of the 'social gospel', who emphasize only the need for the betterment of the human environment through the application of Christian principles. All would agree that the efforts of Christian people towards the amelioration of man's earthly lot are eminently commendable, but God's messengers are not primarily called to 'serve tables', as Peter categorically pointed out. Their chief task is to prepare men for a future life in the kingdom of heaven, and any so-called Gospel which fails to do this is a perversion of the true Gospel.

Paul warned that in the 'last days' there would be many who would have a 'form' of godliness, but who would be devoid of the 'power' thereof, but those who were truly fulfilling the great commission would be carrying the whole Gospel to the whole world. And that Gospel is the unadulterated, undiminished 'faith once delivered unto the saints' with its call for obedience, by grace to all 'the commandments of God'.

'Gifts' appropriate to their need were promised to Christ's witnesses 'severally' as the Spirit should choose, but the great-

Around the world Christianity is spreading hope. The doctor arrives with medicine and a Bible. Children are taught to read in Christian schools. For them and many others there is the delight of finding in the Bible the joy of the Gospel, culminating in the public witness of baptism, a demonstration of their intention to follow Jesus.

est gift of all would be the presence of Jesus, which would be with His people 'all the days, even unto the end of the world'.

As the Gospel messengers fulfilled their God-given task from generation to generation, 'signs' would set the seal of God's approval upon their ministry. 'These signs,' said Jesus, 'shall follow them that believe; In my name shall they cast out devils; they shall speak with new tongues; they shall lay hands on the sick, and they shall recover. . . . They shall take up serpents; and if they drink any deadly thing, it shall not hurt them.' But the greatest 'sign' would be the spiritual transformations wrought by the Gospel in the lives of sinners saved by grace.

The response of the first disciples to this 'total' programme of Christ was the 'total' surrender of themselves to the task, with the result that, in their day, they saw the Gospel preached 'to every creature which is under heaven'. Today the same dedication is carrying God's last message of mercy to 'every nation, and kindred, and tongue, and people'. Soon 'this Gospel of the kingdom' will have been 'preached in all the world for a witness unto all nations;' then the 'end' of this world order will come and God's new world order will be brought in.

This chapter is based on Matthew 28:16-20; Mark 16:15-18.

I will come again!

When Jesus had given His commission to the assembled believers on the mountain in Galilee, He bade His disciples return to Jerusalem, where the proclamation of the Gospel of the risen Christ was to begin. While they awaited further instructions from Him, they met regularly in the upper room. It may have been during these days that Jesus appeared to James, as Paul mentions. Then on the twenty-fifth of the month of Iyyar, just ten days before Pentecost, as the disciples were gathered together, Jesus appeared in their midst and they fell before Him in worship.

This time He did not stay to talk, but at once summoned them to follow Him. Through the streets of Jerusalem they went and out of the city by the Sheep Gate. They descended the Kidron steps, crossed the river, and took the road up the Mount of Olives. Passing the Garden of Gethsemane they soon reached the rough upland on the central summit of the mountain overlooking the village of Bethany.

Here Jesus halted and the disciples gathered around, wondering what word He had for them at this time. Now that Jesus had 'suffered', it surely would not be long before He 'entered into the glory' of His kingdom. One of the disciples, therefore, asked Him plainly, 'Lord, wilt thou at this time restore again the kingdom to Israel?'

Jesus could have told them that a long time would pass before the establishment of His kingdom, but He did not want to discourage them. So He said briefly, 'It is not for you to know the times or the seasons, which the Father hath put in his own power.'

The timing of the kingdom they could well leave to God. What was important was that they should address themselves to the interim task which He had given to them. So Jesus went on, 'Ye shall receive power, after that the Holy Ghost is come upon you: and ye shall be witnesses unto me, both in Jerusalem, and in all Judea, and in Samaria, and unto the uttermost part of the earth.'

Then as He stretched forth His nail-pierced hands in blessing upon the disciples, He began to ascend from the earth. The eyes of the disciples followed Him as He rose higher and higher until a cloud of glorious angels surrounded Him and 'He was parted from them, and carried up into heaven'.

The Bible does not give us sufficient information to identify the exact place of the ascension, and as there are three Gethsemanes there are three suggested spots, all within a quarter of a mile of one another, which are pointed out as the place from which He ascended.

In the fourth century a Rotunda of the Ascension was erected on one of these spots. It had a paved court open to the sky, symbolic of Christ's ascent, and was surrounded by three rows of columns, forming a double portico. In the centre of the court was the supposed rock from which Christ rose. This first structure was destroyed by the Persians, but was rebuilt by the Crusaders in the form of an octagonal building supported on eight double pillars, with arches between, and again open to the sky. When the Crusaders were driven out, the Moslems filled in the arches and added a dome, which form it has retained until the present time. For curiously enough, while the Moslems deny the resurrection of Christ, they believe in His ascension, and a few yards away from the building is a mosque and minaret from which there is a wonderful view towards Jerusalem and down into the

wilderness of Judea.

A short distance from what is now the Chapel of the Ascension, the Russian bell tower, erected in the late nineteenth century, is also identified with the place of the ascension, and so is the residence of the Greek Orthodox patriarch not far away.

Wherever the exact place is, it is significant that Jesus ascended from a mountain when His work was done. It was on a mountain in Galilee that He preached His Sermon on the Mount and ordained His disciples. On the Mount of Transfiguration His eternal glory was for a moment revealed, and on Calvary's mount He wrought His supreme sacrifice for the re-

demption of a lost world. Now it was from the Mount of Olives that He returned to His home in glory, and when He comes finally to establish His kingdom on earth it will be upon this same mountain that He will descend in power and glory.

While the gospels describe the dramatic departure of Christ from the earth, they do not portray His arrival at the gate of heaven. This thrilling scene, however, is prophetically described by the Psalmist. Vividly he tells how, when the triumphal procession reached the heavenly gates the cry went up from the accompanying host, 'Lift up your heads, O ye gates; and be ye lift up ye everlasting doors; and the King of glory shall come in.'

Back from heaven came the answering cry, 'Who is this King of glory?' to which the angel host replied, 'The Lord strong and mighty, the Lord mighty in battle. Lift up your heads, O ye gates, even lift them up, ye everlasting doors, and the King of glory shall come in.'

Again the question came, 'Who is this King of glory?' and the reply was repeated, 'The Lord of hosts, He is the King of glory.'

Then the portals of heaven opened wide, and the procession, led by the glorified Christ, swept through to the

Viewed from the eastern side of the Mount of Olives is the Tower of the Ascension (left) a prominent landmark within the walls of a Russian Orthodox convent. The traditional site of the ascension is show below. It was built by the Crusaders on earlier structures dating back to AD 380.

throne of God, where the victory of Christ was proclaimed. The command went forth, 'Let all the angels of God worship him,' and as all heaven was prostrated in worship, the courts of glory rang with the shouts of praise.

When Jesus ascended we are told that 'he led captivity captive'. Doubtless this refers to the dead who were raised from their graves at His resurrection. These were given an honoured place in the triumphal procession back to heaven, and in the Revelation we glimpse them finally as the twenty-four 'elders', sharing in the worship of the angels round the throne.

As the disciples strained their eyes to catch a last glimpse of their ascending Lord, a voice called to them. Turning in the direction from which it came, they saw two angels. 'Ye men of Galilee, why stand ye gazing up into heaven?' said one of them. 'This same Jesus, which is taken up from you into heaven, shall so come in like manner as ye have seen him go into heaven.'

It was necessary that Jesus should return to heaven to begin His mediatorial ministry as our High Priest on the basis of His vicarious sacrifice. It was necessary also that He should go away in order that He might dispense the 'gifts' His earthly witnesses needed for the prosecution of their great task. Jesus had said, too, 'I go to prepare a place for you . . . that where I am, there ye may be also.' For all these reasons it was expedient that Jesus should leave His followers for a time. But when the last soul has received the invitation of the Gospel, when Jesus has pleaded His blood for the last repentant sinner, and the heavenly 'mansions' are ready for the reception of His faithful people, Jesus will fulfil His promise to 'come again'. Then will the present kingdom of grace give

251

place to His universal and everlasting kingdom of glory.

The ascension of Jesus, the angels declared further, would set the pattern for His return. The very 'same Jesus', who was parted from His disciples, will come back in person to receive His people to Himself. As Jesus ascended visibly from the midst of His disciples into heaven, so 'every eye' will see Him return. Amid a cloud of shining angels, He ascended into heaven, and accompanied by all 'the holy angels' He will return to the earth to 'gather together his elect from the four winds, from one end of heaven to the other.' 'And so', adds the apostle Paul, 'shall we ever be with the Lord.'

When the angels had delivered their message they vanished and the disciples fell to the ground in worship. Then they went back to the city and entered the temple 'praising and blessing God'.

Ten days later, at Pentecost, the promised 'power from on high' descended upon them in flaming fire, and they went forth to begin their great missionary task. Soon persecution broke out against the rapidly growing Church and the believers were scattered. But this only accelerated the work of the Gospel, for, as they had been commanded, 'they went forth, and preached everywhere, the Lord working with them, and confirming the word'.

Here the story of these pages must perforce end. We have followed the footprints of Jesus until His feet left the earth at His ascension, and space does not permit us to follow the footsteps of the ascended Christ in the story of His Church through the centuries.

Suffice it to say that the fervent hope of the aged John in the closing sentences of the last gospel to be written has been abundantly fulfilled. 'These are written,' he declared, 'that ye might believe that Jesus is the Christ, the Son of God; and that believing ye might have life through his name,' and in every generation since, multitudes have found that 'life' in a look at the crucified and risen Saviour. The changes wrought in the lives of men by the Gospel have conclusively shown that the 'testimony' of the inspired penmen is no ordinary word, no mere philosophy of life, but the very Word of our salvation.

In spite of persecution and apostasy, the message of the Gospel has gone forth 'conquering and to conquer' until in our day, through the unparalleled means of communication God's providence has provided, we have seen its miraculous extension into all the world, and in the hearts of God's people everywhere the conviction is deepening that the 'end' long foretold is near.

True, the great majority of men 'see not the bright light' behind 'the clouds' of darkness which cover the earth, but we know that He is there, eagerly waiting for the day of His final manifestation. Soon He will fulfil His promise and come again the 'second time', not in humiliation but in glory, not to be rejected of men but for the establishment of His universal and everlasting kingdom.

If therefore in our hearts we can pray the last prayer of the Bible, 'Even so, come, Lord Jesus', we may be assured that in the great day of His coming we will be among those who will look up and say, 'This is our God; we have waited for him, and he will save us: this is the Lord; we have waited for him, we will be glad and rejoice in his salvation.' God grant that this glorious company may include you.

This chapter is based on Luke 24:50-53; Mark 16:19, 20; John 20:30, 31; 21:24, 25; Acts 1:6-12.

INDEX

Figures in **bold** refer to volume number. Figures in *italic* refer to illustrations. Figures in roman refer to textual page numbers.

SUBJECT INDEX

Figures in **bold** refer to volume number.

PHOTOGRAPHERS

ARTISTS